Spell on ★ Wheels™

JUST TO
GET TO YOU

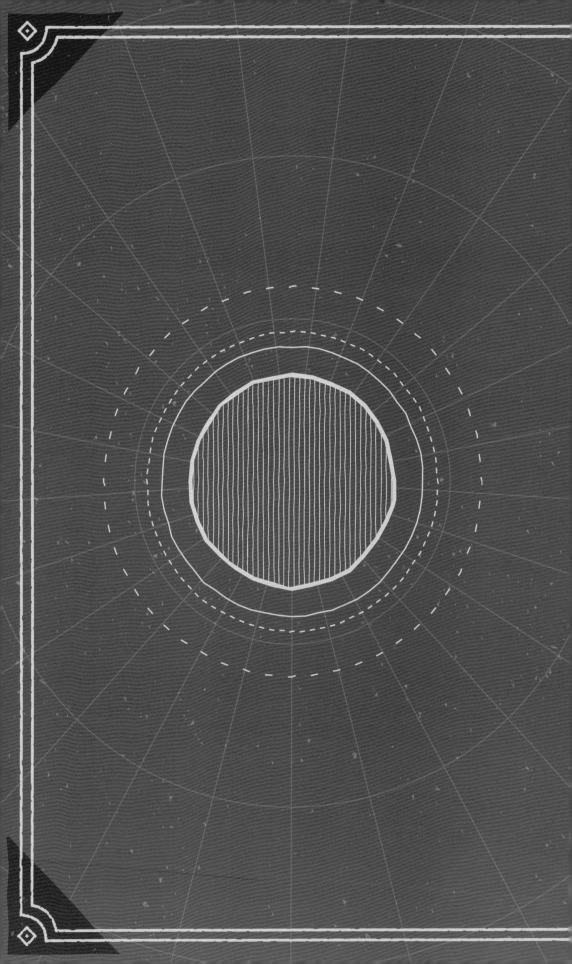

Spell on Wheels ™

JUST TO GET TO YOU

Story by ★ **KATE LETH**

Art by ★ **MEGAN LEVENS**

Colors by ★ **MARISSA LOUISE**

Letters by ★ **RACHEL DEERING**

Cover Art by ★ **MEGAN LEVENS** with **MARISSA LOUISE**

DARK HORSE BOOKS

President and Publisher **Mike Richardson**
Editor **Shantel LaRocque** | *Assistant Editor* **Brett Israel**
Designer **Brennan Thome** | *Digital Art Technician* **Allyson Haller**

Published by Dark Horse Books
A division of Dark Horse Comics LLC
10956 SE Main Street | Milwaukie, OR 97222

DarkHorse.com

To find a comics shop in your area, visit ComicShopLocator.com.

First edition: December 2020
Ebook ISBN 978-1-50671-478-3
Trade Paperback ISBN 978-1-50671-477-6

1 3 5 7 9 10 8 6 4 2
Printed in China

Library of Congress Cataloging-in-Publication Data

Names: Leth, Kate, author. | Levens, Megan, artist. | Louise, Marissa,
   colourist. | Piekos, Nate, letterer. | Bartel, Jen, artist. | Doyle, Ming,
   artist. | Ganucheau, Paulina, artist. | Sauvage, Marguerite, artist. |
   Quinones, Joe, artist.
Title: Spell on wheels / script by Kate Leth ; art by Megan Levens ; colors
   by Marissa Louise ; letters by Nate Piekos of Blambot ; cover by Jen
   Bartel ; chapter break art by Ming Doyle, Paulina Ganucheau, Marguerite
   Sauvage, Jen Bartel, and Joe Quinones.
Description: First edition. | Milwaukie, OR : Dark Horse Books, 2017. | "This
   volume collects Spell on Wheels #1–#5"
Identifiers: LCCN 2016056237 | ISBN 9781506701837 (paperback)
Subjects: LCSH: Comic books, strips, etc. | BISAC: COMICS & GRAPHIC NOVELS /
   Science Fiction. | FICTION / Fantasy / Paranormal. | COMICS & GRAPHIC
   NOVELS / Fantasy.
Classification: LCC PN6728.S596 L48 2017 | DDC 741.5/973--dc23
LC record available at https://lccn.loc.gov/2016056237

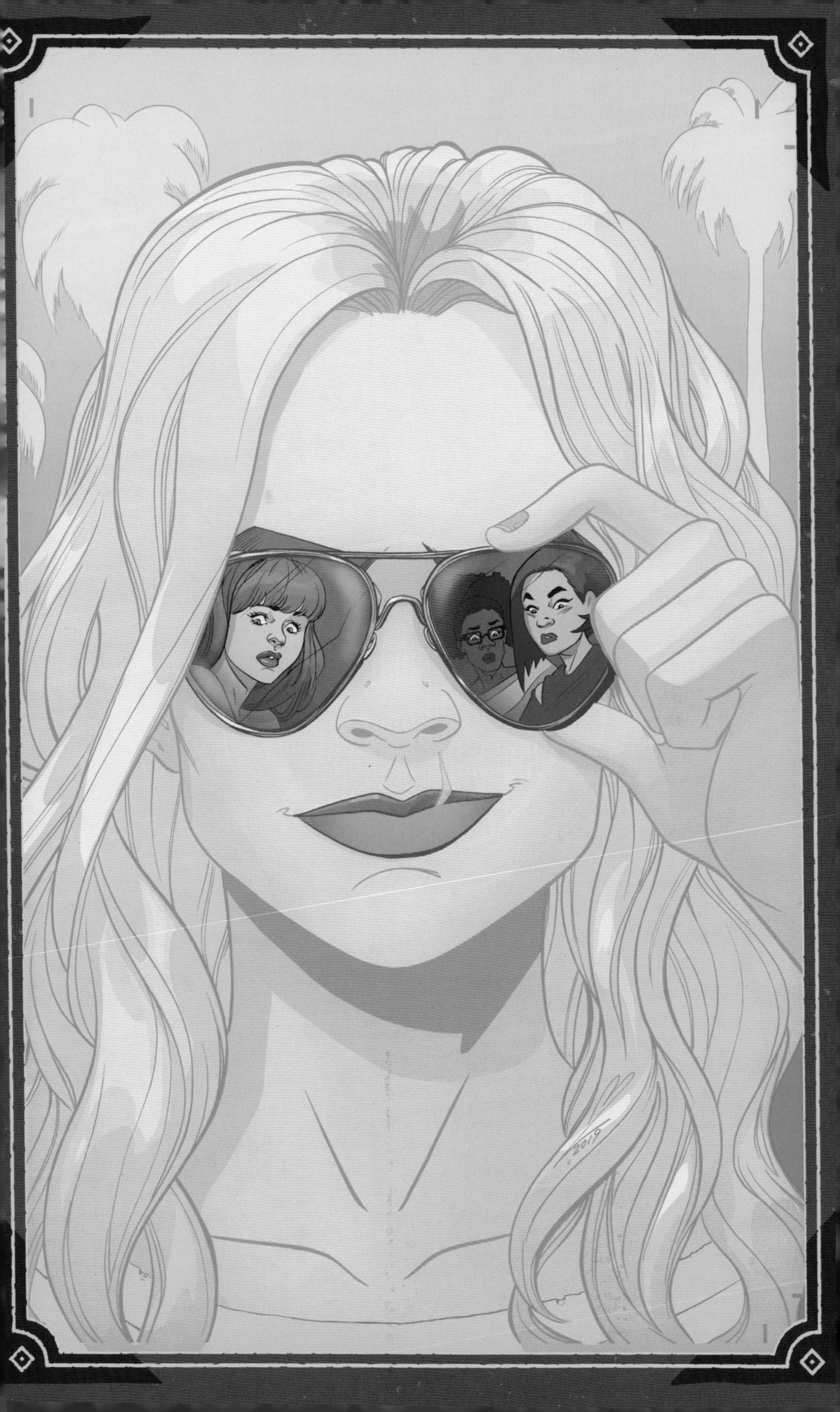
2019

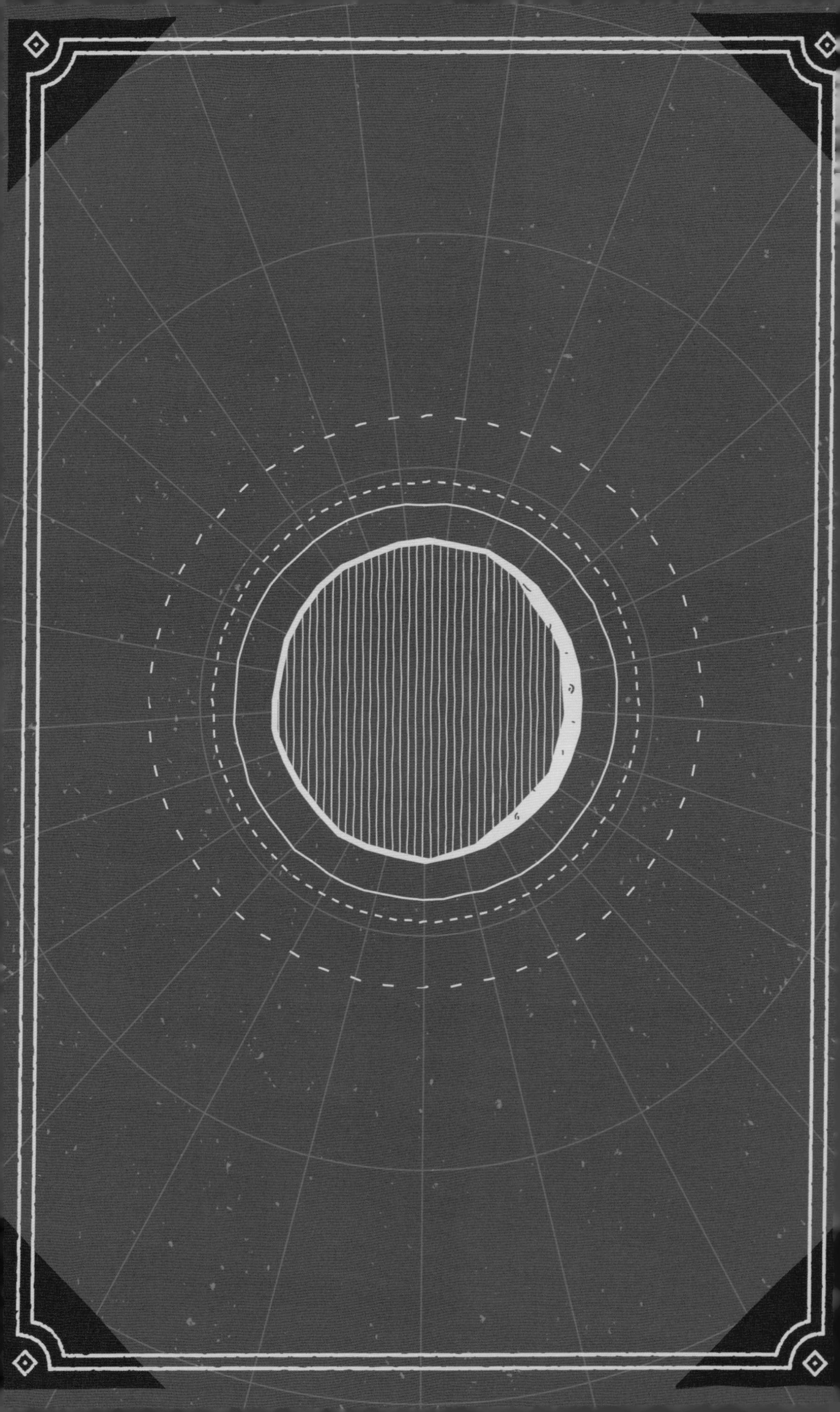

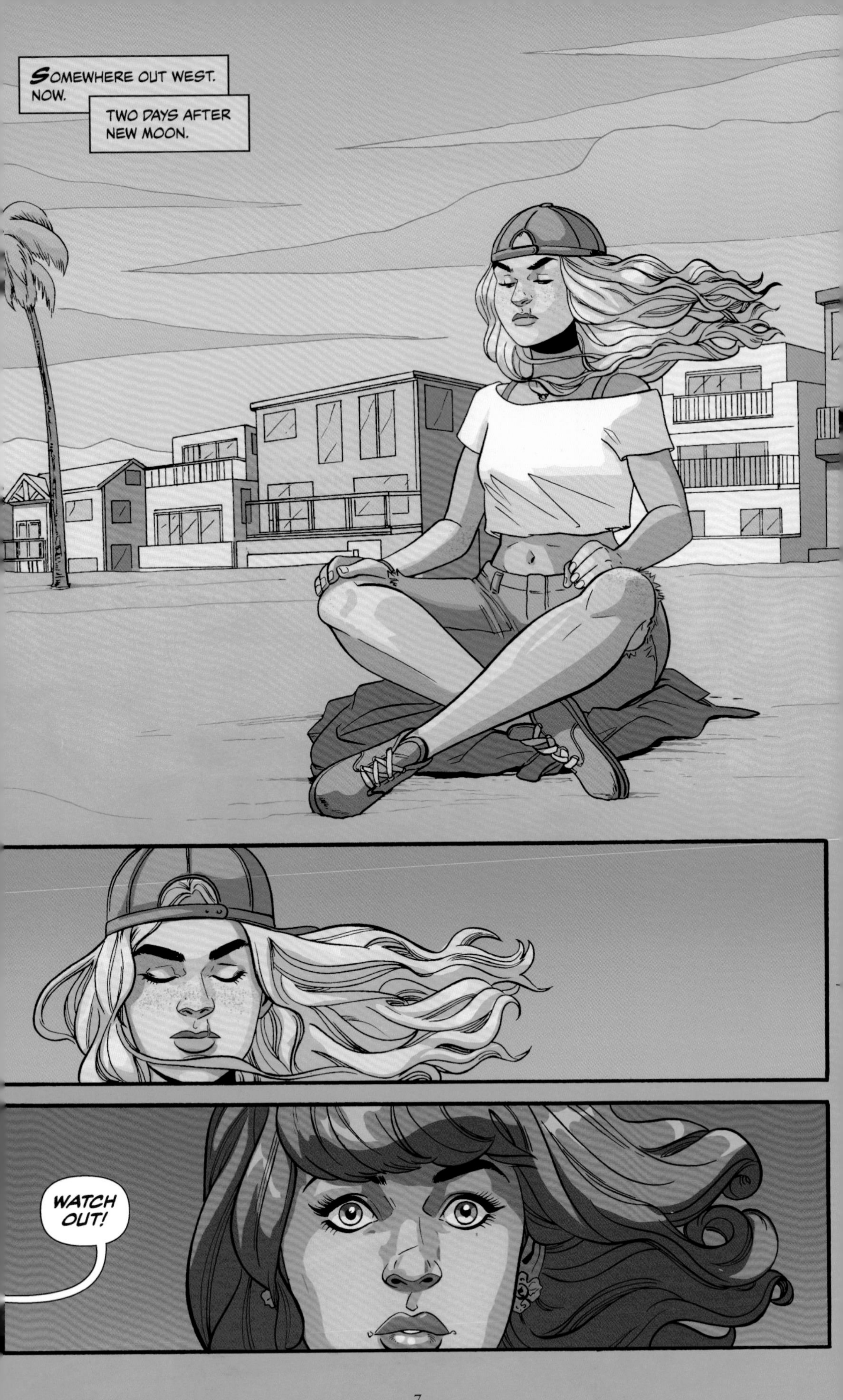

SOMEWHERE OUT WEST. NOW.
TWO DAYS AFTER NEW MOON.
WATCH OUT!

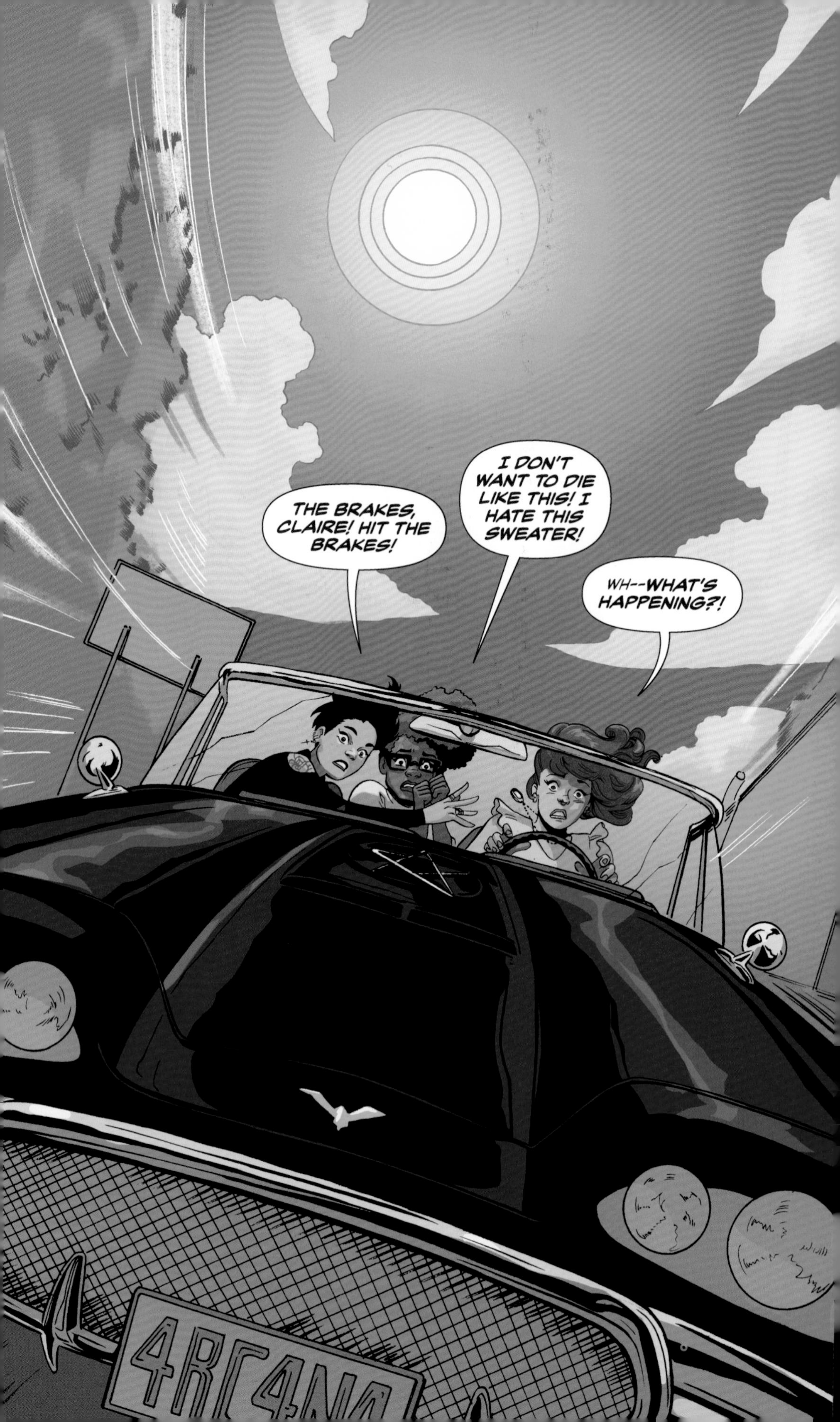
THE BRAKES, CLAIRE! HIT THE BRAKES!
I DON'T WANT TO DIE LIKE THIS! I HATE THIS SWEATER!
WH--WHAT'S HAPPENING?!
4RC4NA

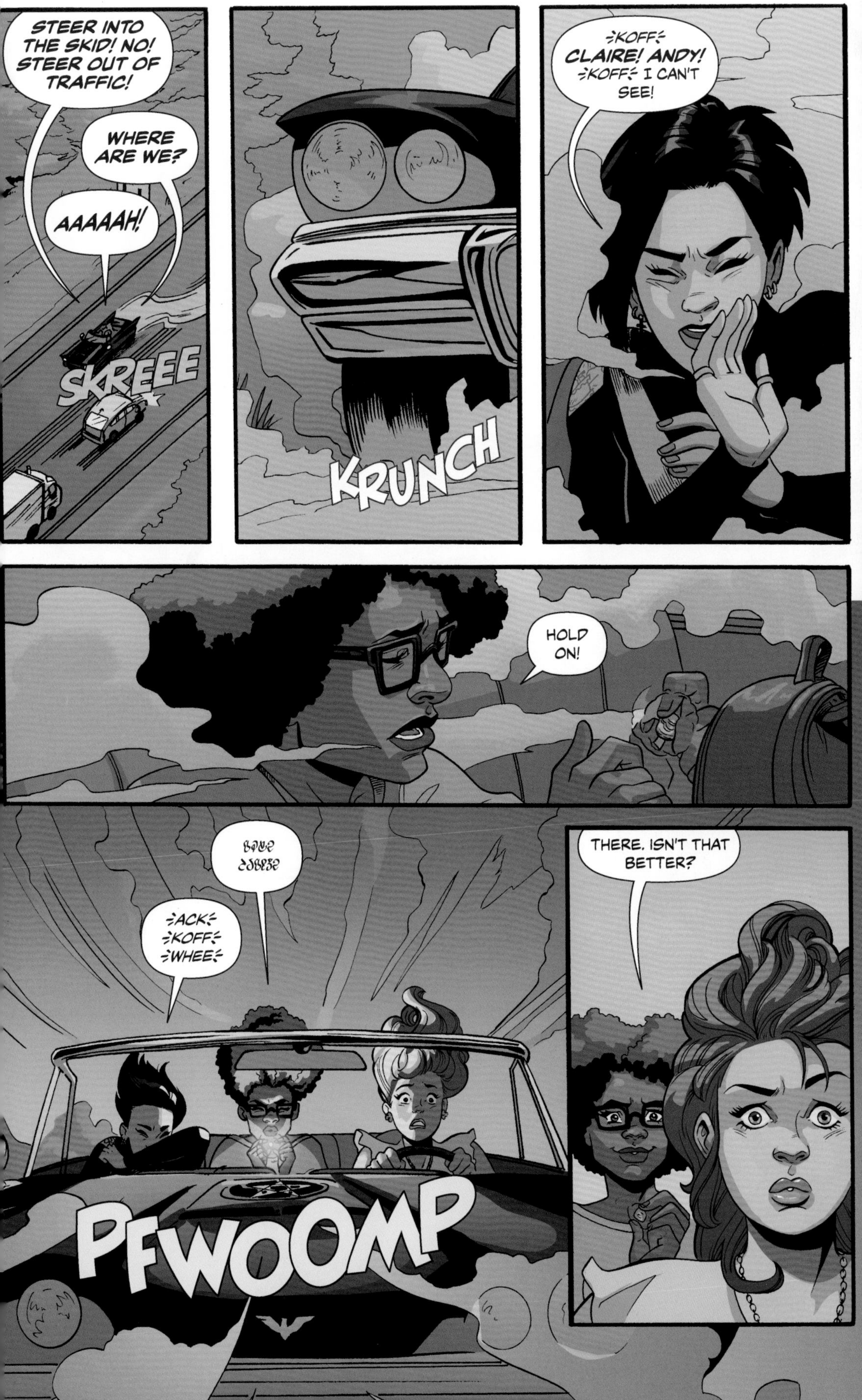
STEER INTO THE SKID! NO! STEER OUT OF TRAFFIC!
WHERE ARE WE?
AAAAAH!
SKREEE
KRUNCH
KOFF
CLAIRE! ANDY!
KOFF I CAN'T SEE!
HOLD ON!
ACK
KOFF
WHEE
PFWOOMP
THERE. ISN'T THAT BETTER?

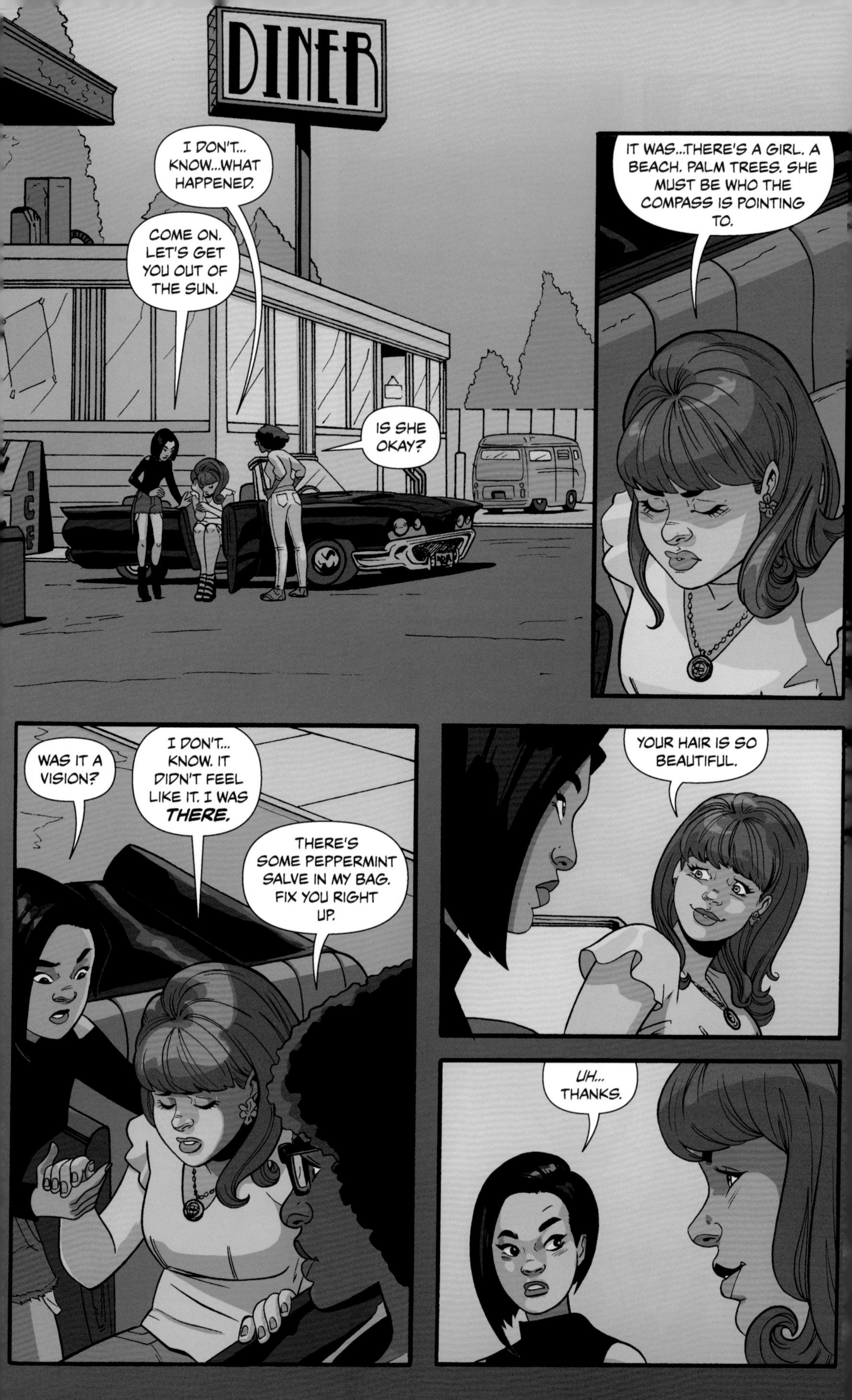
DINER
I DON'T... KNOW...WHAT HAPPENED.
COME ON. LET'S GET YOU OUT OF THE SUN.
IS SHE OKAY?
ICE
IT WAS...THERE'S A GIRL. A BEACH. PALM TREES. SHE MUST BE WHO THE COMPASS IS POINTING TO.
WAS IT A VISION?
I DON'T... KNOW. IT DIDN'T FEEL LIKE IT. I WAS *THERE.*
THERE'S SOME PEPPERMINT SALVE IN MY BAG. FIX YOU RIGHT UP.
YOUR HAIR IS SO BEAUTIFUL.
UH... THANKS.

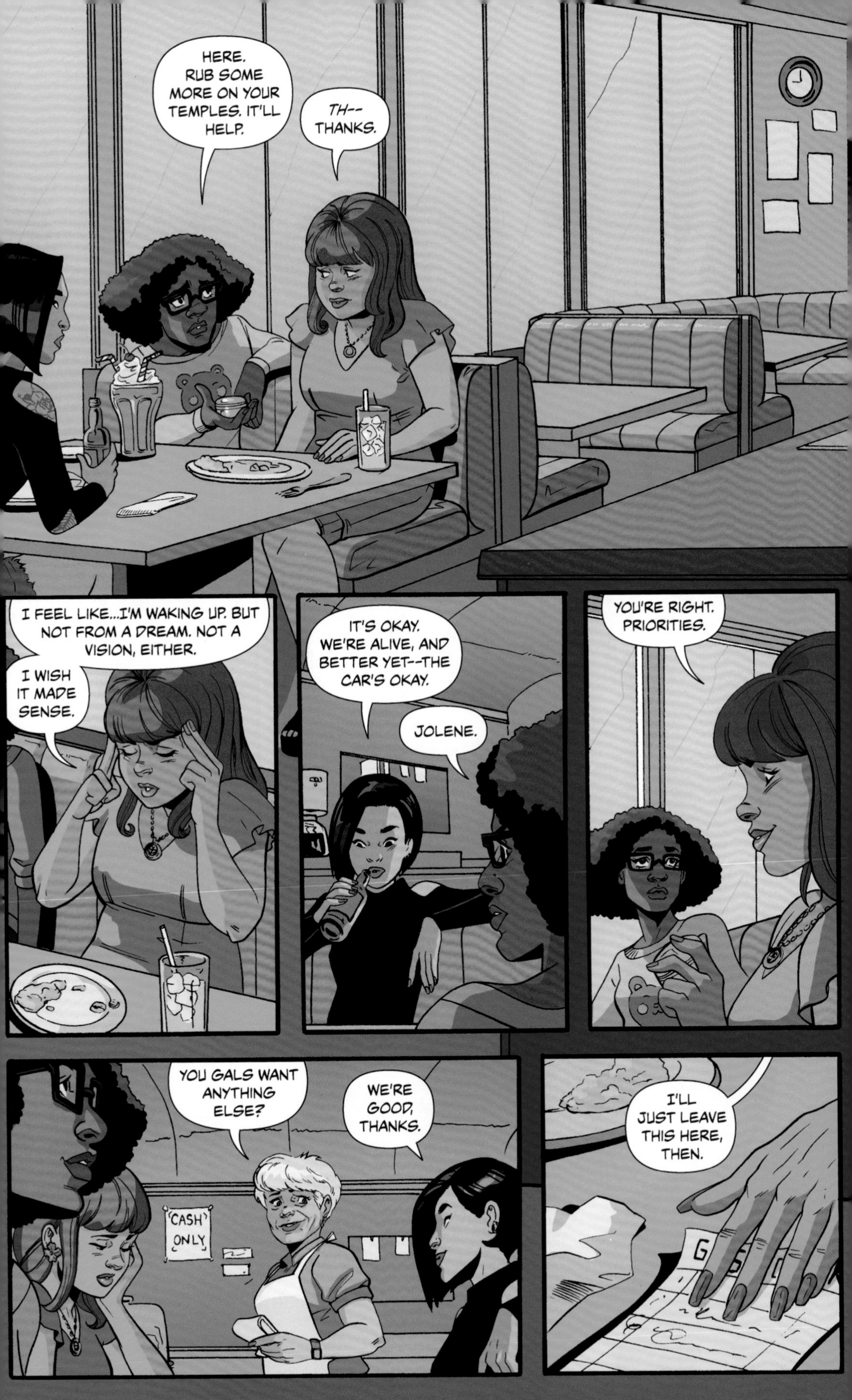
HERE. RUB SOME MORE ON YOUR TEMPLES. IT'LL HELP.
TH-- THANKS.
I FEEL LIKE...I'M WAKING UP. BUT NOT FROM A DREAM. NOT A VISION, EITHER.
I WISH IT MADE SENSE.
IT'S OKAY. WE'RE ALIVE, AND BETTER YET--THE CAR'S OKAY.
JOLENE.
YOU'RE RIGHT. PRIORITIES.
YOU GALS WANT ANYTHING ELSE?
WE'RE GOOD, THANKS.
CASH ONLY
I'LL JUST LEAVE THIS HERE, THEN.

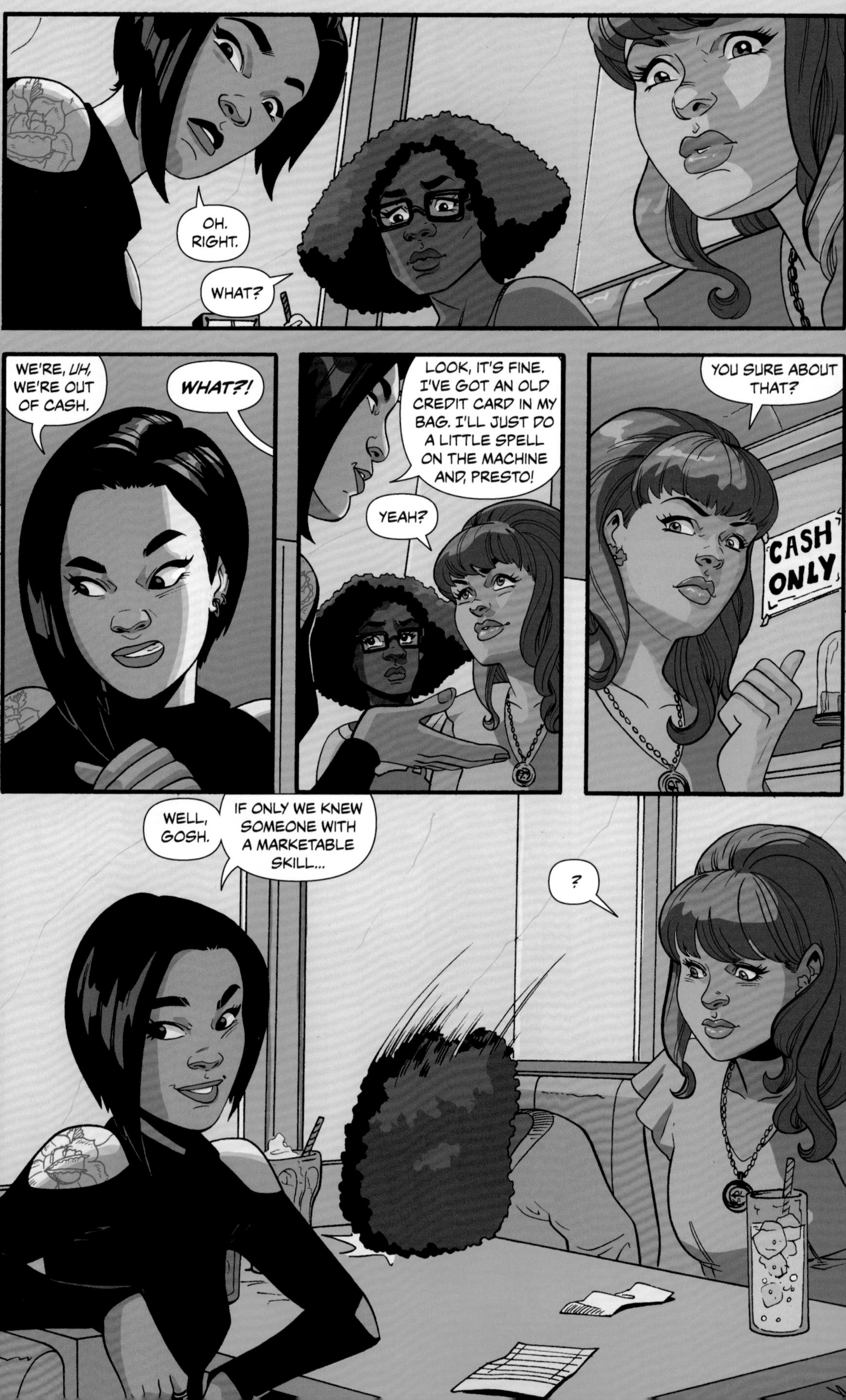
OH. RIGHT.
WHAT?
WE'RE, *UH*, WE'RE OUT OF CASH.
WHAT?!
LOOK, IT'S FINE. I'VE GOT AN OLD CREDIT CARD IN MY BAG. I'LL JUST DO A LITTLE SPELL ON THE MACHINE AND, PRESTO!
YEAH?
YOU SURE ABOUT THAT?
CASH ONLY
WELL, GOSH.
IF ONLY WE KNEW SOMEONE WITH A MARKETABLE SKILL...
?

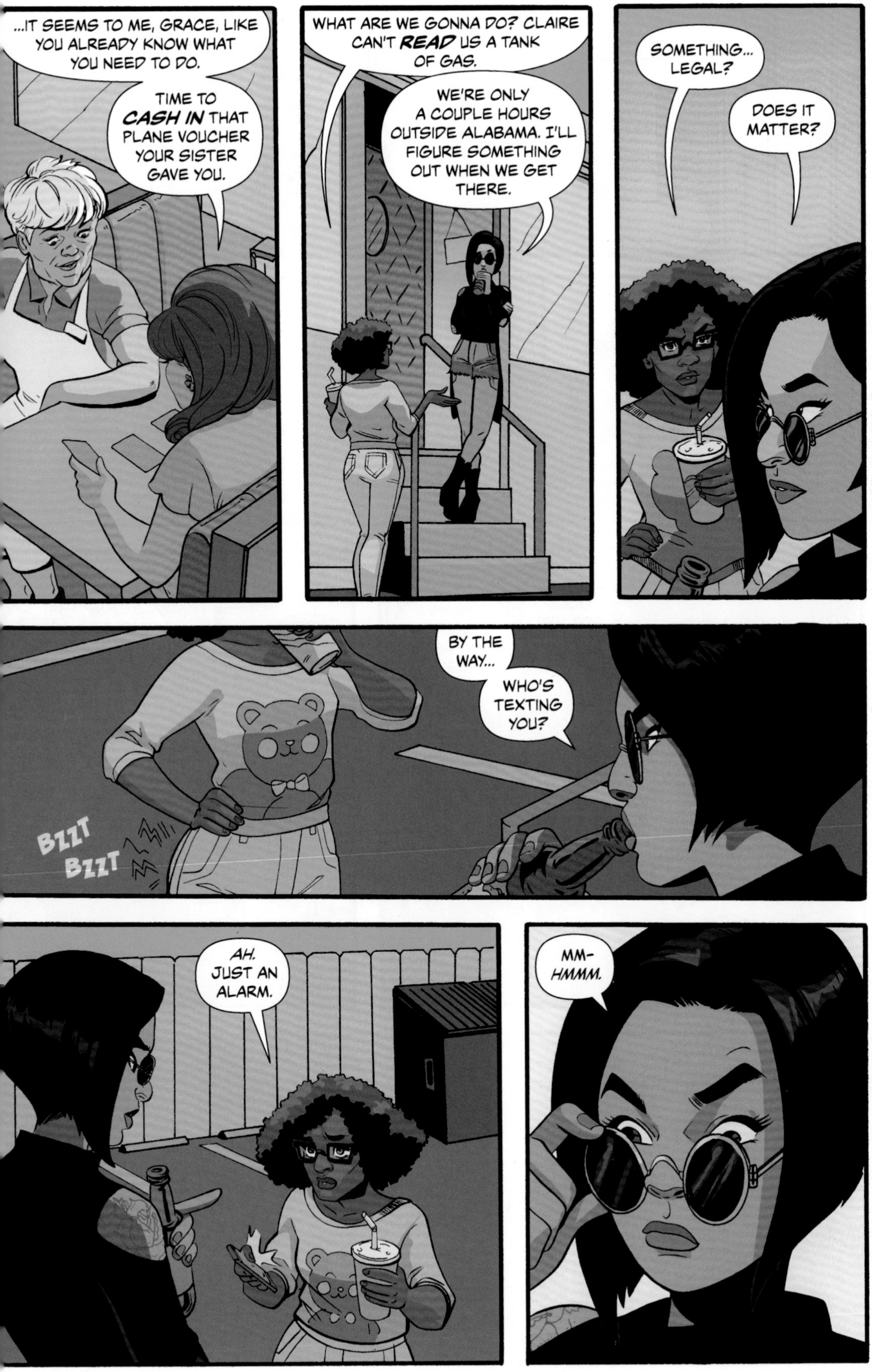

...IT SEEMS TO ME, GRACE, LIKE YOU ALREADY KNOW WHAT YOU NEED TO DO.
TIME TO **CASH IN** THAT PLANE VOUCHER YOUR SISTER GAVE YOU.
WHAT ARE WE GONNA DO? CLAIRE CAN'T **READ** US A TANK OF GAS.
WE'RE ONLY A COUPLE HOURS OUTSIDE ALABAMA. I'LL FIGURE SOMETHING OUT WHEN WE GET THERE.
SOMETHING... LEGAL?
DOES IT MATTER?
BY THE WAY...
WHO'S TEXTING YOU?
BZZT BZZT
AH. JUST AN ALARM.
MM-*HMMM.*

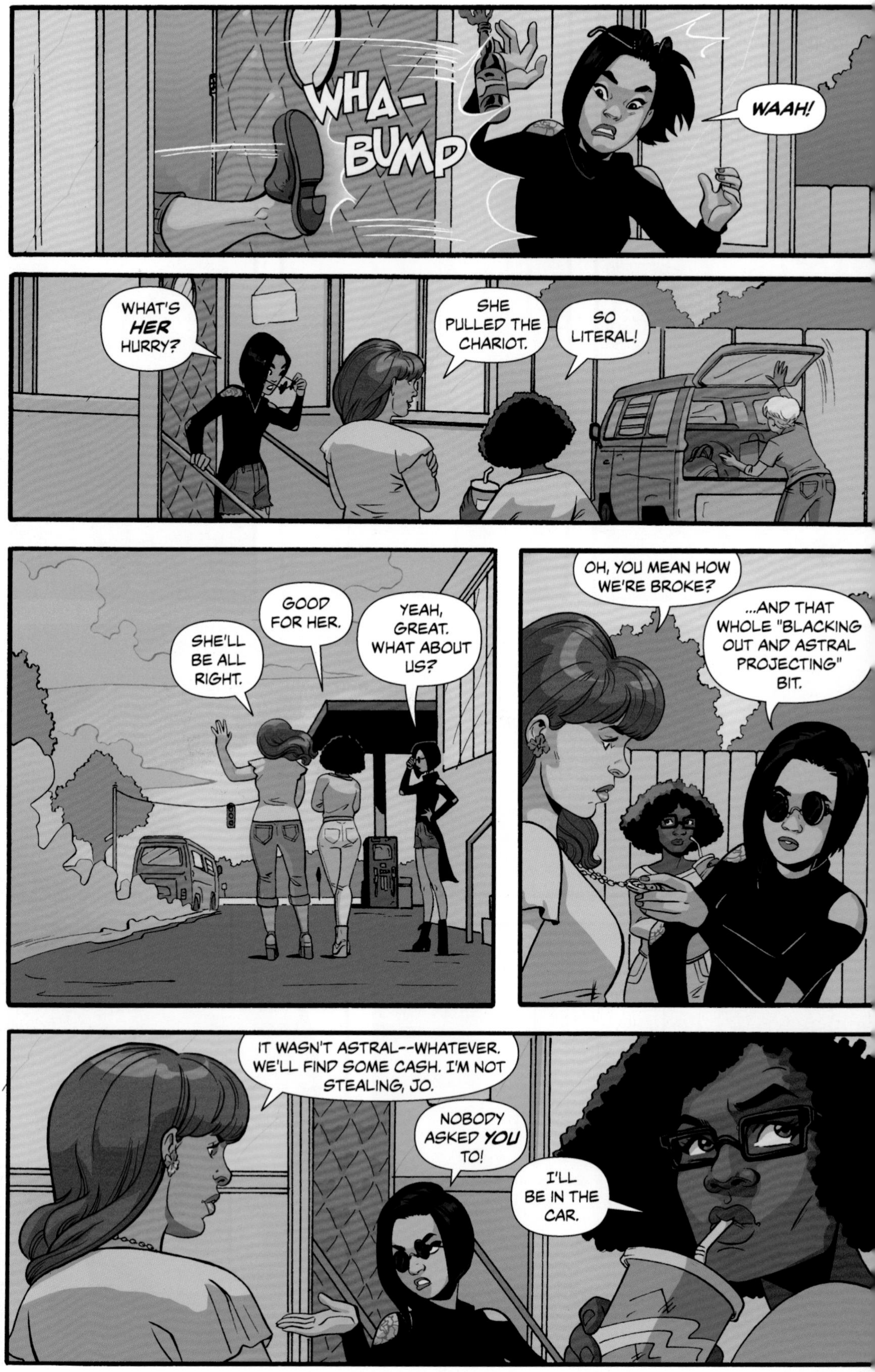
WHA-BUMP
WAAH!
WHAT'S HER HURRY?
SHE PULLED THE CHARIOT.
SO LITERAL!
SHE'LL BE ALL RIGHT.
GOOD FOR HER.
YEAH, GREAT. WHAT ABOUT US?
OH, YOU MEAN HOW WE'RE BROKE?
...AND THAT WHOLE "BLACKING OUT AND ASTRAL PROJECTING" BIT.
IT WASN'T ASTRAL--WHATEVER. WE'LL FIND SOME CASH. I'M NOT STEALING, JO.
NOBODY ASKED YOU TO!
I'LL BE IN THE CAR.

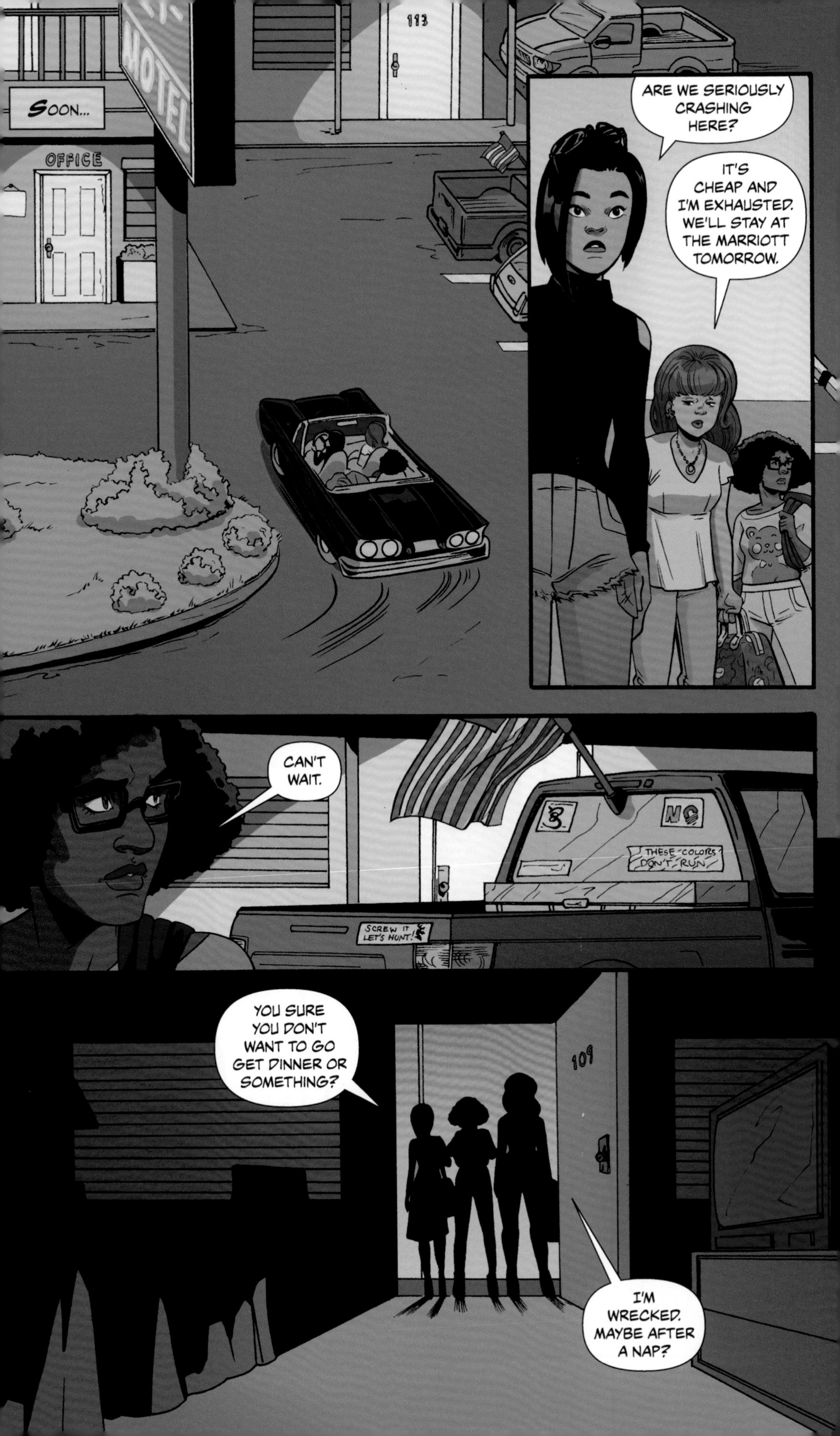

MOTEL
OFFICE
113
SOON...
ARE WE SERIOUSLY CRASHING HERE?
IT'S CHEAP AND I'M EXHAUSTED. WE'LL STAY AT THE MARRIOTT TOMORROW.
CAN'T WAIT.
THESE COLORS DON'T RUN
SCREW IT LET'S HUNT!
109
YOU SURE YOU DON'T WANT TO GO GET DINNER OR SOMETHING?
I'M WRECKED. MAYBE AFTER A NAP?

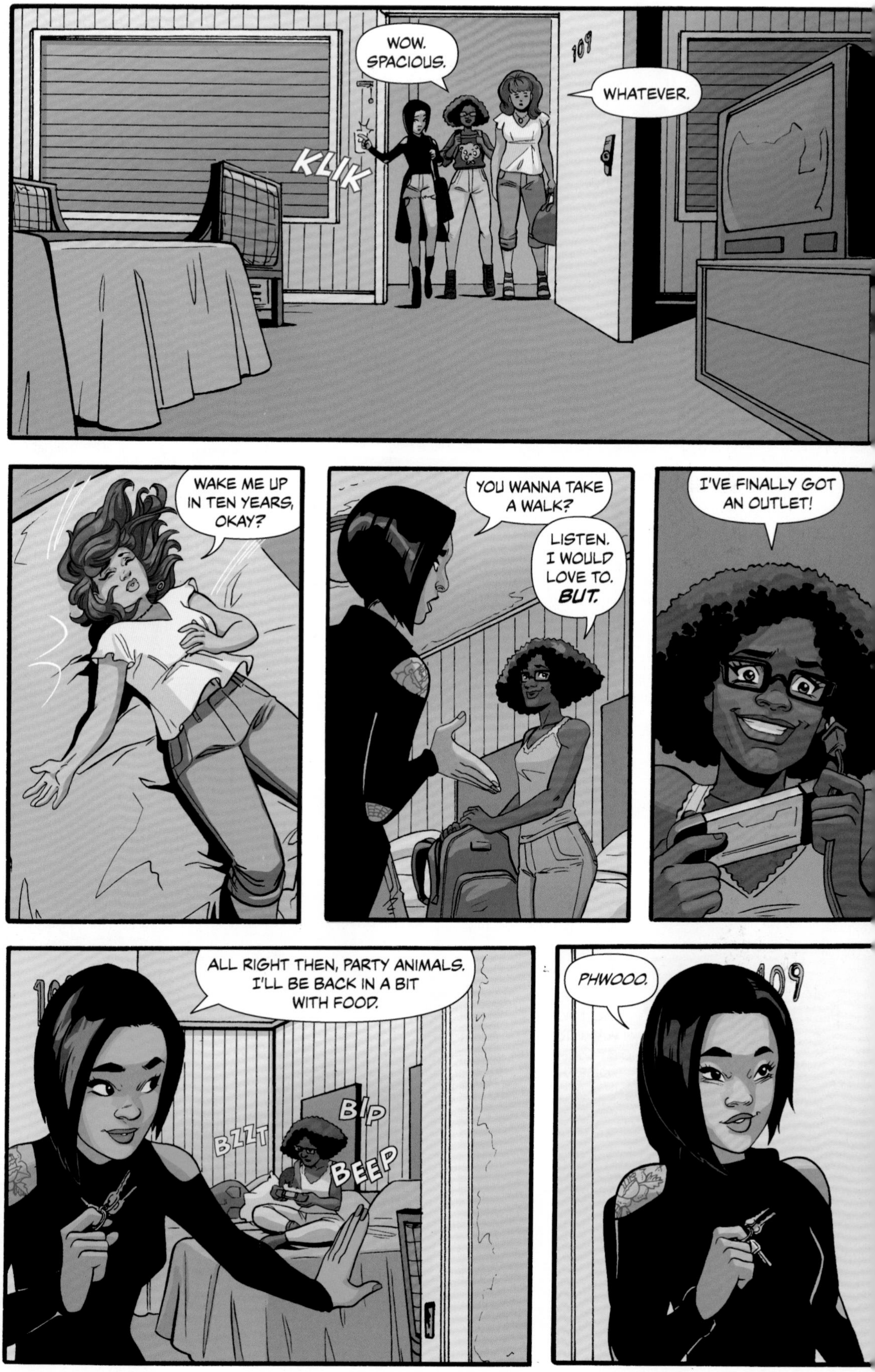
WOW. SPACIOUS.
KLIK
109
WHATEVER.
WAKE ME UP IN TEN YEARS, OKAY?
YOU WANNA TAKE A WALK?
LISTEN. I WOULD LOVE TO. BUT.
I'VE FINALLY GOT AN OUTLET!
ALL RIGHT THEN, PARTY ANIMALS. I'LL BE BACK IN A BIT WITH FOOD.
BZZT
BIP
BEEP
PHWOOO.
109

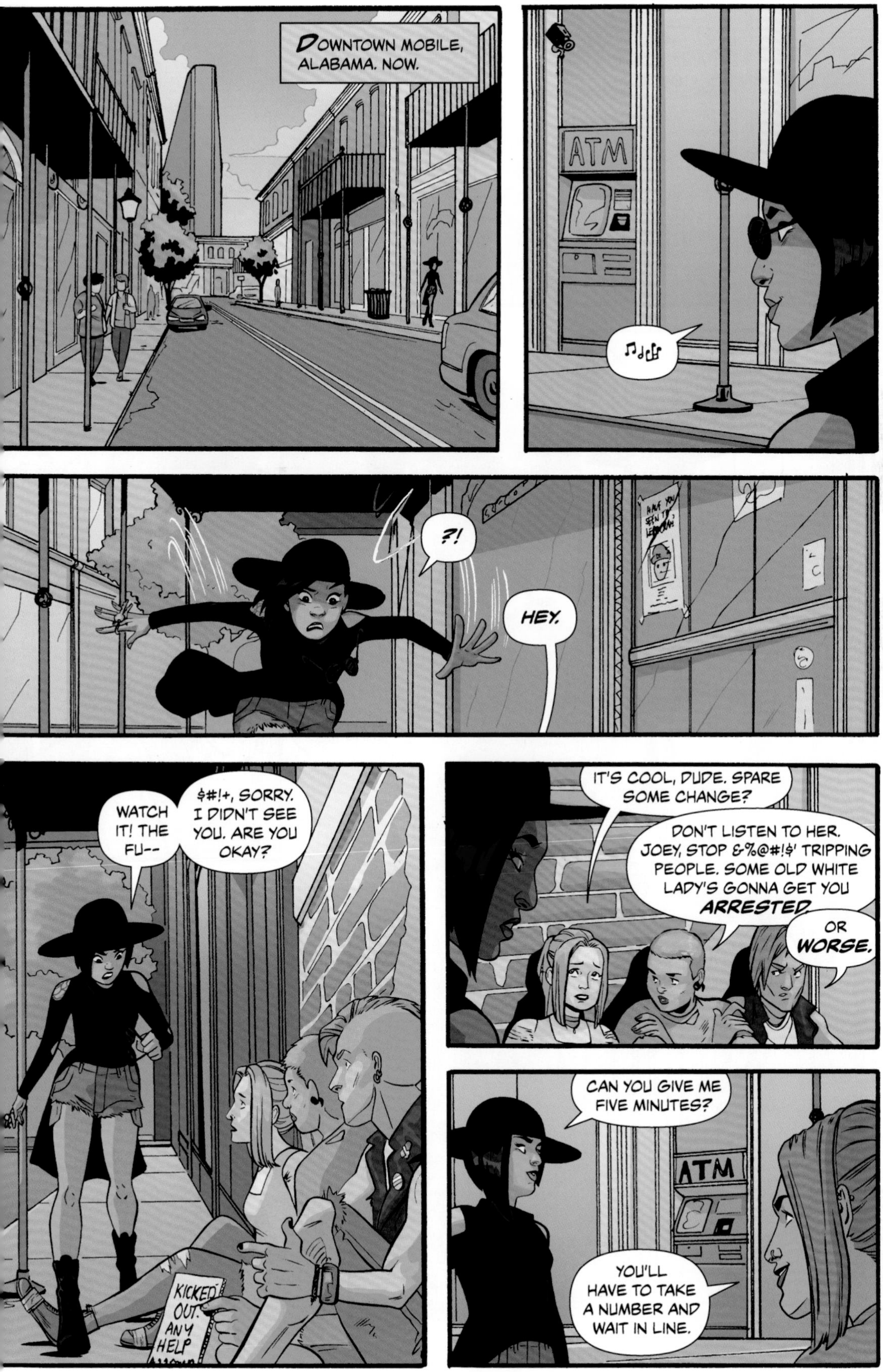

DOWNTOWN MOBILE, ALABAMA. NOW.
ATM
♫♩♫
?!
HEY.
WATCH IT! THE FU--
$#!+, SORRY. I DIDN'T SEE YOU. ARE YOU OKAY?
KICKED OUT. ANY HELP
IT'S COOL, DUDE. SPARE SOME CHANGE?
DON'T LISTEN TO HER. JOEY, STOP &%@#!$' TRIPPING PEOPLE. SOME OLD WHITE LADY'S GONNA GET YOU ARRESTED.
OR WORSE.
CAN YOU GIVE ME FIVE MINUTES?
ATM
YOU'LL HAVE TO TAKE A NUMBER AND WAIT IN LINE.

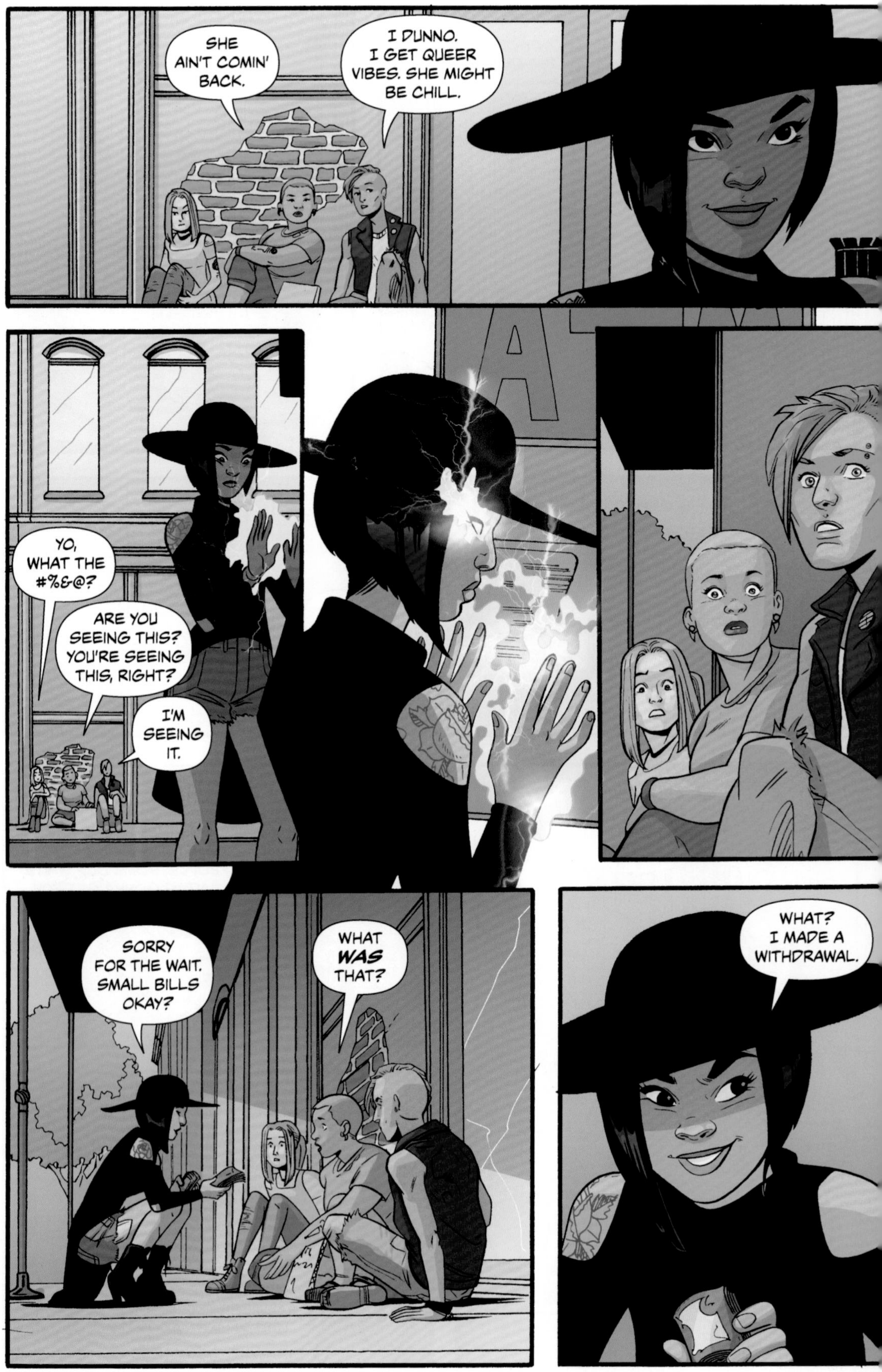
SHE AIN'T COMIN' BACK.
I DUNNO. I GET QUEER VIBES. SHE MIGHT BE CHILL.
YO, WHAT THE #%&@?
ARE YOU SEEING THIS? YOU'RE SEEING THIS, RIGHT?
I'M SEEING IT.
SORRY FOR THE WAIT. SMALL BILLS OKAY?
WHAT *WAS* THAT?
WHAT? I MADE A WITHDRAWAL.

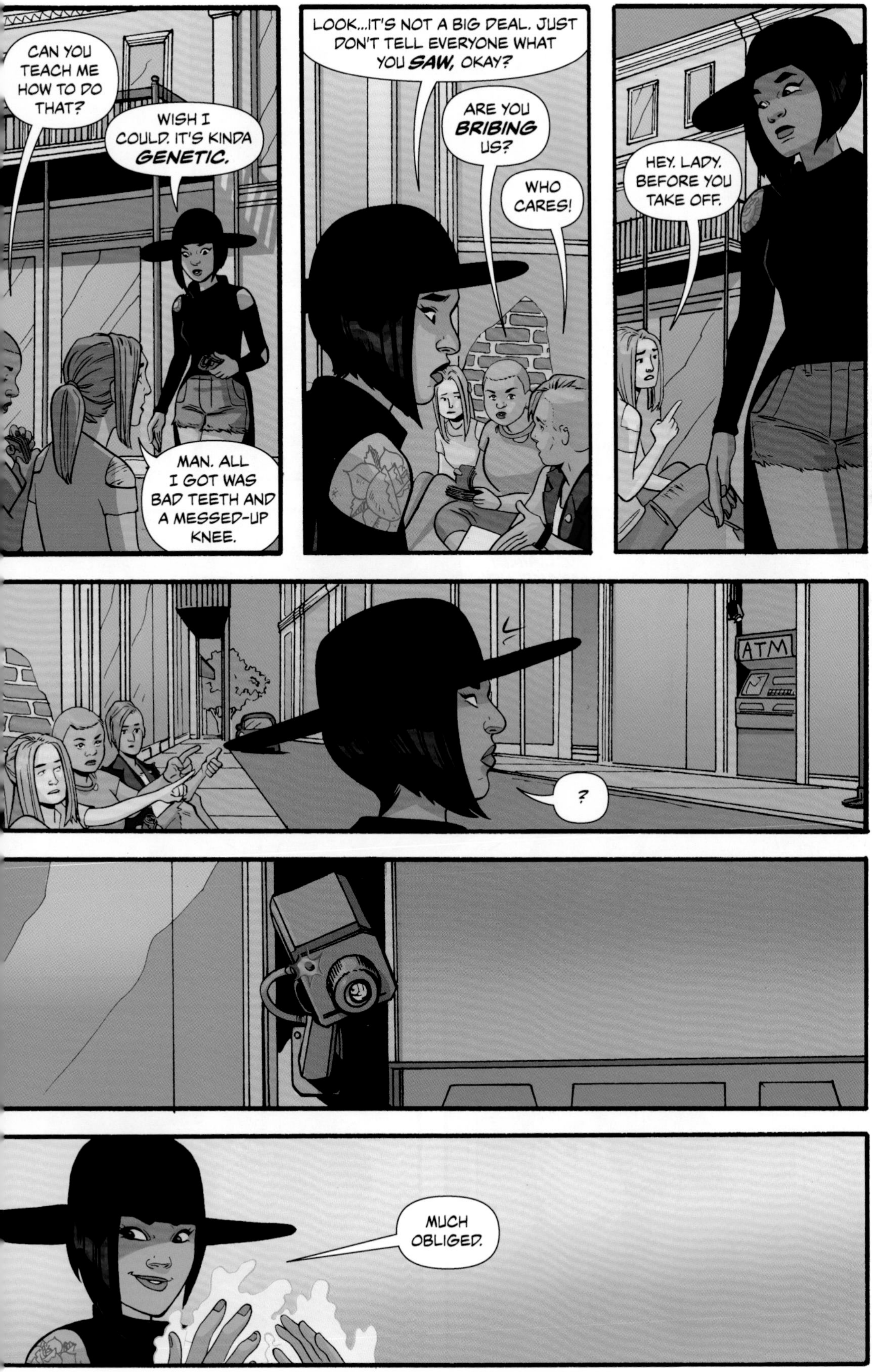
CAN YOU TEACH ME HOW TO DO THAT?
WISH I COULD. IT'S KINDA GENETIC.
MAN. ALL I GOT WAS BAD TEETH AND A MESSED-UP KNEE.
LOOK...IT'S NOT A BIG DEAL. JUST DON'T TELL EVERYONE WHAT YOU SAW, OKAY?
ARE YOU BRIBING US?
WHO CARES!
HEY. LADY. BEFORE YOU TAKE OFF.
ATM
?
MUCH OBLIGED.

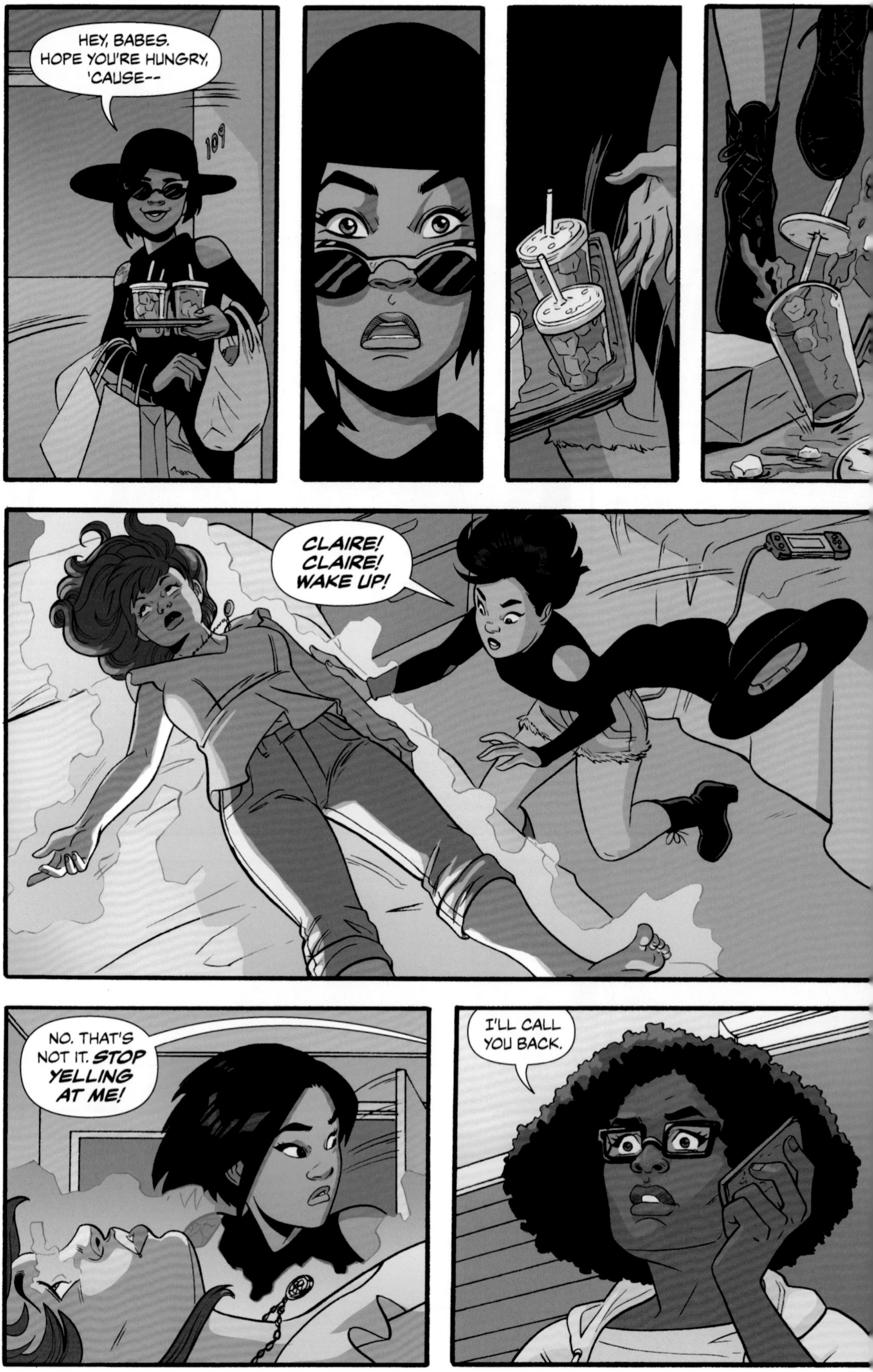
HEY, BABES. HOPE YOU'RE HUNGRY, 'CAUSE--
109
CLAIRE! CLAIRE! WAKE UP!
NO. THAT'S NOT IT. STOP YELLING AT ME!
I'LL CALL YOU BACK.

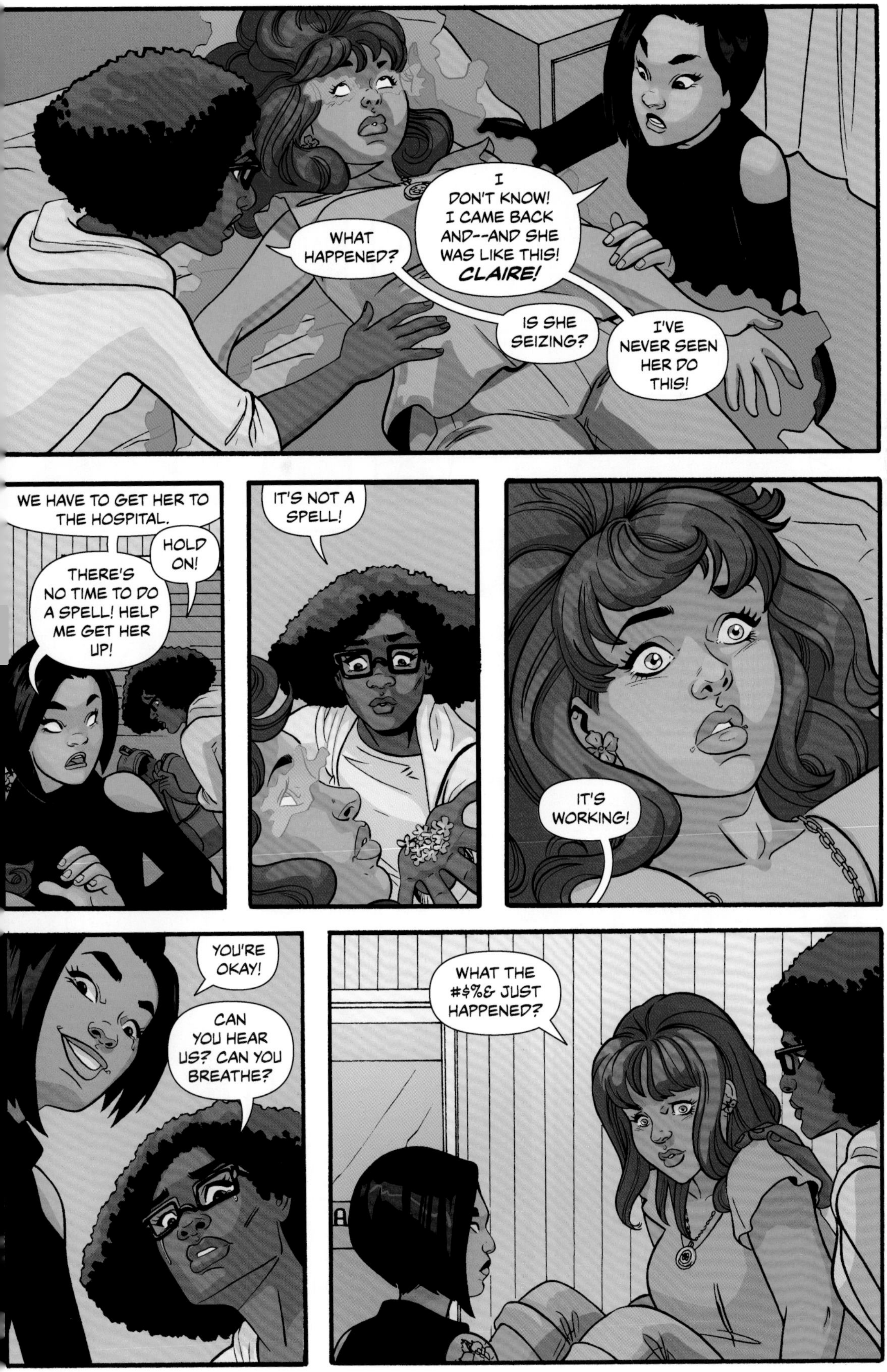
WHAT HAPPENED?
I DON'T KNOW! I CAME BACK AND--AND SHE WAS LIKE THIS! ***CLAIRE!***
IS SHE SEIZING?
I'VE NEVER SEEN HER DO THIS!
WE HAVE TO GET HER TO THE HOSPITAL.
HOLD ON!
THERE'S NO TIME TO DO A SPELL! HELP ME GET HER UP!
IT'S NOT A SPELL!
IT'S WORKING!
YOU'RE OKAY!
CAN YOU HEAR US? CAN YOU BREATHE?
WHAT THE #$%& JUST HAPPENED?

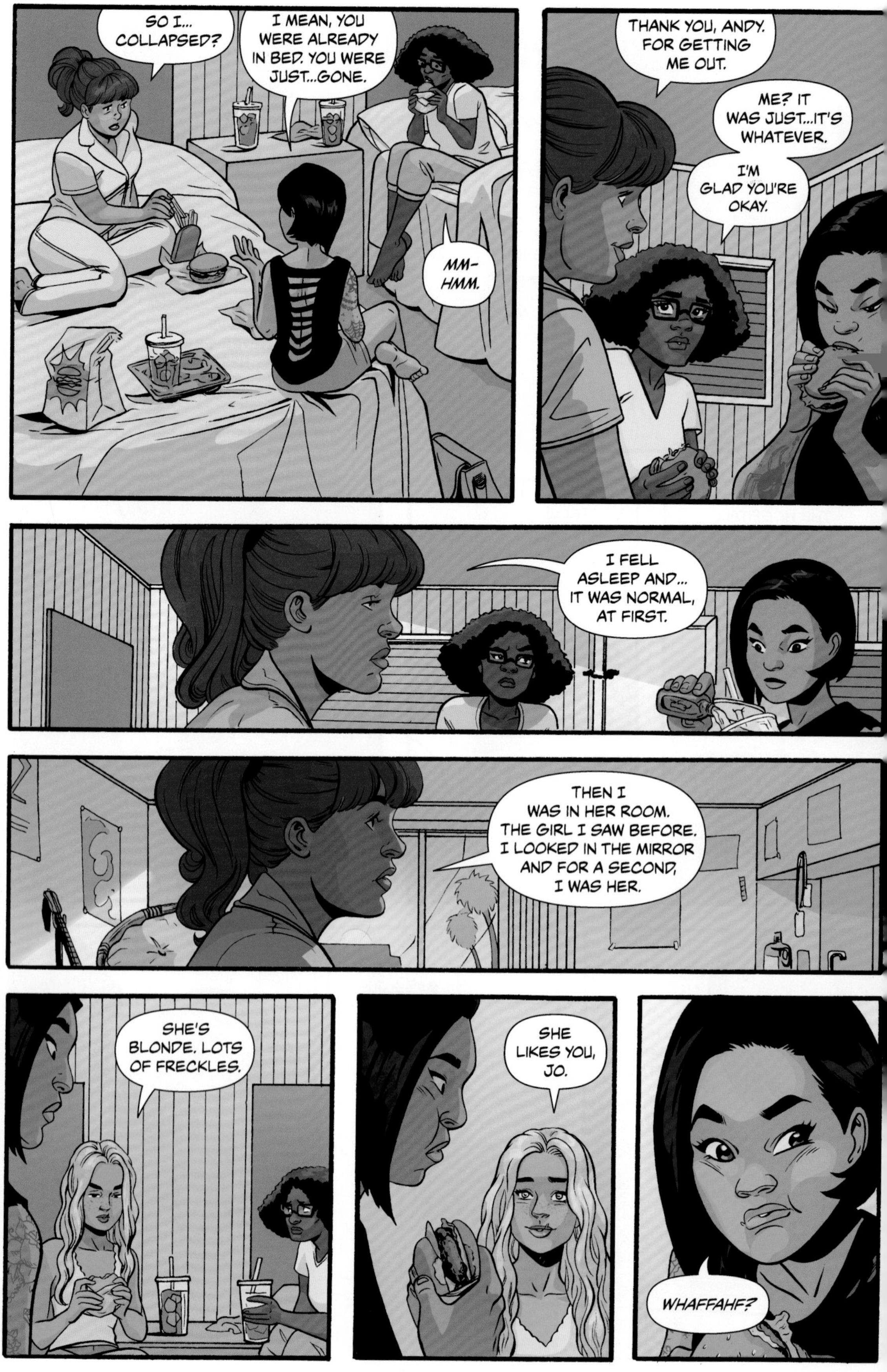
SO I... COLLAPSED?
I MEAN, YOU WERE ALREADY IN BED. YOU WERE JUST...GONE.
MM-HMM.
THANK YOU, ANDY. FOR GETTING ME OUT.
ME? IT WAS JUST...IT'S WHATEVER.
I'M GLAD YOU'RE OKAY.
I FELL ASLEEP AND... IT WAS NORMAL, AT FIRST.
THEN I WAS IN HER ROOM. THE GIRL I SAW BEFORE. I LOOKED IN THE MIRROR AND FOR A SECOND, I WAS HER.
SHE'S BLONDE. LOTS OF FRECKLES.
SHE LIKES YOU, JO.
WHAFFAHF?

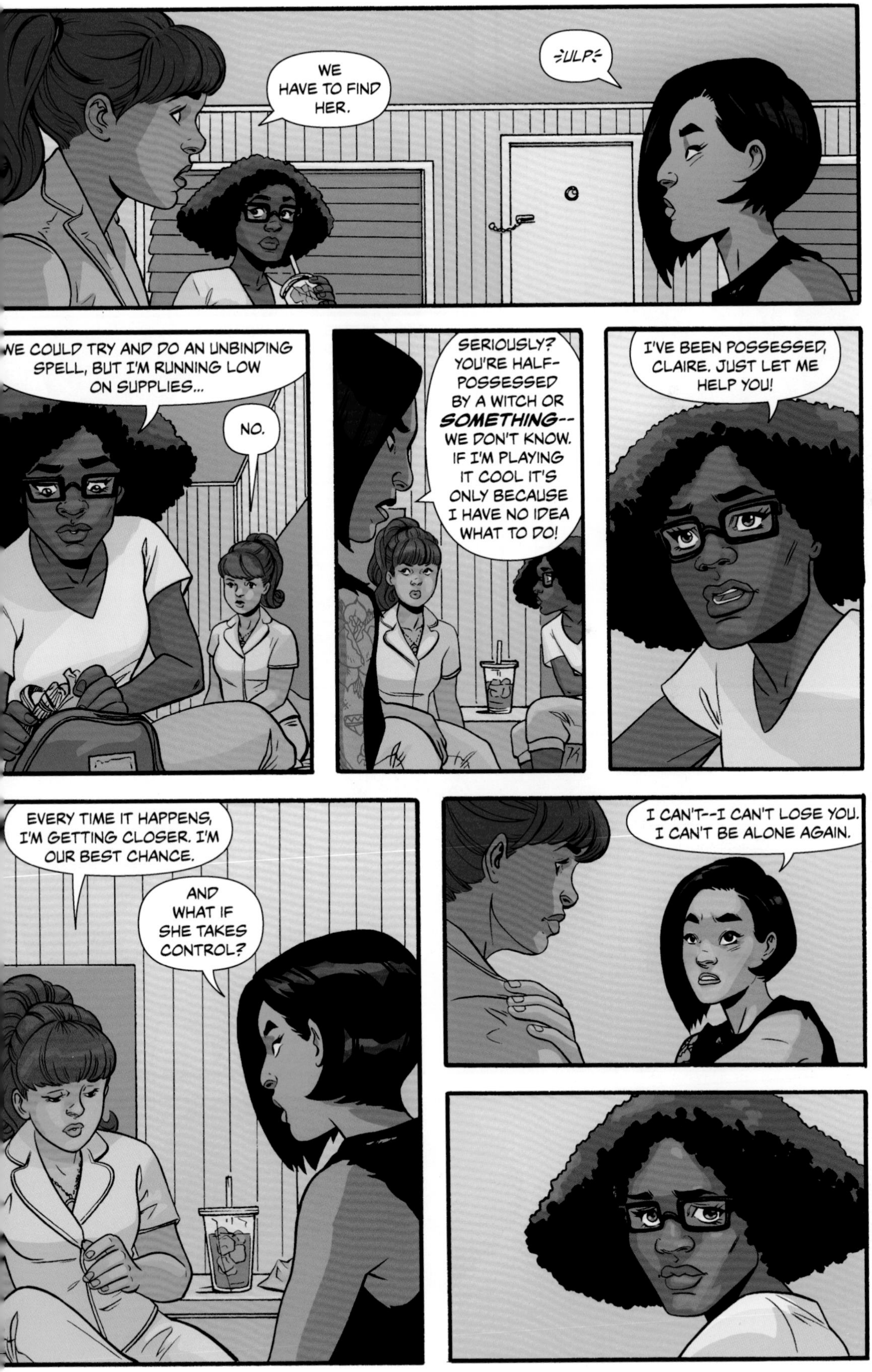
WE HAVE TO FIND HER.
≈ULP≈
WE COULD TRY AND DO AN UNBINDING SPELL, BUT I'M RUNNING LOW ON SUPPLIES...
NO.
SERIOUSLY? YOU'RE HALF-POSSESSED BY A WITCH OR SOMETHING-- WE DON'T KNOW. IF I'M PLAYING IT COOL IT'S ONLY BECAUSE I HAVE NO IDEA WHAT TO DO!
I'VE BEEN POSSESSED, CLAIRE. JUST LET ME HELP YOU!
EVERY TIME IT HAPPENS, I'M GETTING CLOSER. I'M OUR BEST CHANCE.
AND WHAT IF SHE TAKES CONTROL?
I CAN'T--I CAN'T LOSE YOU. I CAN'T BE ALONE AGAIN.

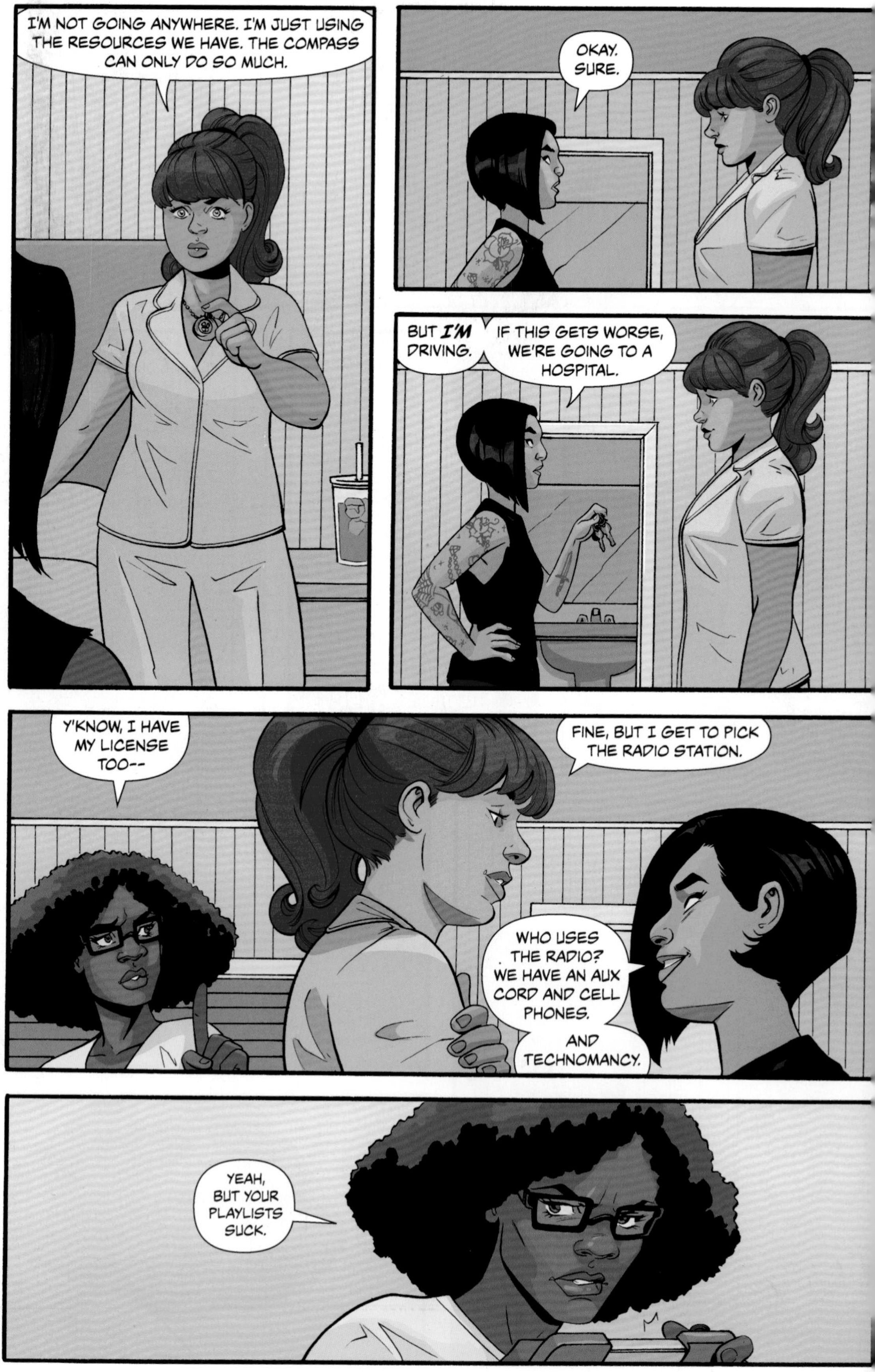
I'M NOT GOING ANYWHERE. I'M JUST USING THE RESOURCES WE HAVE. THE COMPASS CAN ONLY DO SO MUCH.
OKAY. SURE.
IF THIS GETS WORSE, WE'RE GOING TO A HOSPITAL.
BUT *I'M* DRIVING.
Y'KNOW, I HAVE MY LICENSE TOO--
FINE, BUT I GET TO PICK THE RADIO STATION.
WHO USES THE RADIO? WE HAVE AN AUX CORD AND CELL PHONES.
AND TECHNOMANCY.
YEAH, BUT YOUR PLAYLISTS SUCK.

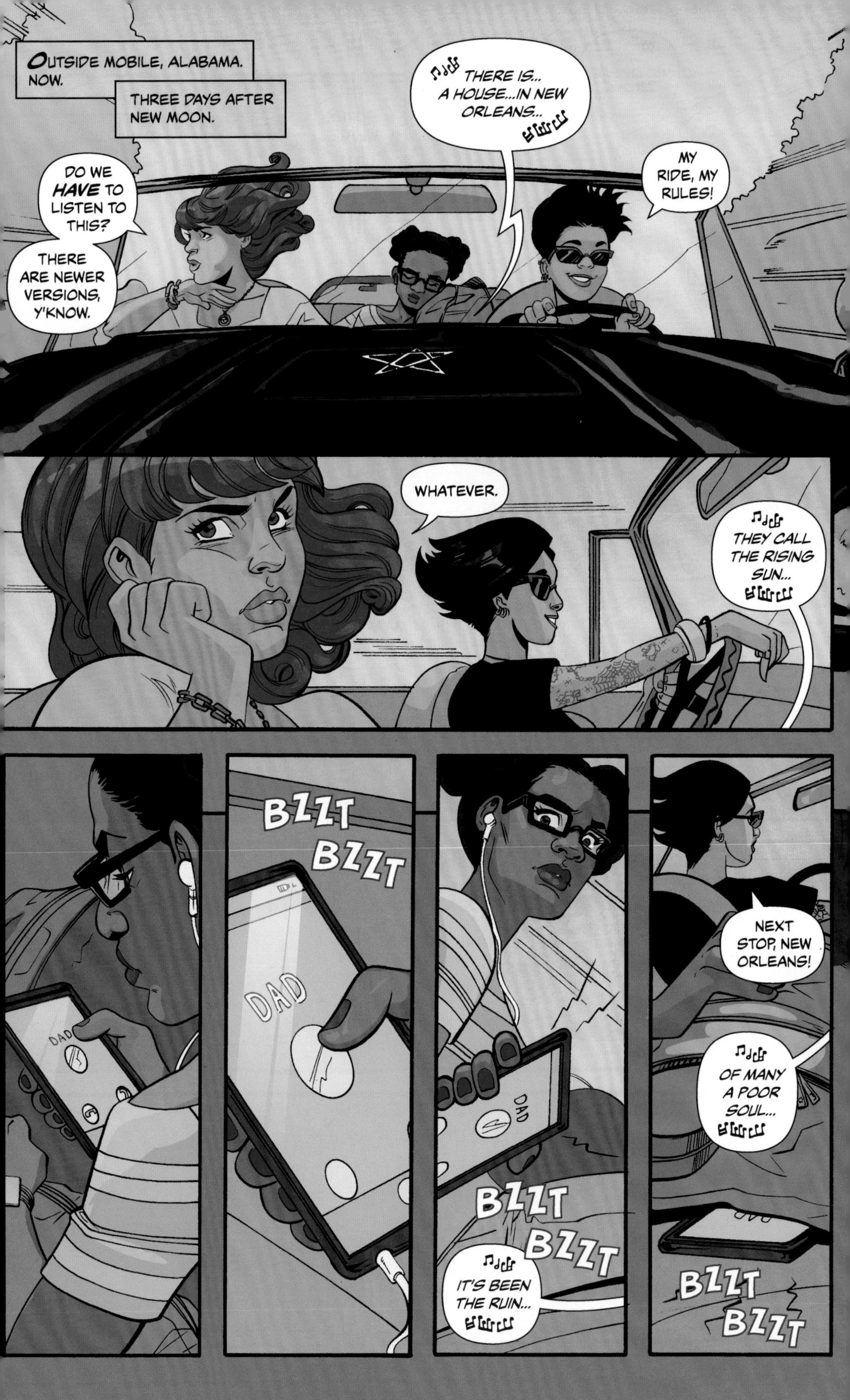
OUTSIDE MOBILE, ALABAMA. NOW.
THREE DAYS AFTER NEW MOON.
THERE IS... A HOUSE...IN NEW ORLEANS...
DO WE HAVE TO LISTEN TO THIS?
THERE ARE NEWER VERSIONS, Y'KNOW.
MY RIDE, MY RULES!
WHATEVER.
THEY CALL THE RISING SUN...
DAD
BZZT BZZT
DAD
DAD
BZZT BZZT
IT'S BEEN THE RUIN...
NEXT STOP, NEW ORLEANS!
OF MANY A POOR SOUL...
BZZT BZZT

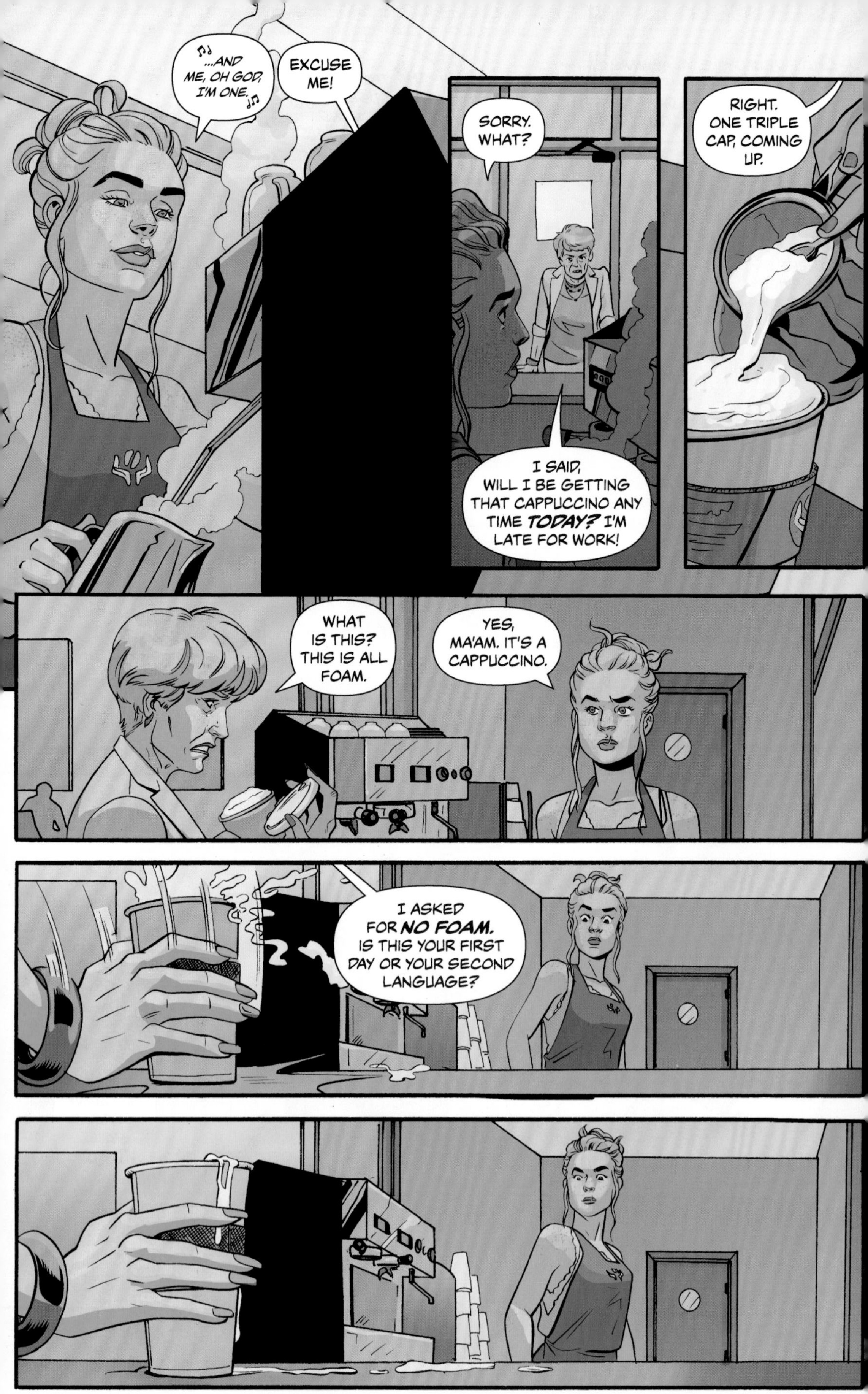
...AND ME, OH GOD, I'M ONE.
EXCUSE ME!
SORRY. WHAT?
I SAID, WILL I BE GETTING THAT CAPPUCCINO ANY TIME TODAY? I'M LATE FOR WORK!
RIGHT. ONE TRIPLE CAP, COMING UP.
WHAT IS THIS? THIS IS ALL FOAM.
YES, MA'AM. IT'S A CAPPUCCINO.
I ASKED FOR NO FOAM. IS THIS YOUR FIRST DAY OR YOUR SECOND LANGUAGE?

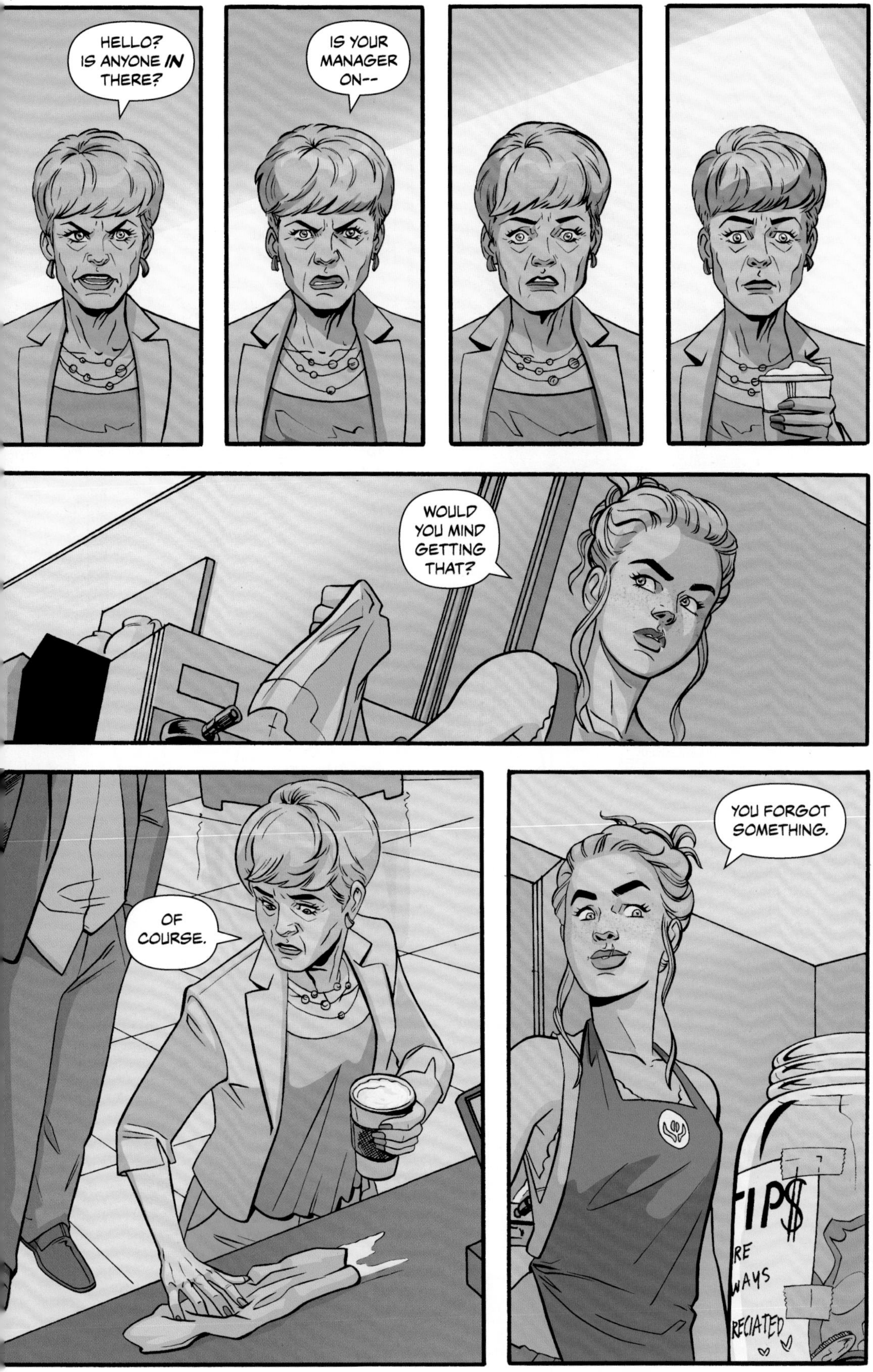
HELLO? IS ANYONE *IN* THERE?
IS YOUR MANAGER ON--
WOULD YOU MIND GETTING THAT?
OF COURSE.
YOU FORGOT SOMETHING.
TIP$
RE
WAYS
RECIATED

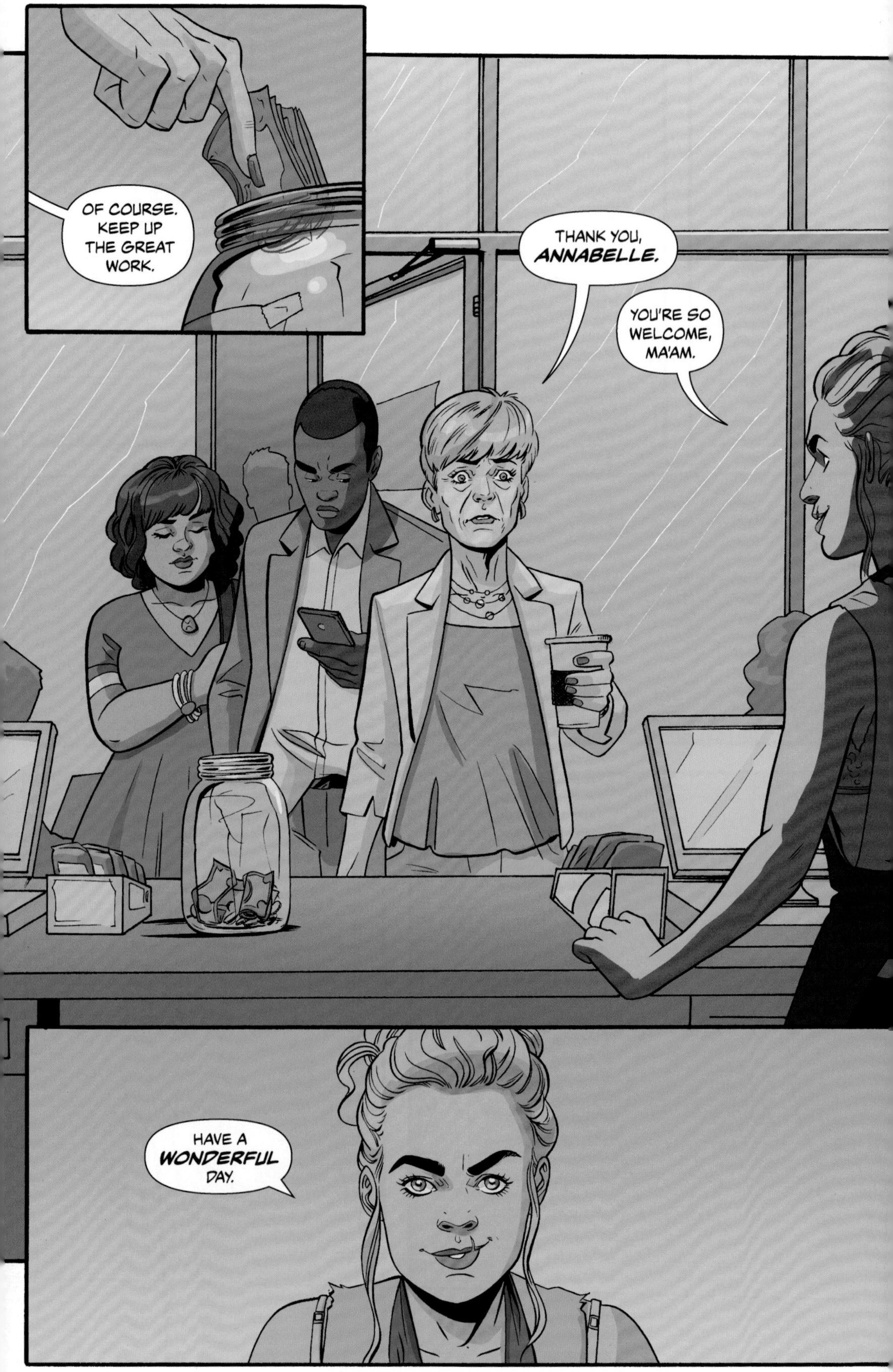
OF COURSE. KEEP UP THE GREAT WORK.
THANK YOU, ANNABELLE.
YOU'RE SO WELCOME, MA'AM.
HAVE A WONDERFUL DAY.

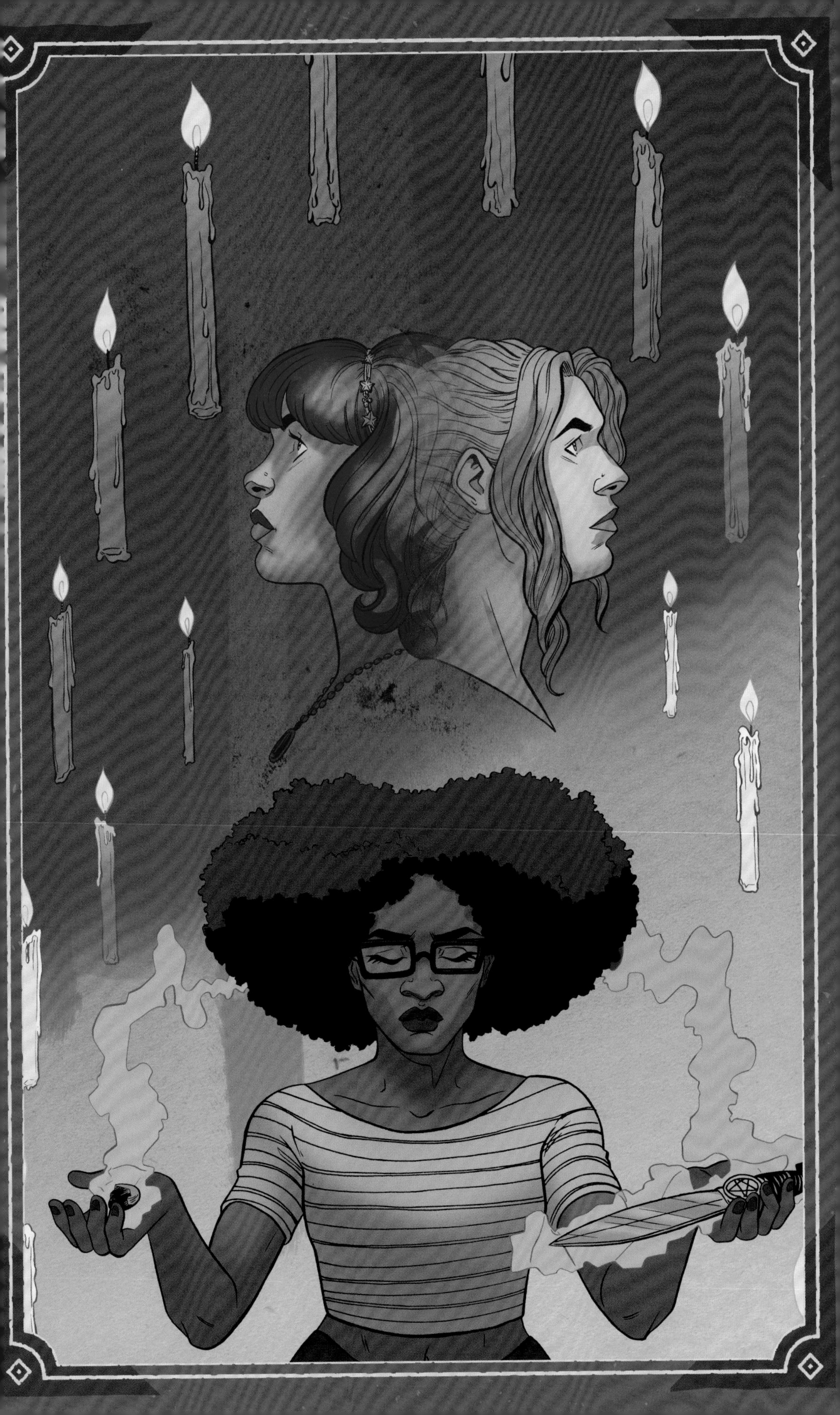

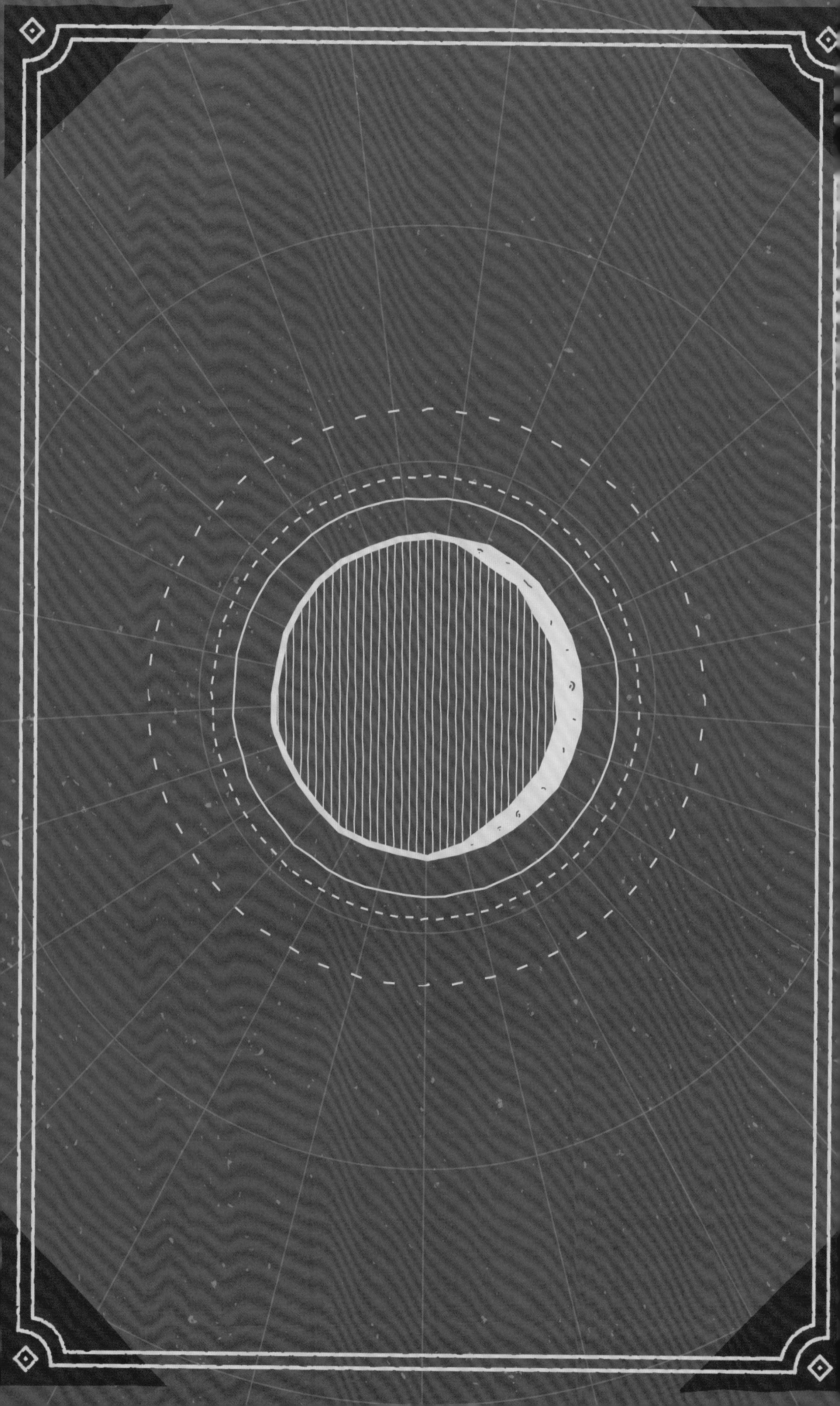

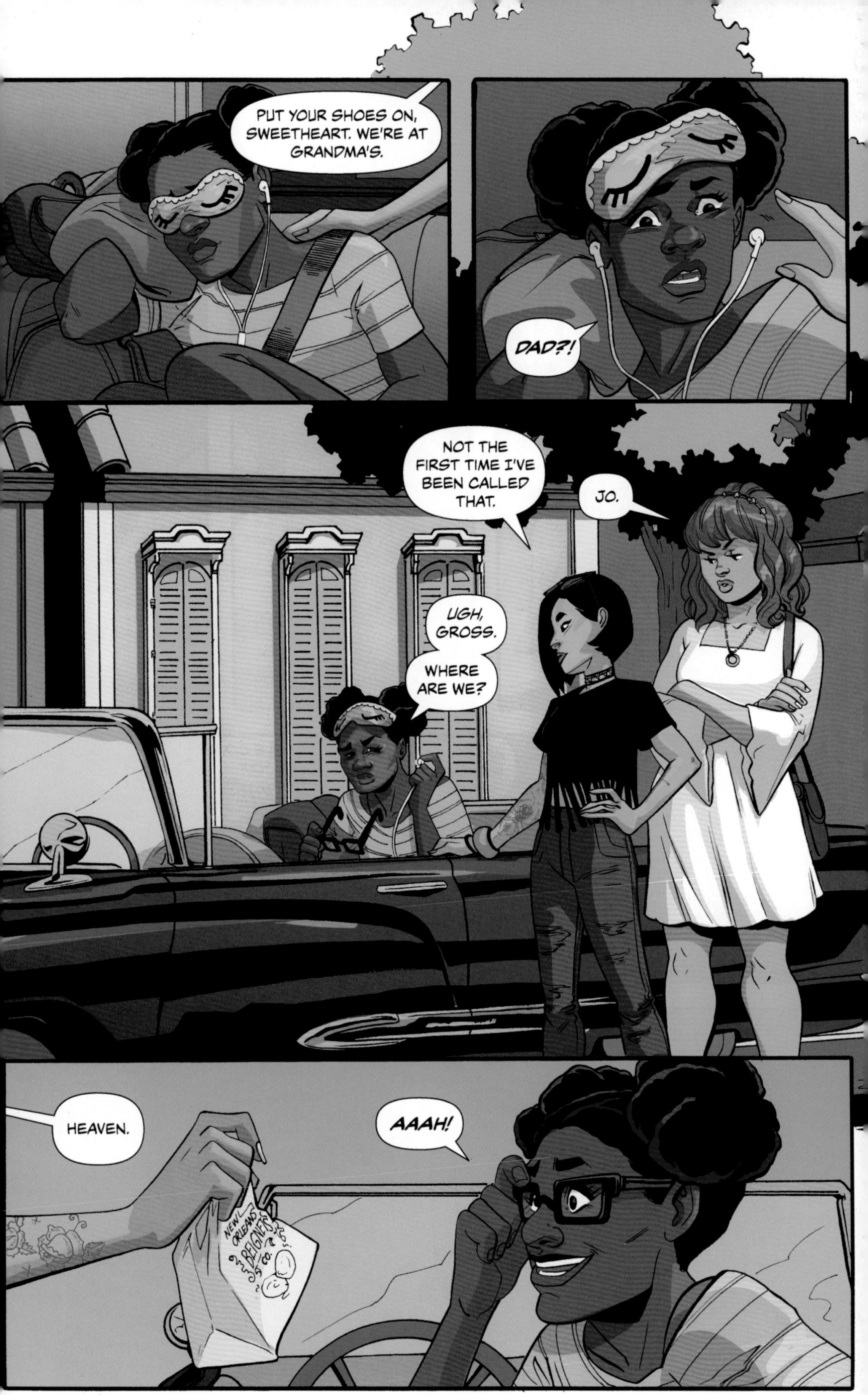
PUT YOUR SHOES ON, SWEETHEART. WE'RE AT GRANDMA'S.
DAD?!
NOT THE FIRST TIME I'VE BEEN CALLED THAT.
JO.
UGH, GROSS.
WHERE ARE WE?
HEAVEN.
AAAH!
NEW ORLEANS BEIGNETS CO.

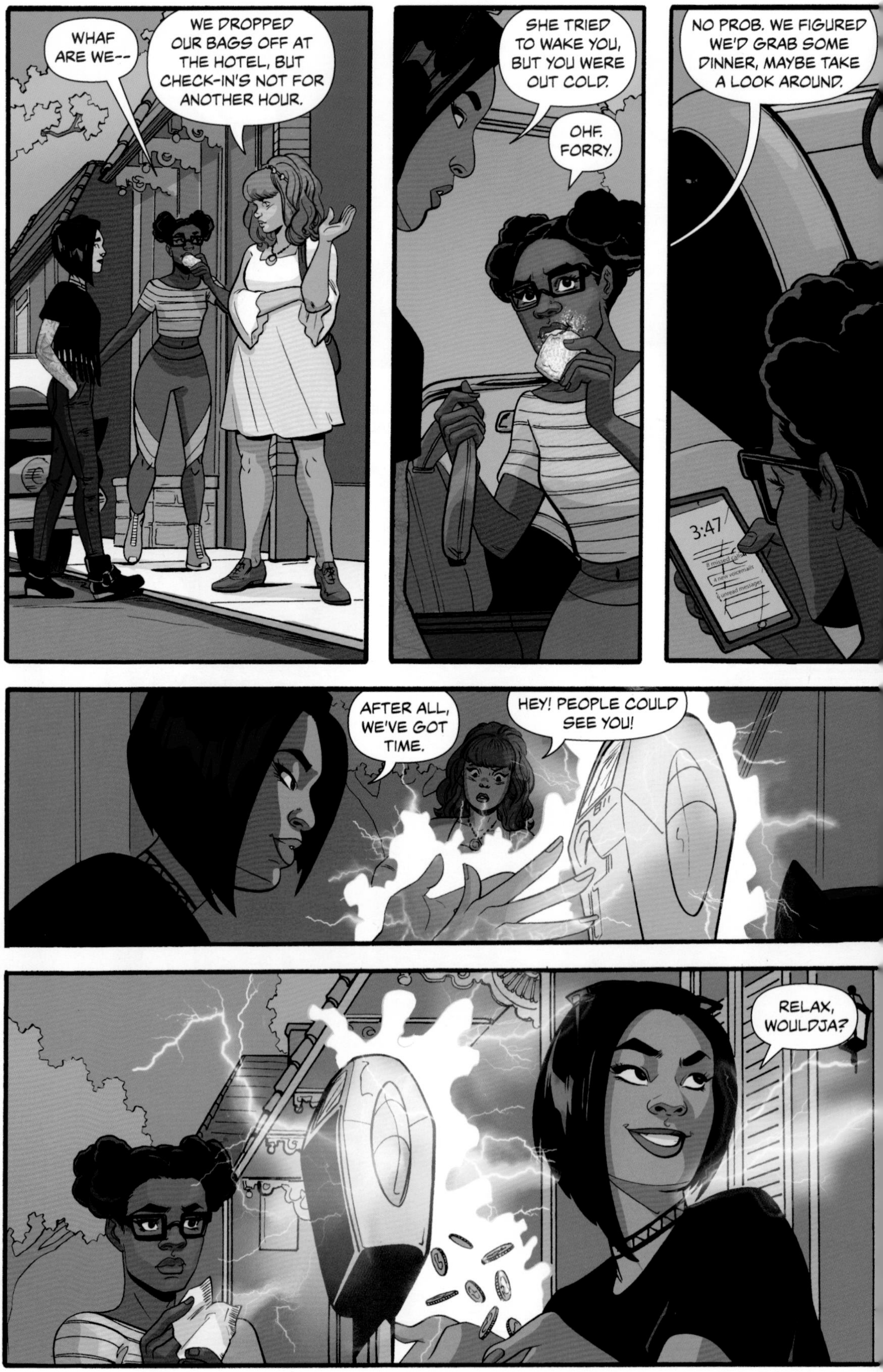
WHAF ARE WE--
WE DROPPED OUR BAGS OFF AT THE HOTEL, BUT CHECK-IN'S NOT FOR ANOTHER HOUR.
SHE TRIED TO WAKE YOU, BUT YOU WERE OUT COLD.
OHF. FORRY.
NO PROB. WE FIGURED WE'D GRAB SOME DINNER, MAYBE TAKE A LOOK AROUND.
3:47
8 missed calls
4 new voicemails
unread messages
AFTER ALL, WE'VE GOT TIME.
HEY! PEOPLE COULD SEE YOU!
RELAX, WOULDJA?

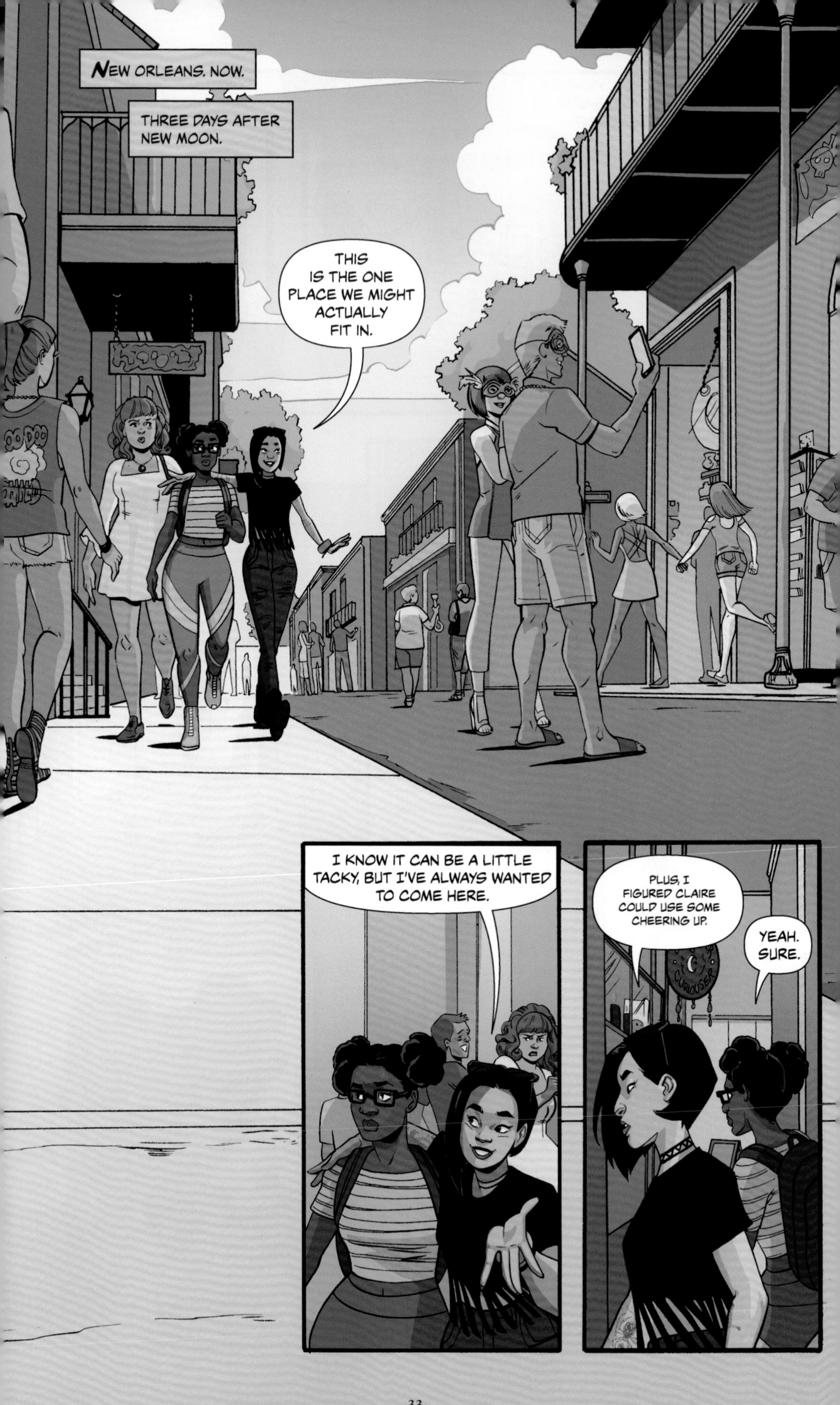
NEW ORLEANS. NOW.
THREE DAYS AFTER NEW MOON.
THIS IS THE ONE PLACE WE MIGHT ACTUALLY FIT IN.
I KNOW IT CAN BE A LITTLE TACKY, BUT I'VE ALWAYS WANTED TO COME HERE.
PLUS, I FIGURED CLAIRE COULD USE SOME CHEERING UP.
YEAH. SURE.
CURIOUSER

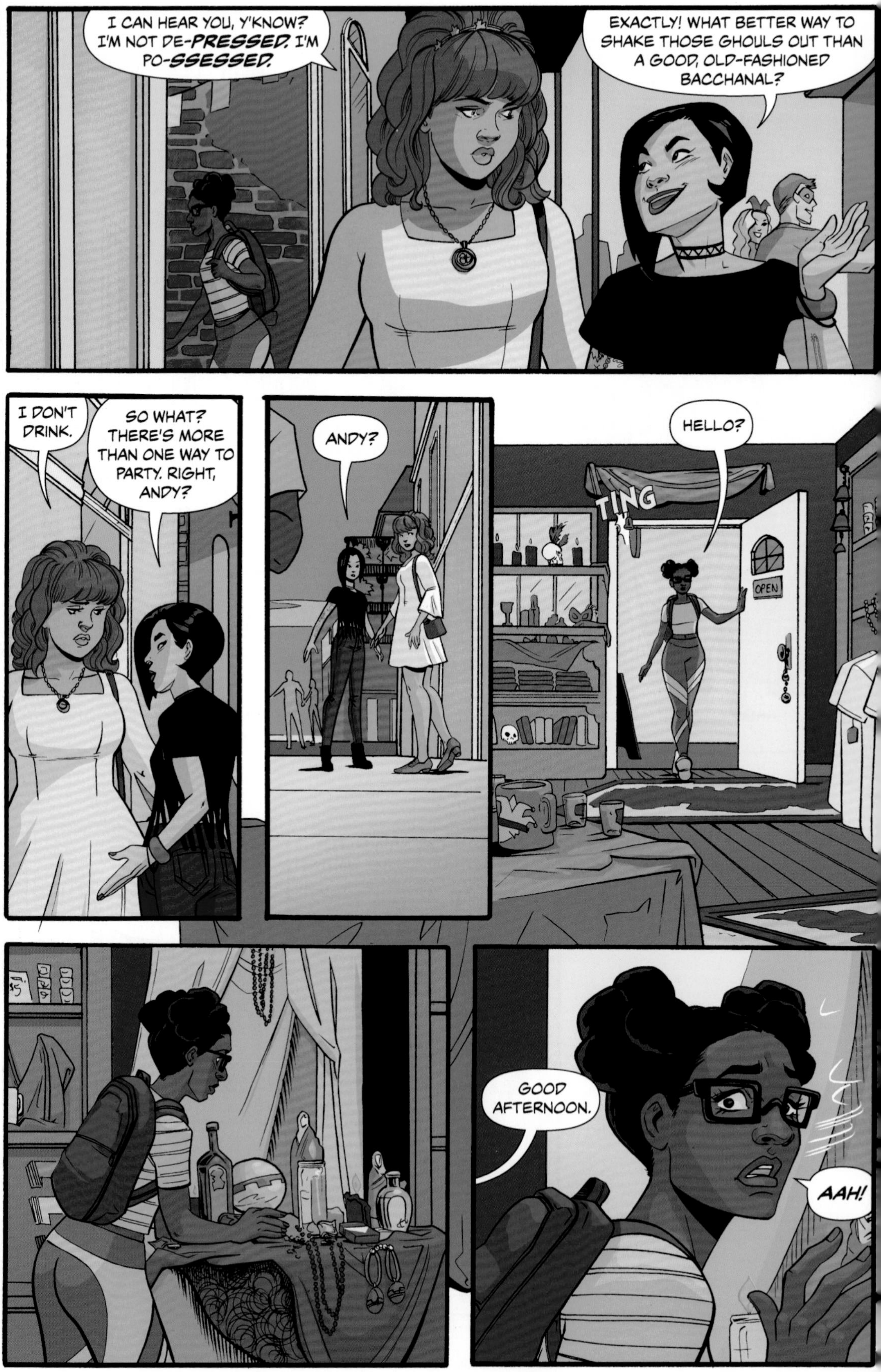
I CAN HEAR YOU, Y'KNOW? I'M NOT DE-**PRESSED.** I'M PO-**SSESSED.**
EXACTLY! WHAT BETTER WAY TO SHAKE THOSE GHOULS OUT THAN A GOOD, OLD-FASHIONED BACCHANAL?
I DON'T DRINK.
SO WHAT? THERE'S MORE THAN ONE WAY TO PARTY. RIGHT, ANDY?
ANDY?
HELLO?
TING
OPEN
GOOD AFTERNOON.
AAH!

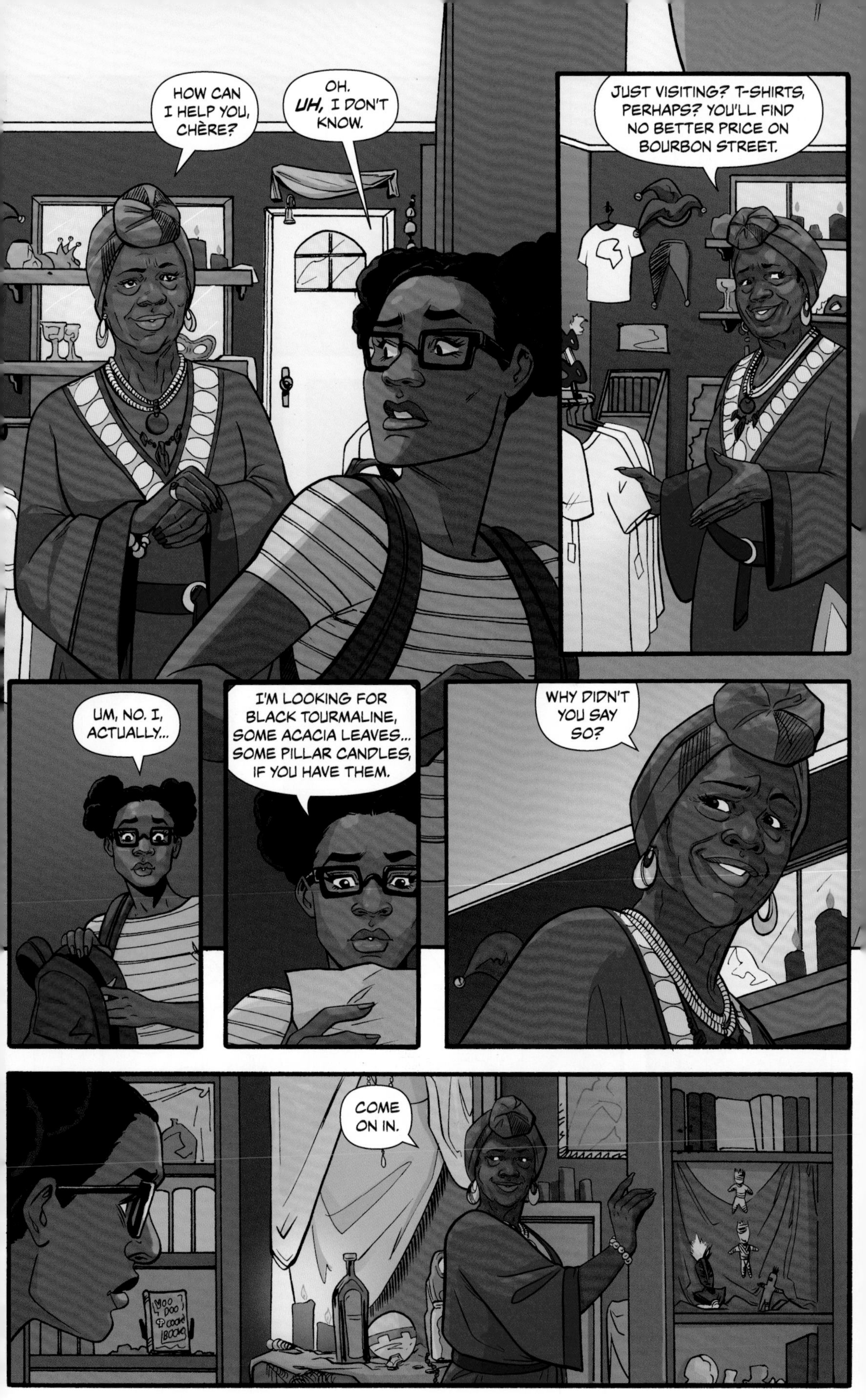
HOW CAN I HELP YOU, CHÈRE?
OH. UH, I DON'T KNOW.
JUST VISITING? T-SHIRTS, PERHAPS? YOU'LL FIND NO BETTER PRICE ON BOURBON STREET.
UM, NO. I, ACTUALLY...
I'M LOOKING FOR BLACK TOURMALINE, SOME ACACIA LEAVES... SOME PILLAR CANDLES, IF YOU HAVE THEM.
WHY DIDN'T YOU SAY SO?
COME ON IN.

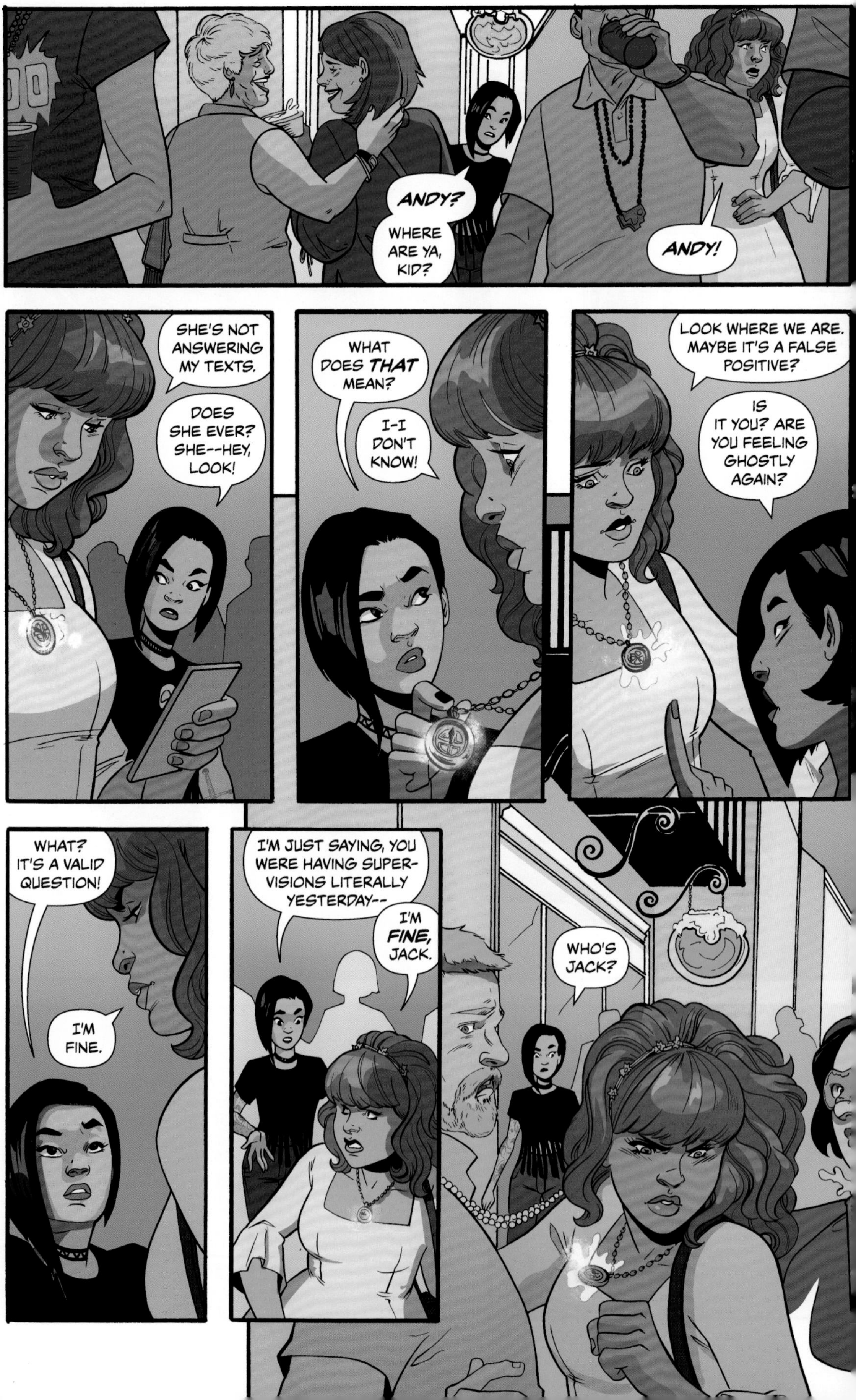
ANDY?
WHERE ARE YA, KID?
ANDY!
SHE'S NOT ANSWERING MY TEXTS.
DOES SHE EVER? SHE--HEY, LOOK!
WHAT DOES THAT MEAN?
I-I DON'T KNOW!
LOOK WHERE WE ARE. MAYBE IT'S A FALSE POSITIVE?
IS IT YOU? ARE YOU FEELING GHOSTLY AGAIN?
WHAT? IT'S A VALID QUESTION!
I'M FINE.
I'M JUST SAYING, YOU WERE HAVING SUPER-VISIONS LITERALLY YESTERDAY--
I'M FINE, JACK.
WHO'S JACK?

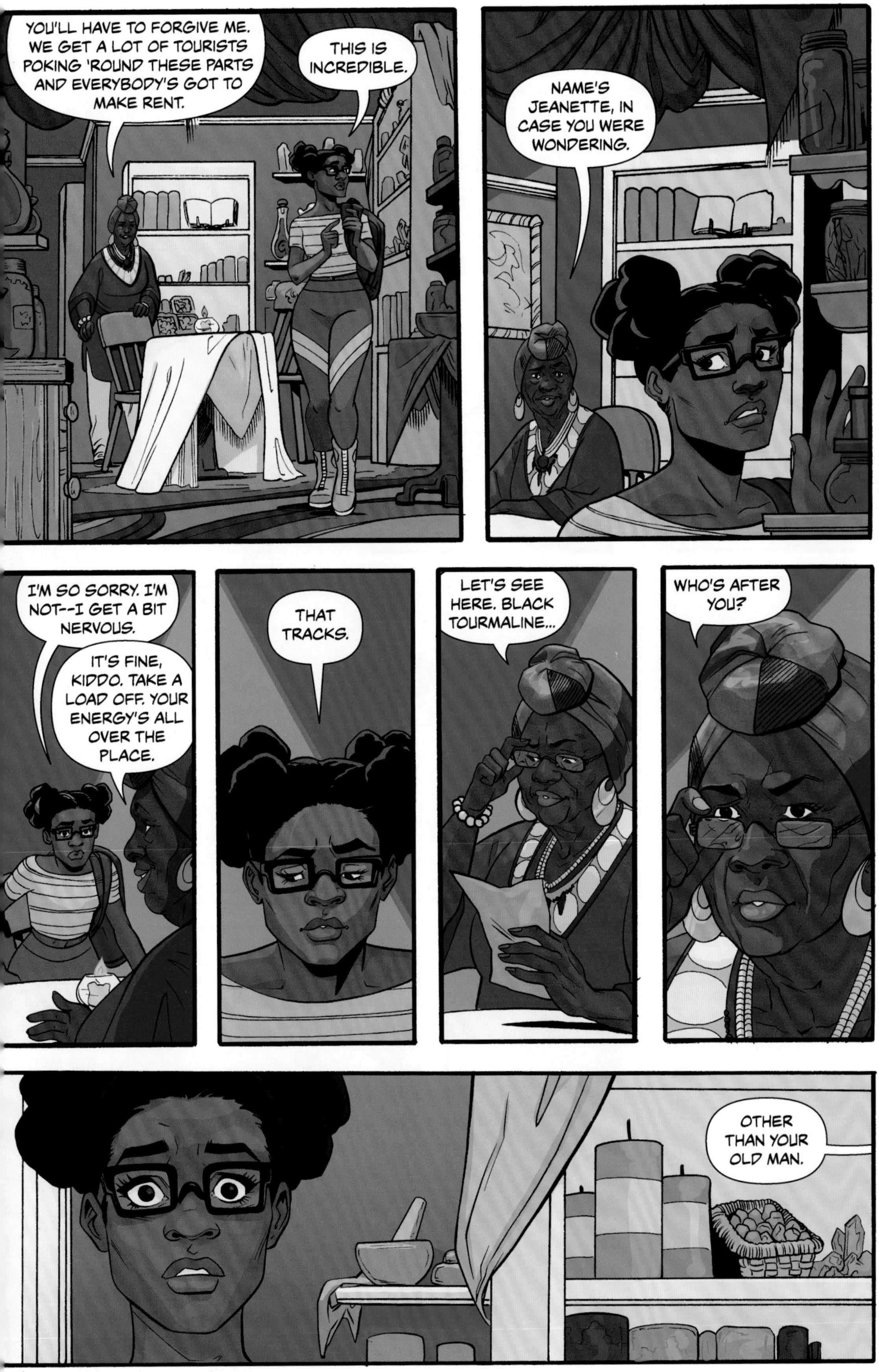
YOU'LL HAVE TO FORGIVE ME. WE GET A LOT OF TOURISTS POKING 'ROUND THESE PARTS AND EVERYBODY'S GOT TO MAKE RENT.
THIS IS INCREDIBLE.
NAME'S JEANETTE, IN CASE YOU WERE WONDERING.
I'M SO SORRY. I'M NOT--I GET A BIT NERVOUS.
IT'S FINE, KIDDO. TAKE A LOAD OFF. YOUR ENERGY'S ALL OVER THE PLACE.
THAT TRACKS.
LET'S SEE HERE. BLACK TOURMALINE...
WHO'S AFTER YOU?
OTHER THAN YOUR OLD MAN.

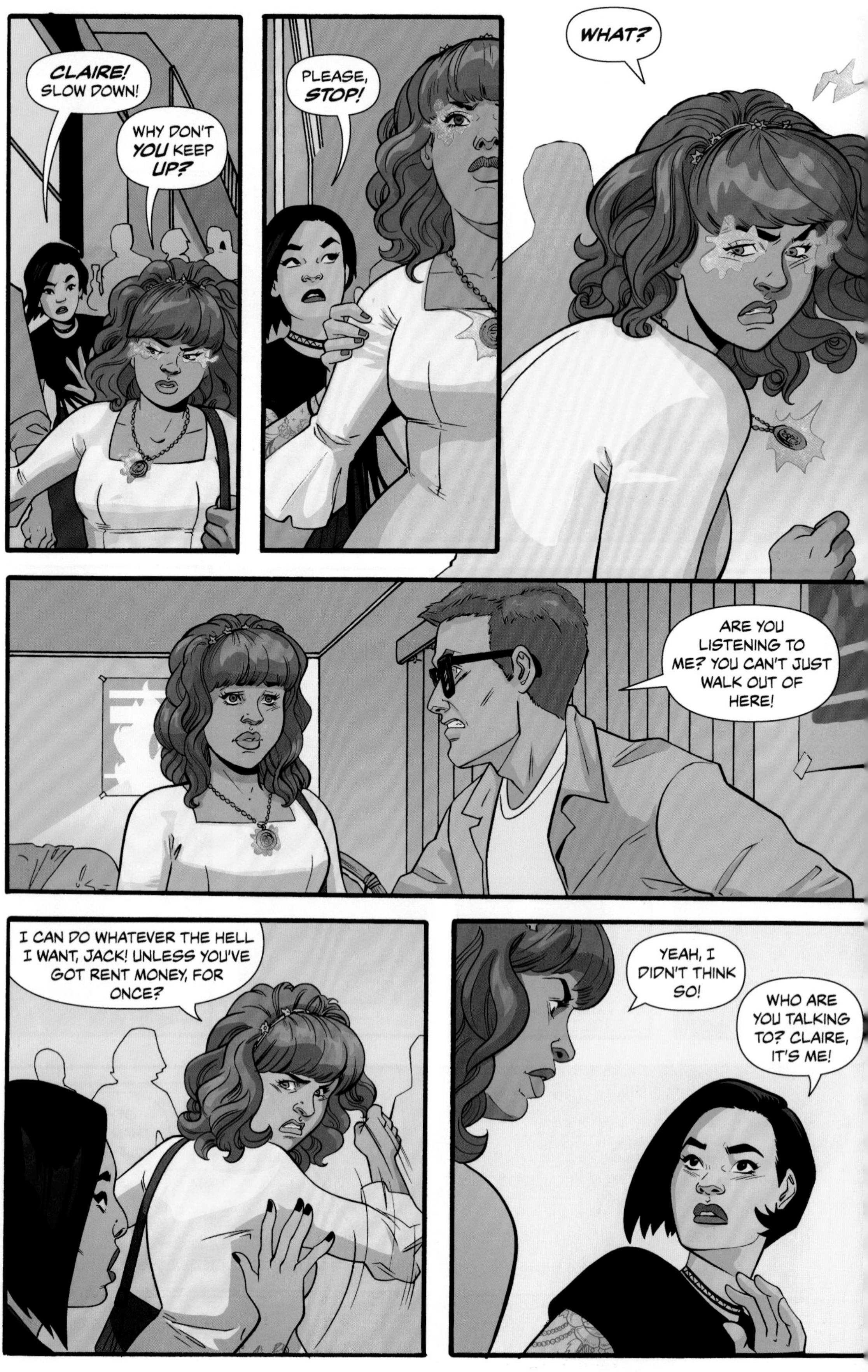
CLAIRE! SLOW DOWN!
WHY DON'T YOU KEEP UP?
PLEASE, STOP!
WHAT?
ARE YOU LISTENING TO ME? YOU CAN'T JUST WALK OUT OF HERE!
I CAN DO WHATEVER THE HELL I WANT, JACK! UNLESS YOU'VE GOT RENT MONEY, FOR ONCE?
YEAH, I DIDN'T THINK SO!
WHO ARE YOU TALKING TO? CLAIRE, IT'S ME!

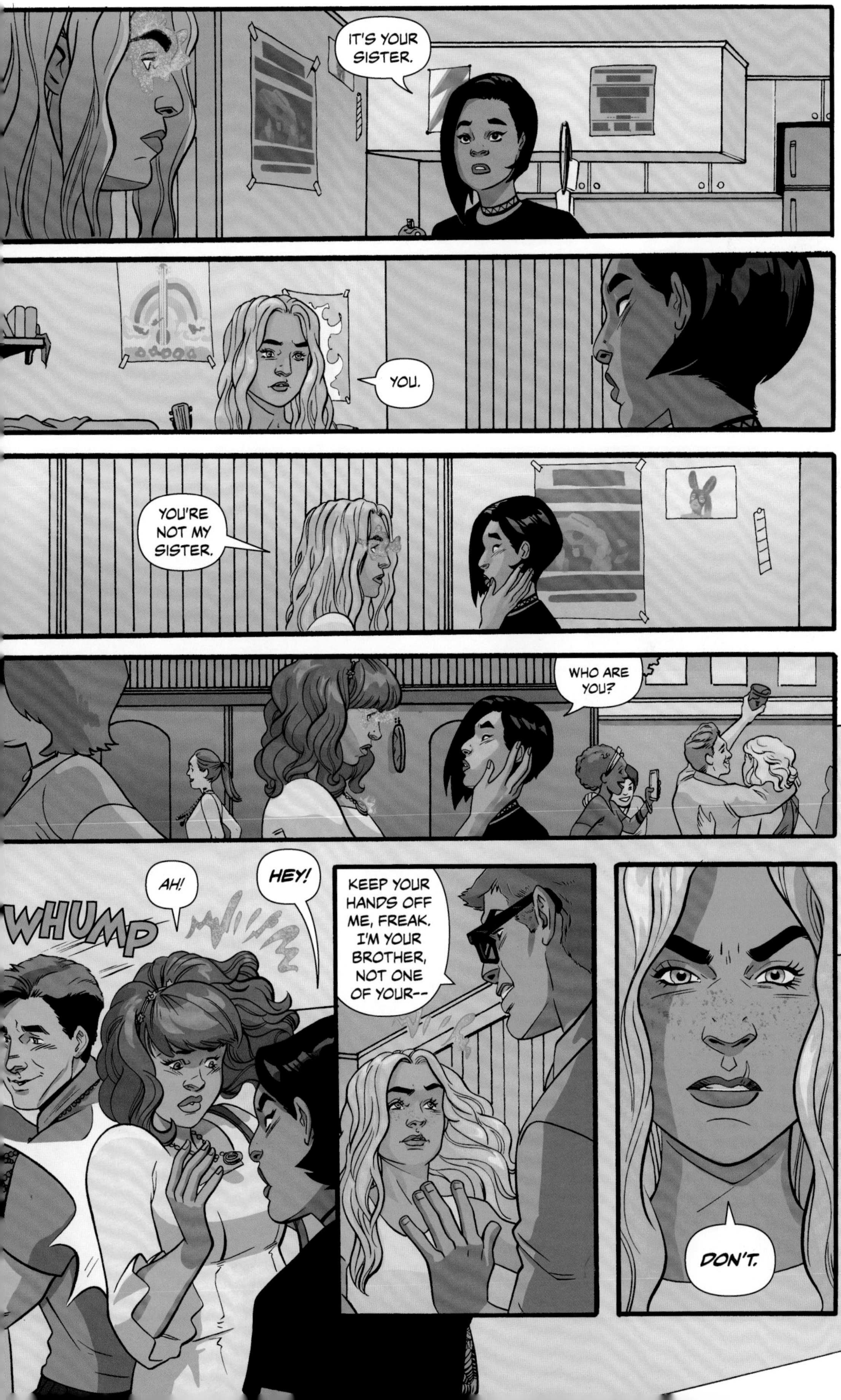
IT'S YOUR SISTER.
YOU.
YOU'RE NOT MY SISTER.
WHO ARE YOU?
WHUMP
AH!
HEY!
KEEP YOUR HANDS OFF ME, FREAK. I'M YOUR BROTHER, NOT ONE OF YOUR--
DON'T.

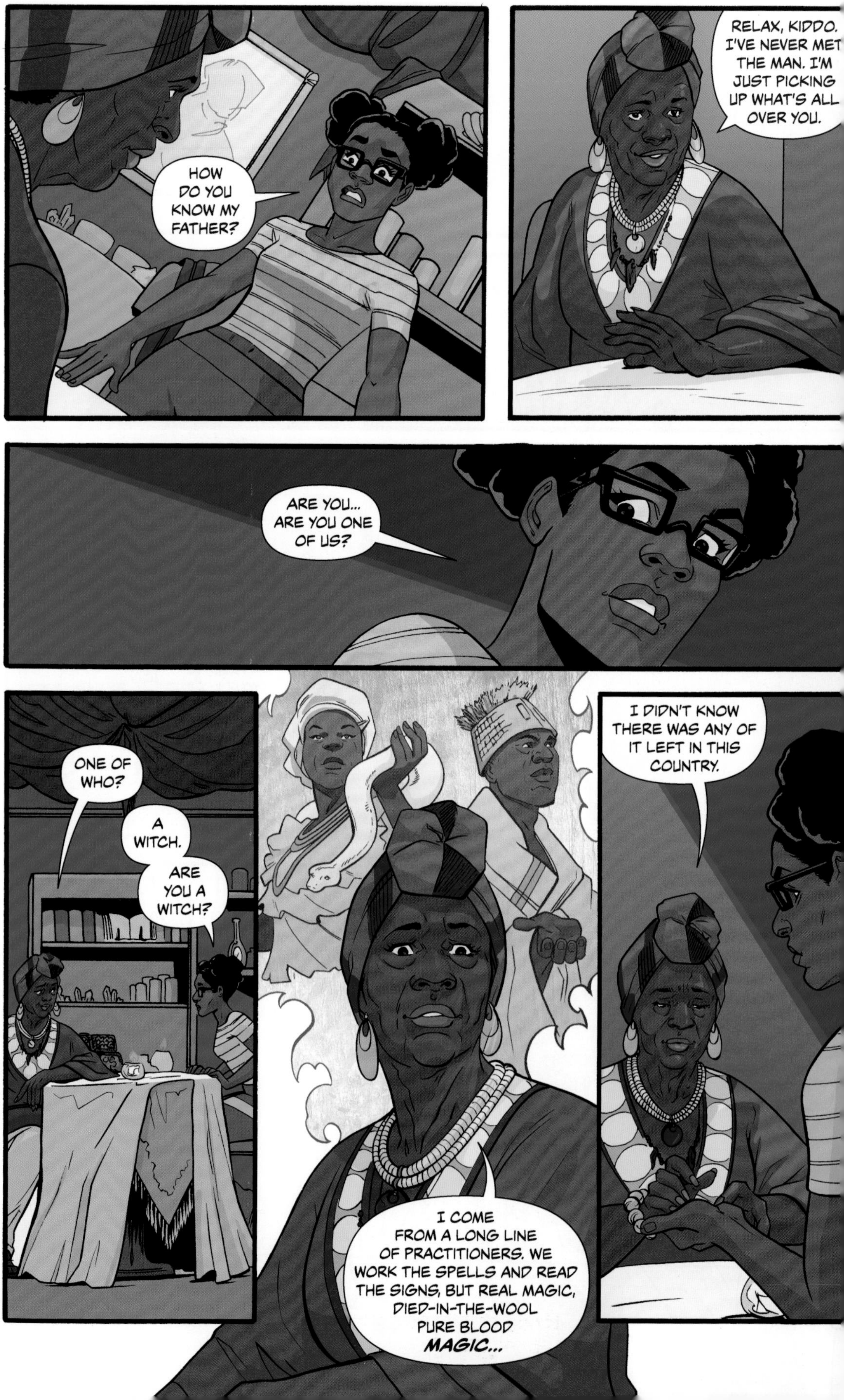
HOW DO YOU KNOW MY FATHER?
RELAX, KIDDO. I'VE NEVER MET THE MAN. I'M JUST PICKING UP WHAT'S ALL OVER YOU.
ARE YOU... ARE YOU ONE OF US?
ONE OF WHO?
A WITCH.
ARE YOU A WITCH?
I COME FROM A LONG LINE OF PRACTITIONERS. WE WORK THE SPELLS AND READ THE SIGNS, BUT REAL MAGIC, DIED-IN-THE-WOOL PURE BLOOD MAGIC...
I DIDN'T KNOW THERE WAS ANY OF IT LEFT IN THIS COUNTRY.

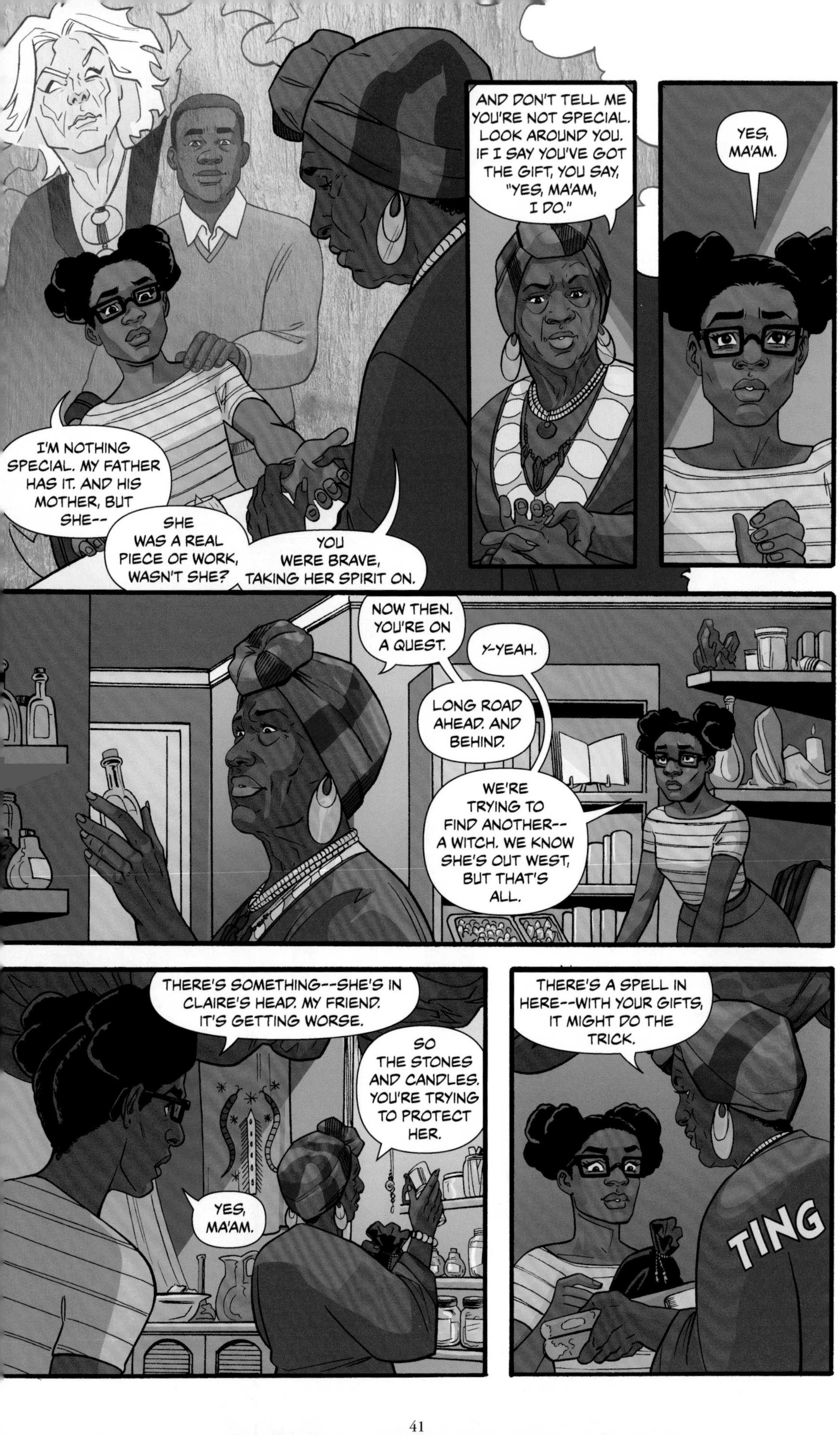

AND DON'T TELL ME YOU'RE NOT SPECIAL. LOOK AROUND YOU. IF I SAY YOU'VE GOT THE GIFT, YOU SAY, "YES, MA'AM, I DO."
YES, MA'AM.
I'M NOTHING SPECIAL. MY FATHER HAS IT. AND HIS MOTHER, BUT SHE--
SHE WAS A REAL PIECE OF WORK, WASN'T SHE?
YOU WERE BRAVE, TAKING HER SPIRIT ON.
NOW THEN. YOU'RE ON A QUEST.
Y-YEAH.
LONG ROAD AHEAD. AND BEHIND.
WE'RE TRYING TO FIND ANOTHER-- A WITCH. WE KNOW SHE'S OUT WEST, BUT THAT'S ALL.
THERE'S SOMETHING--SHE'S IN CLAIRE'S HEAD. MY FRIEND. IT'S GETTING WORSE.
SO THE STONES AND CANDLES. YOU'RE TRYING TO PROTECT HER.
YES, MA'AM.
THERE'S A SPELL IN HERE--WITH YOUR GIFTS, IT MIGHT DO THE TRICK.
TING

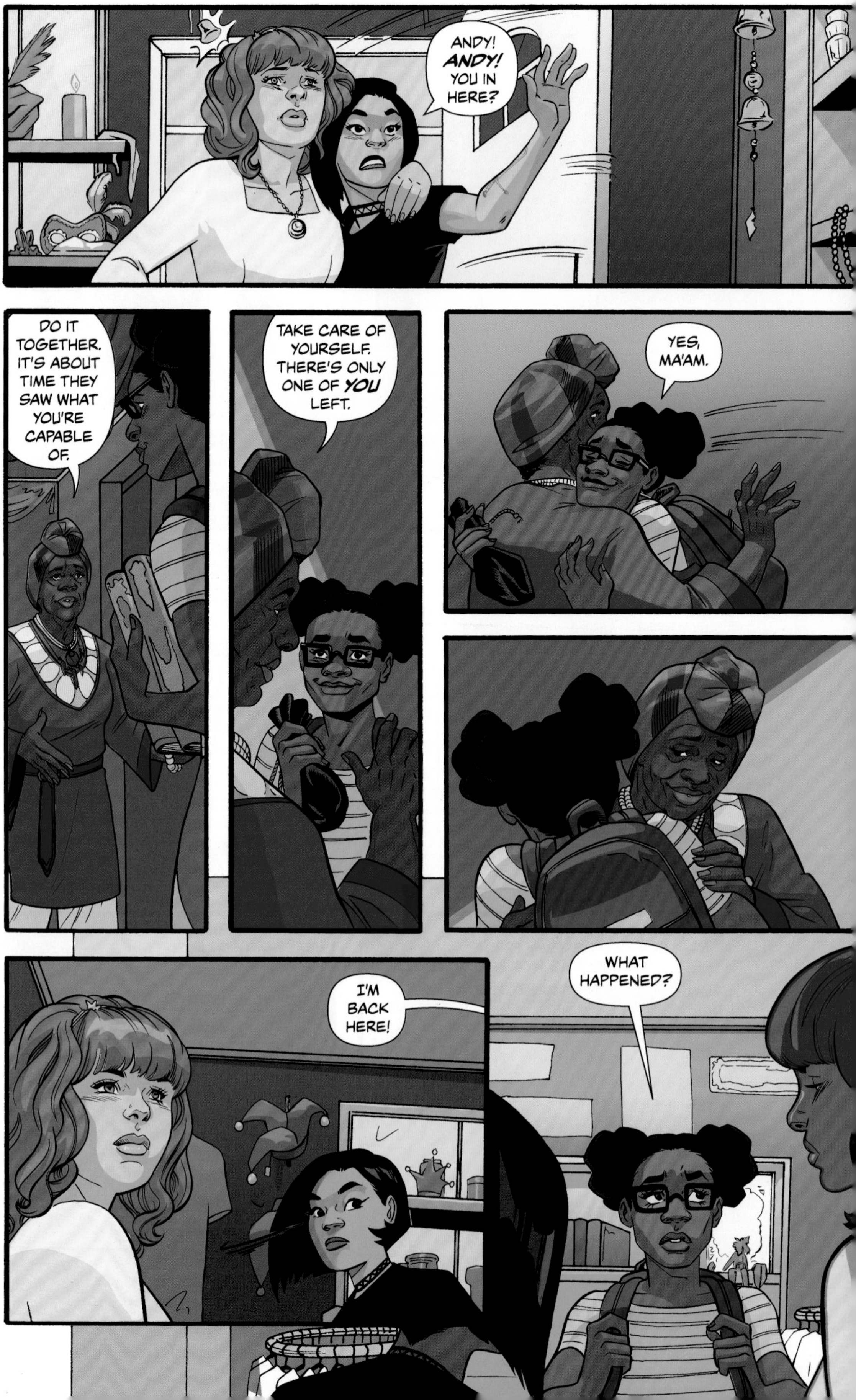
ANDY!
ANDY!
YOU IN
HERE?
DO IT
TOGETHER.
IT'S ABOUT
TIME THEY
SAW WHAT
YOU'RE
CAPABLE
OF.
TAKE CARE OF
YOURSELF.
THERE'S ONLY
ONE OF YOU
LEFT.
YES,
MA'AM.
I'M
BACK
HERE!
WHAT
HAPPENED?

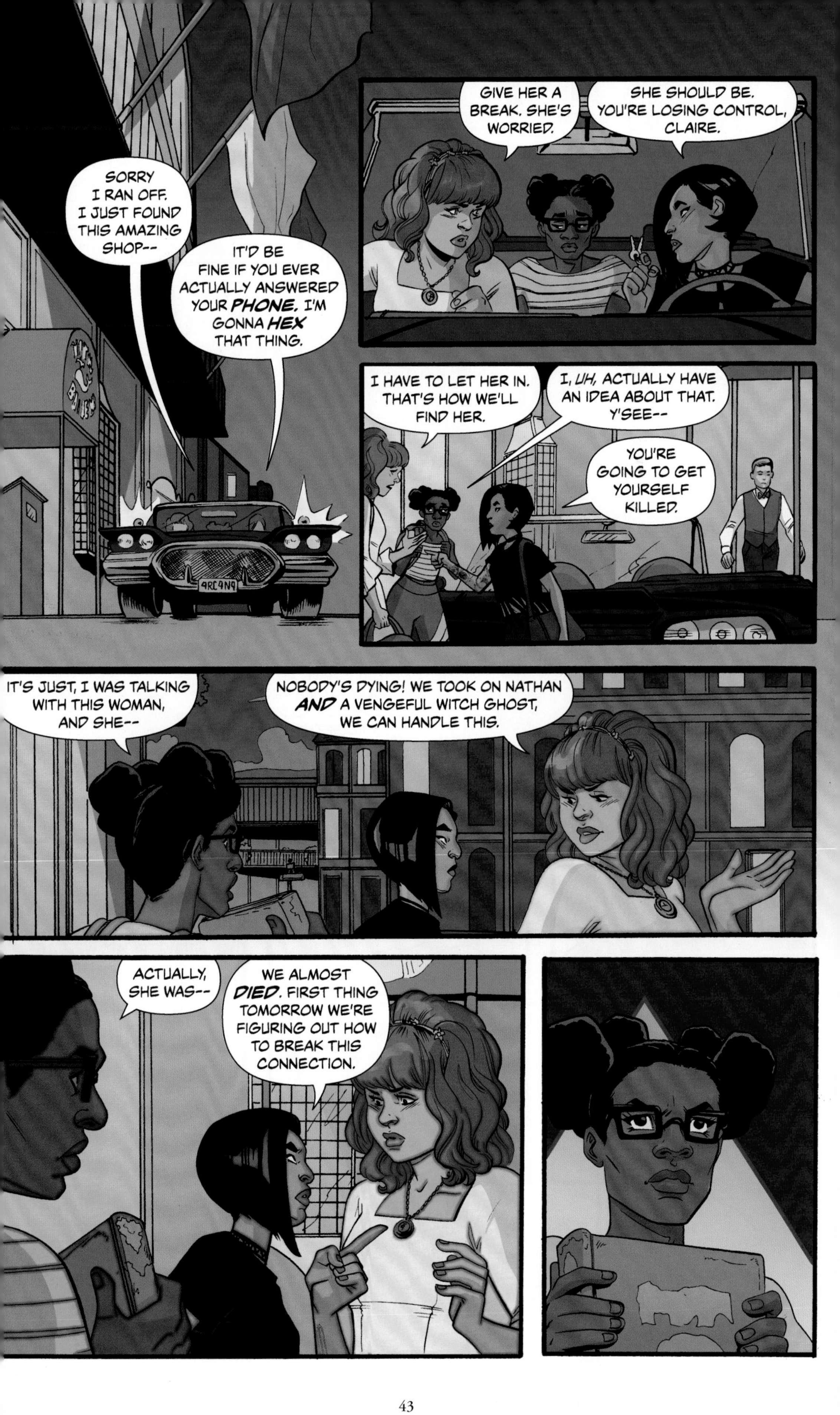
SORRY I RAN OFF. I JUST FOUND THIS AMAZING SHOP--
IT'D BE FINE IF YOU EVER ACTUALLY ANSWERED YOUR PHONE. I'M GONNA HEX THAT THING.
GIVE HER A BREAK. SHE'S WORRIED.
SHE SHOULD BE. YOU'RE LOSING CONTROL, CLAIRE.
I HAVE TO LET HER IN. THAT'S HOW WE'LL FIND HER.
I, UH, ACTUALLY HAVE AN IDEA ABOUT THAT. Y'SEE--
YOU'RE GOING TO GET YOURSELF KILLED.
IT'S JUST, I WAS TALKING WITH THIS WOMAN, AND SHE--
NOBODY'S DYING! WE TOOK ON NATHAN AND A VENGEFUL WITCH GHOST, WE CAN HANDLE THIS.
ACTUALLY, SHE WAS--
WE ALMOST DIED. FIRST THING TOMORROW WE'RE FIGURING OUT HOW TO BREAK THIS CONNECTION.

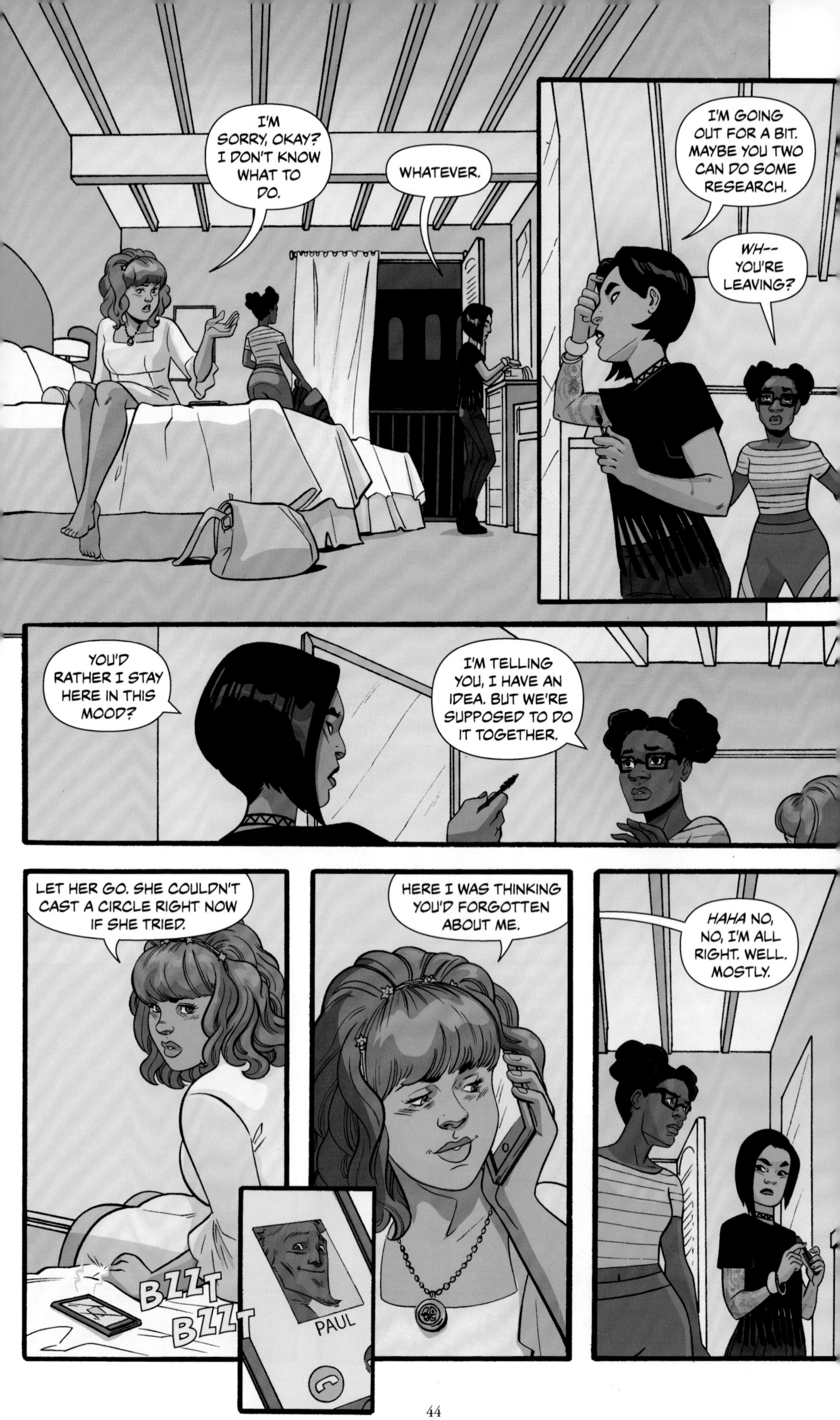
I'M SORRY, OKAY? I DON'T KNOW WHAT TO DO.
WHATEVER.
I'M GOING OUT FOR A BIT. MAYBE YOU TWO CAN DO SOME RESEARCH.
WH-- YOU'RE LEAVING?
YOU'D RATHER I STAY HERE IN THIS MOOD?
I'M TELLING YOU, I HAVE AN IDEA. BUT WE'RE SUPPOSED TO DO IT TOGETHER.
LET HER GO. SHE COULDN'T CAST A CIRCLE RIGHT NOW IF SHE TRIED.
BZZT BZZT
PAUL
HERE I WAS THINKING YOU'D FORGOTTEN ABOUT ME.
HAHA NO, NO, I'M ALL RIGHT. WELL. MOSTLY.

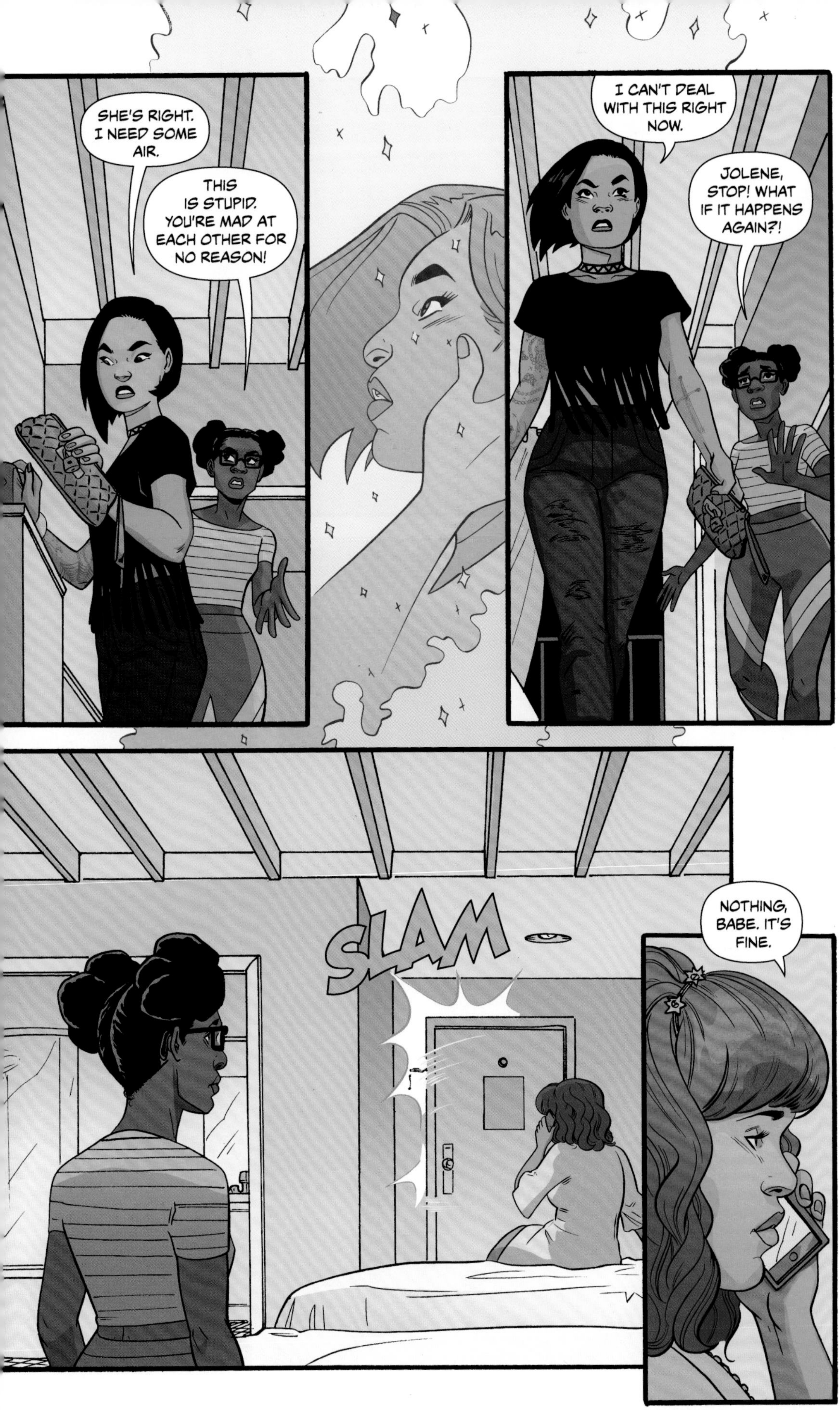
SHE'S RIGHT. I NEED SOME AIR.
THIS IS STUPID. YOU'RE MAD AT EACH OTHER FOR NO REASON!
I CAN'T DEAL WITH THIS RIGHT NOW.
JOLENE, STOP! WHAT IF IT HAPPENS AGAIN?!
SLAM
NOTHING, BABE. IT'S FINE.

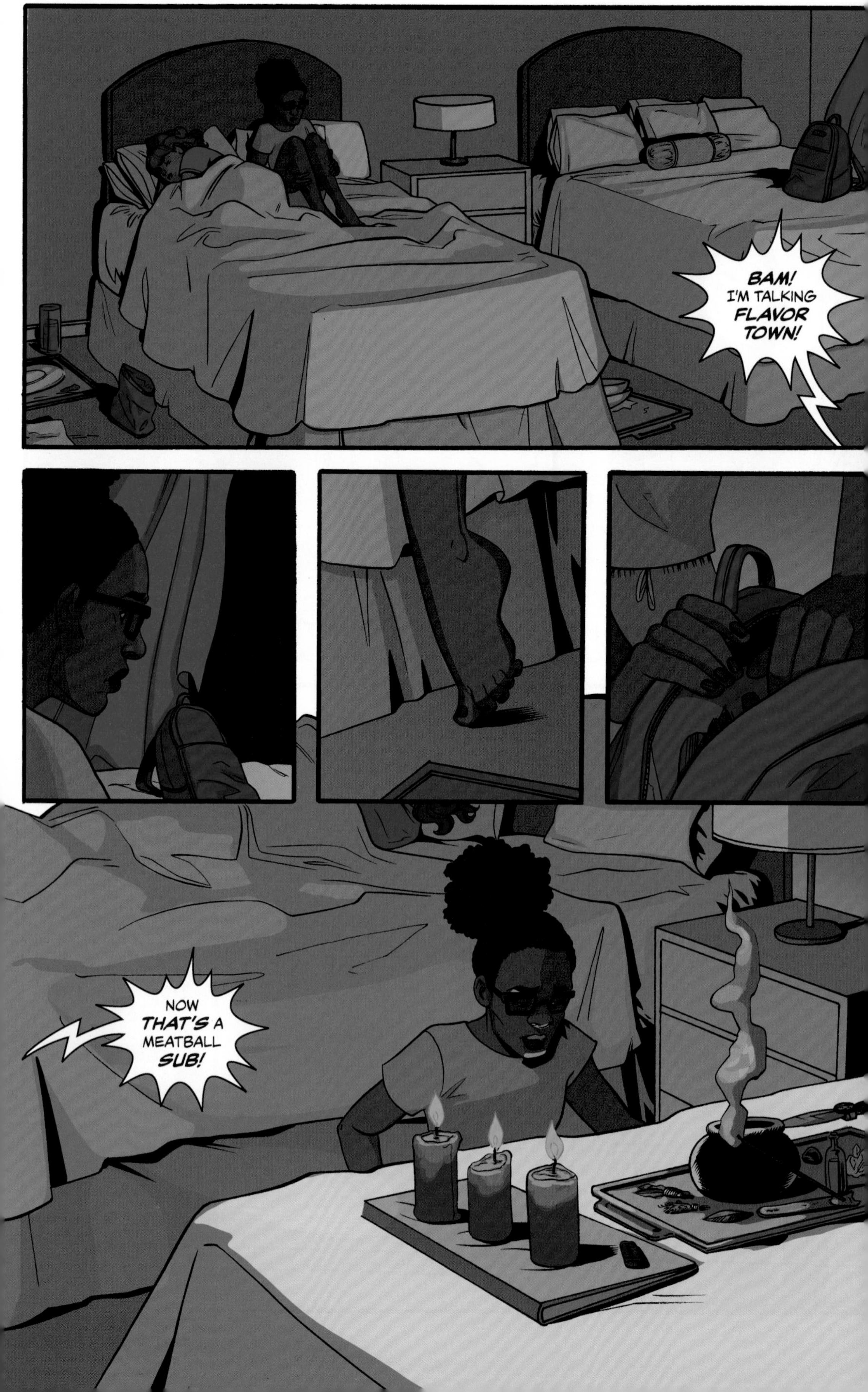
BAM! I'M TALKING FLAVOR TOWN!
NOW THAT'S A MEATBALL SUB!

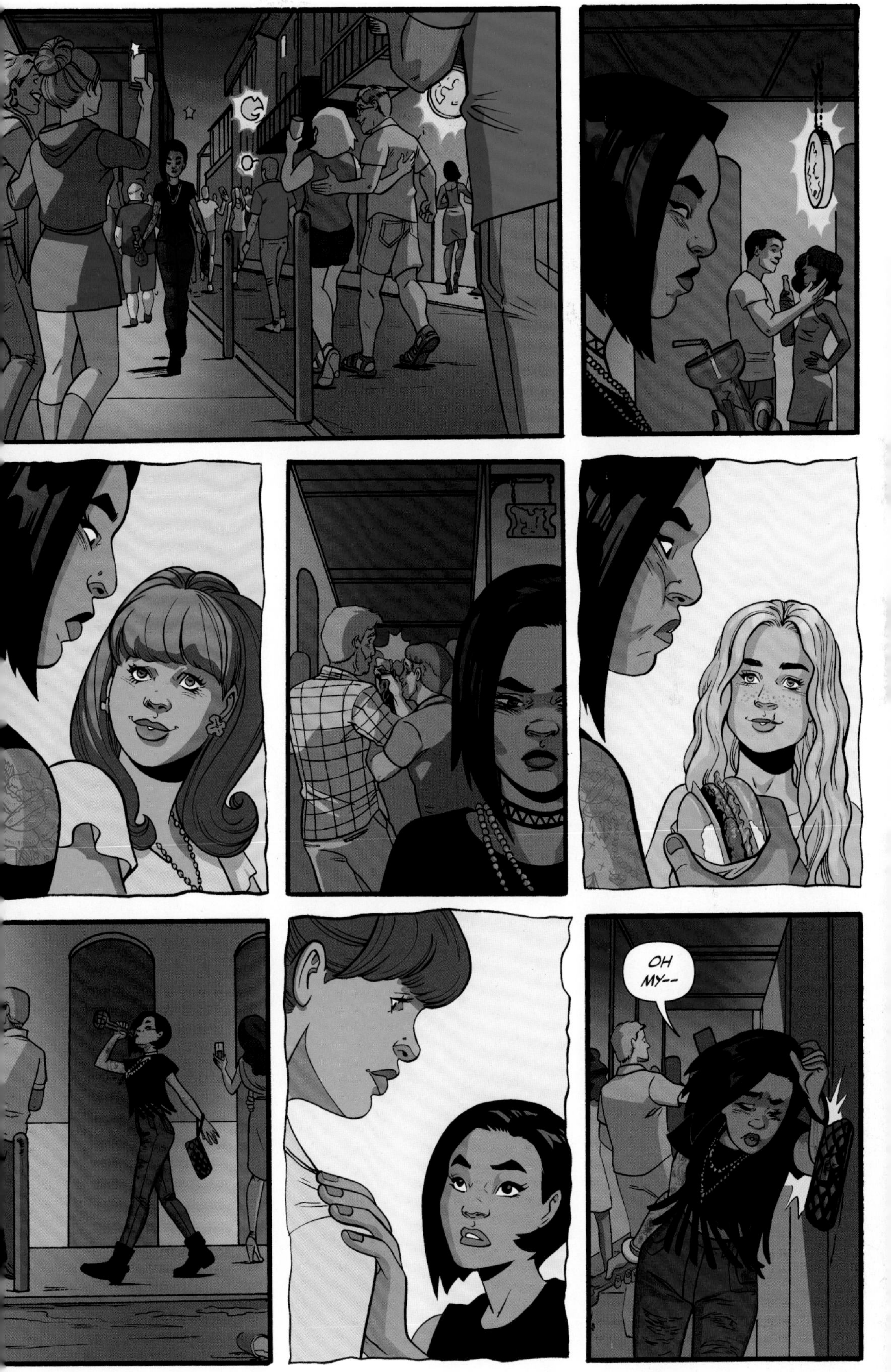
OH
MY--

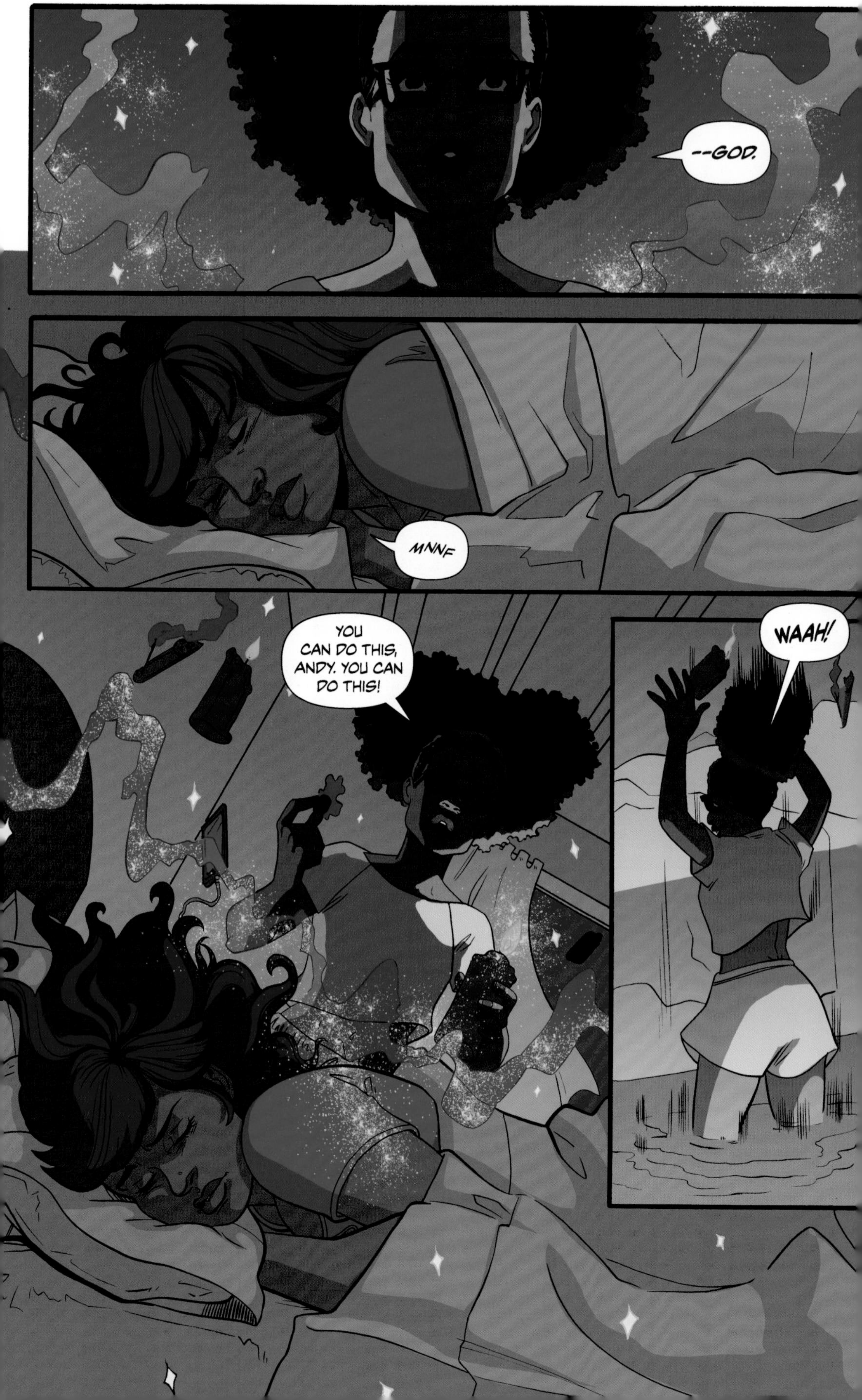
--GOD.
MNNF
YOU CAN DO THIS, ANDY. YOU CAN DO THIS!
WAAH!

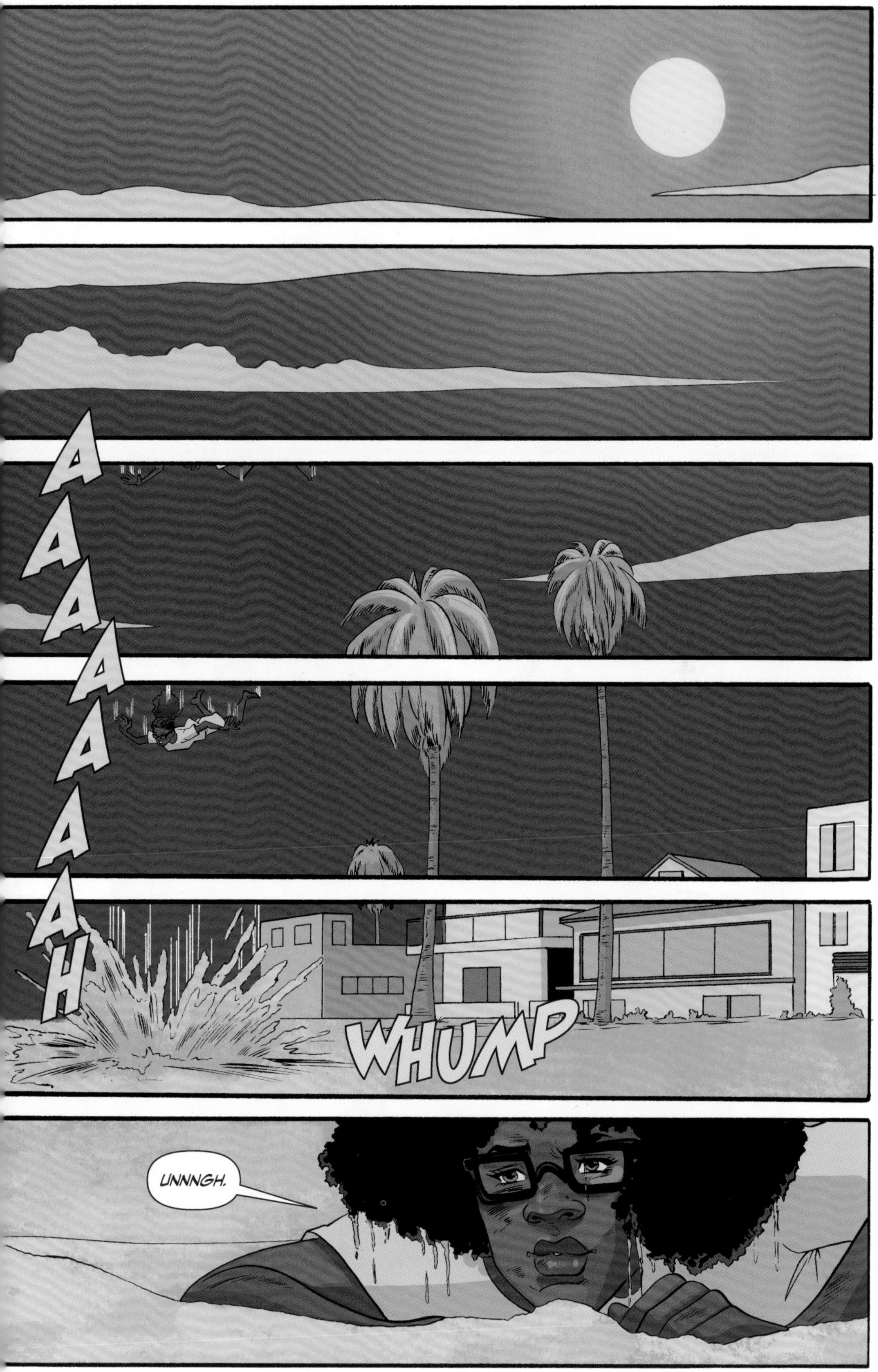
AAAAAAAAAH
WHUMP
UNNNGH.

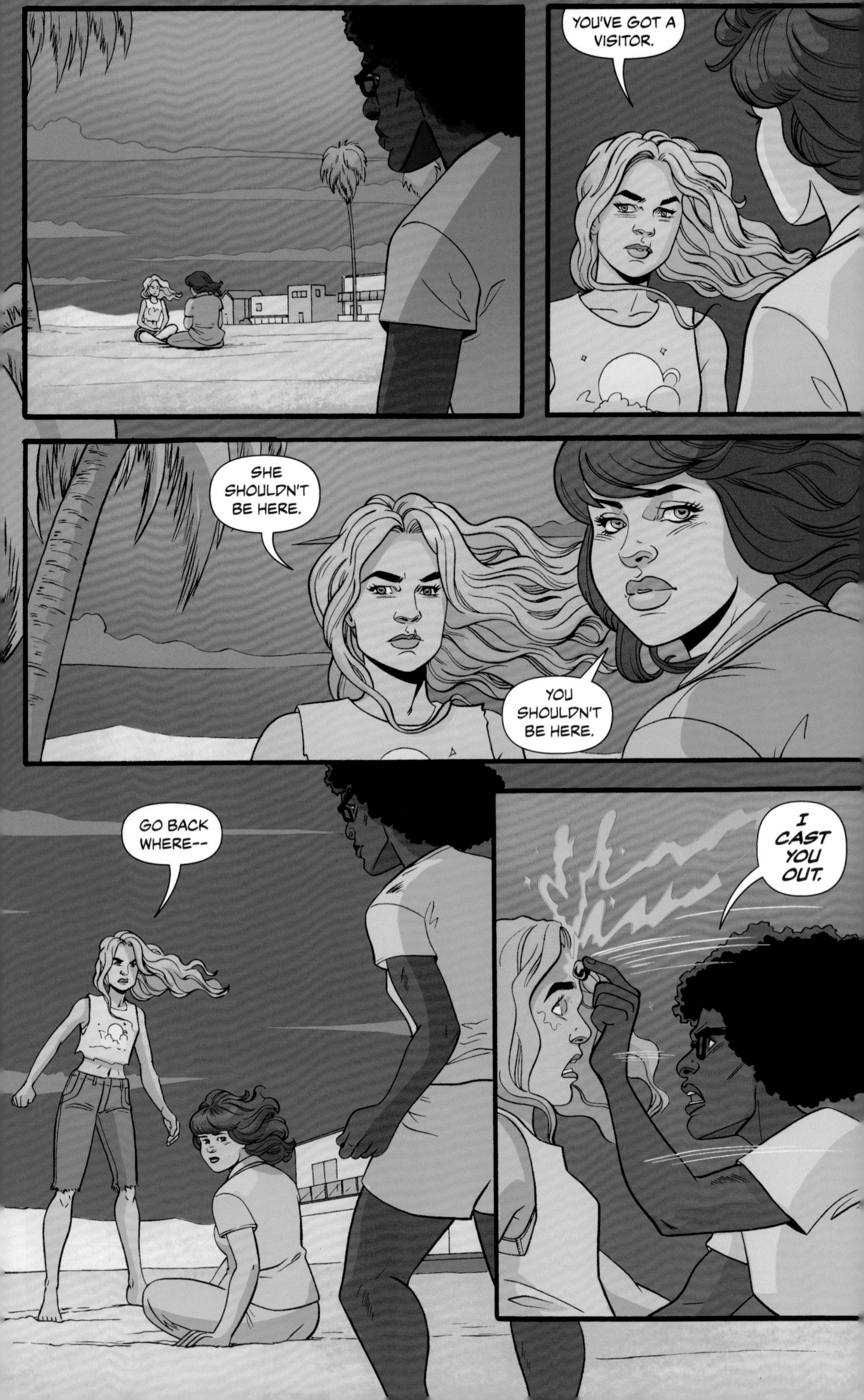
YOU'VE GOT A VISITOR.
SHE SHOULDN'T BE HERE.
YOU SHOULDN'T BE HERE.
GO BACK WHERE--
I CAST YOU OUT.

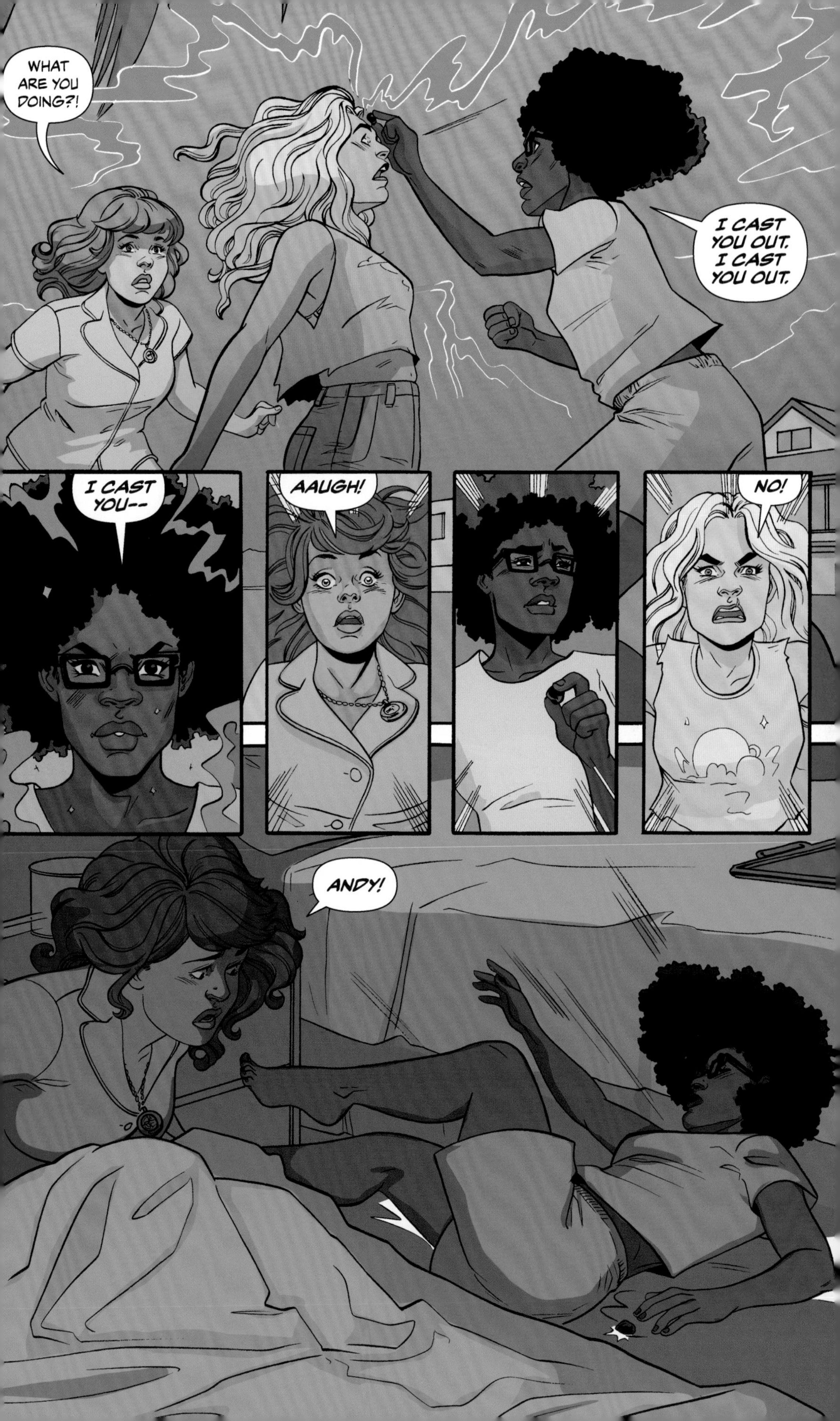
WHAT ARE YOU DOING?!
I CAST YOU OUT. I CAST YOU OUT.
I CAST YOU--
AAUGH!
NO!
ANDY!

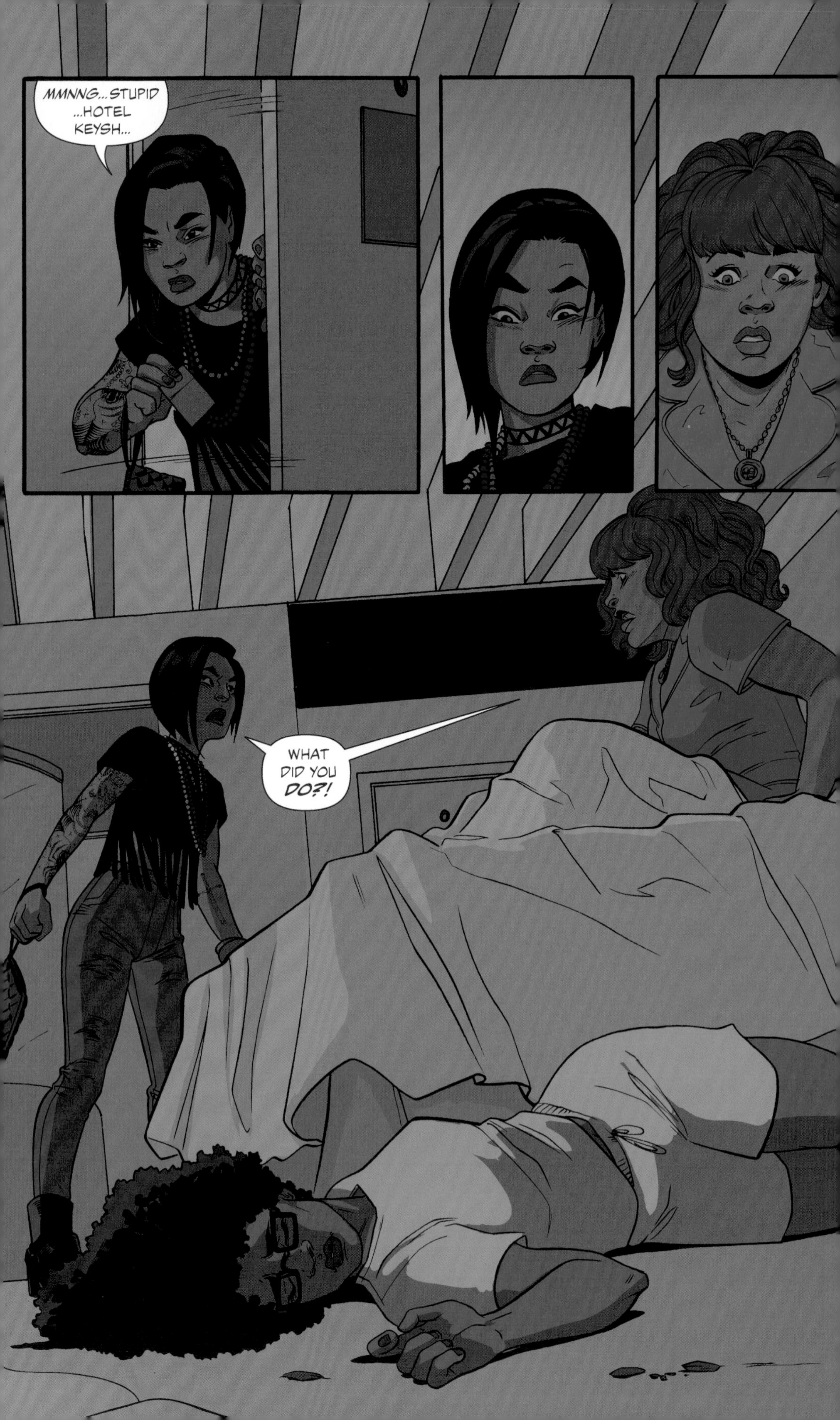
MMNNG... STUPID ...HOTEL KEYSH...
WHAT DID YOU *DO?!*

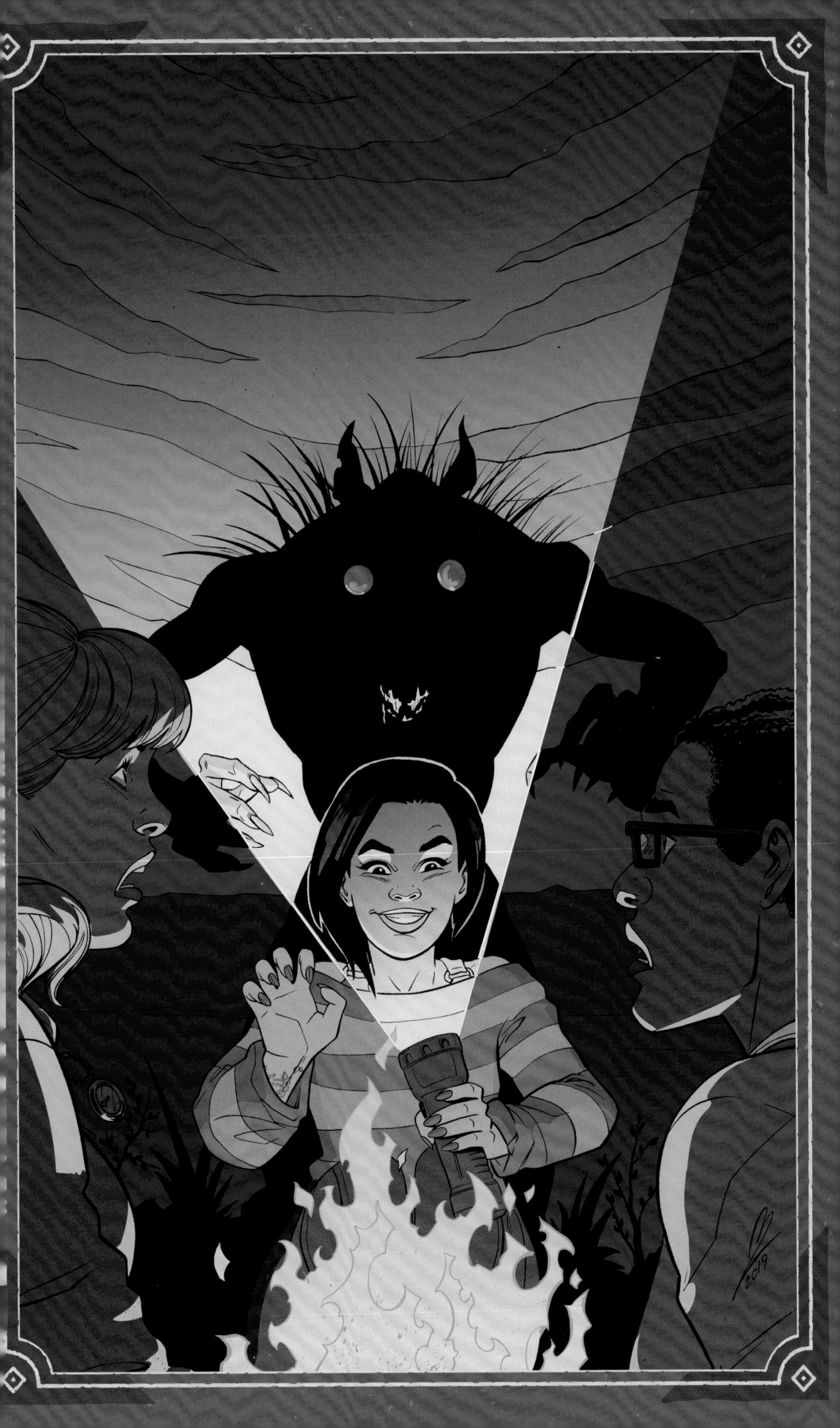

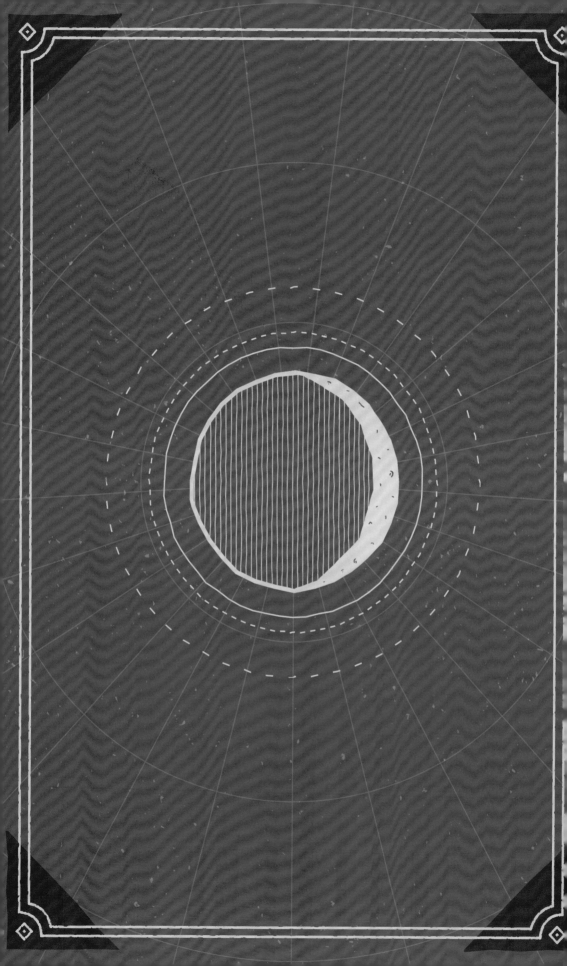

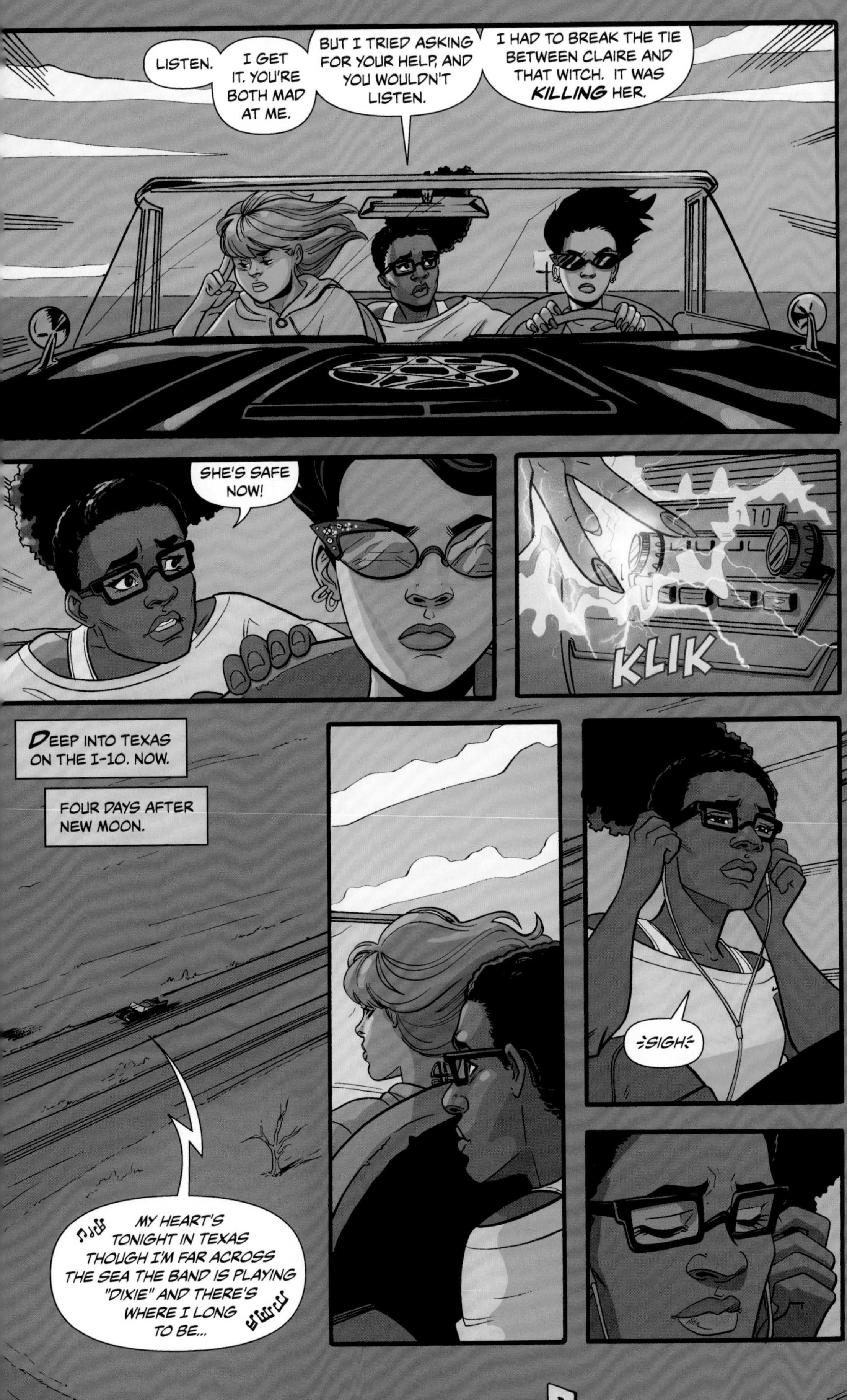
LISTEN.
I GET IT. YOU'RE BOTH MAD AT ME.
BUT I TRIED ASKING FOR YOUR HELP, AND YOU WOULDN'T LISTEN.
I HAD TO BREAK THE TIE BETWEEN CLAIRE AND THAT WITCH. IT WAS *KILLING* HER.
SHE'S SAFE NOW!
KLIK
DEEP INTO TEXAS ON THE I-10. NOW.
FOUR DAYS AFTER NEW MOON.
MY HEART'S TONIGHT IN TEXAS THOUGH I'M FAR ACROSS THE SEA THE BAND IS PLAYING "DIXIE" AND THERE'S WHERE I LONG TO BE...
SIGH

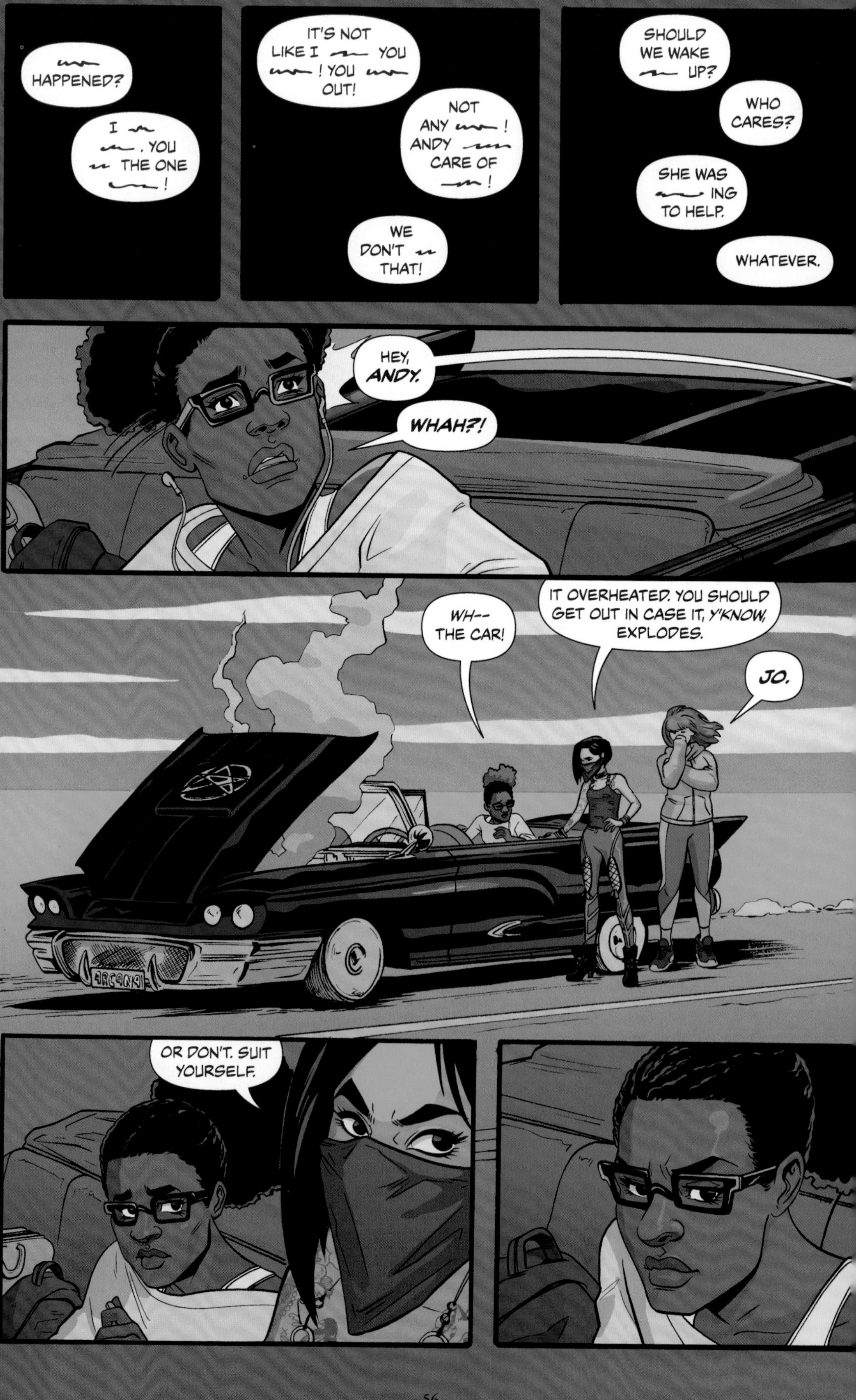

HAPPENED?
I . YOU THE ONE !
IT'S NOT LIKE I YOU ! YOU OUT!
NOT ANY ! ANDY CARE OF !
WE DON'T THAT!
SHOULD WE WAKE UP?
WHO CARES?
SHE WAS ING TO HELP.
WHATEVER.
HEY, ANDY.
WHAH?!
WH-- THE CAR!
IT OVERHEATED. YOU SHOULD GET OUT IN CASE IT, Y'KNOW, EXPLODES.
JO.
OR DON'T. SUIT YOURSELF.

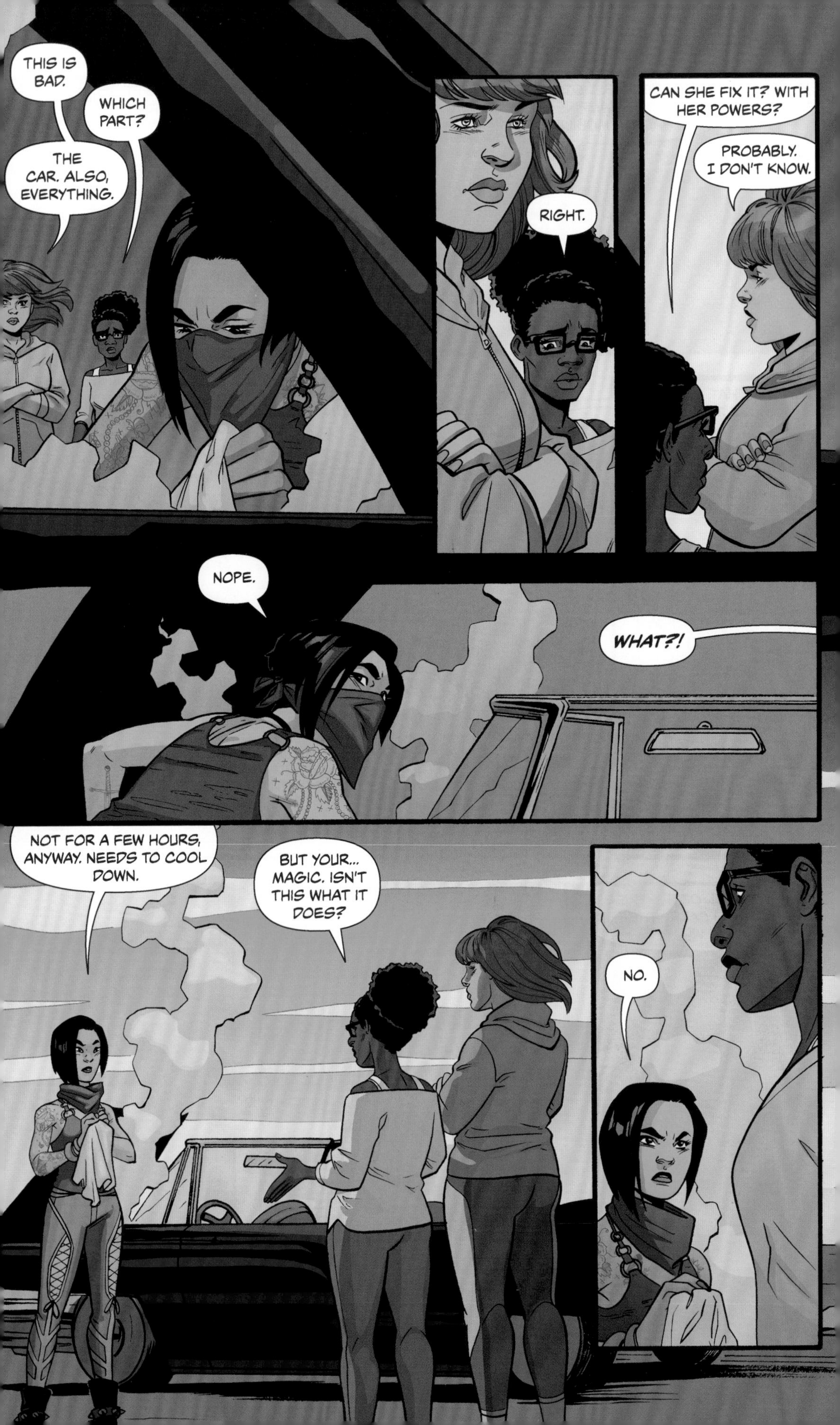
THIS IS BAD.
WHICH PART?
THE CAR. ALSO, EVERYTHING.
RIGHT.
CAN SHE FIX IT? WITH HER POWERS?
PROBABLY. I DON'T KNOW.
NOPE.
WHAT?!
NOT FOR A FEW HOURS, ANYWAY. NEEDS TO COOL DOWN.
BUT YOUR... MAGIC. ISN'T THIS WHAT IT DOES?
NO.

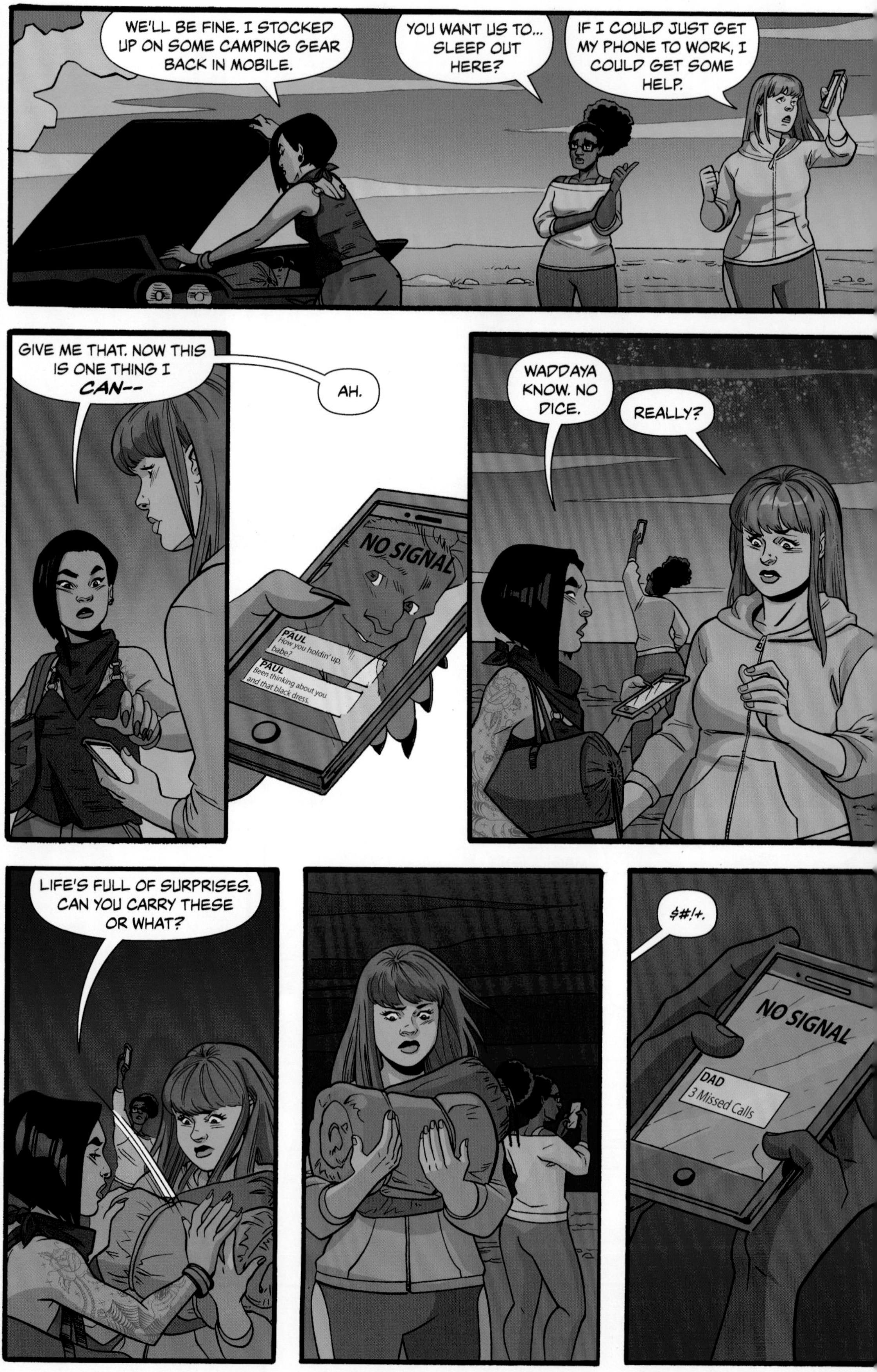
WE'LL BE FINE. I STOCKED UP ON SOME CAMPING GEAR BACK IN MOBILE.
YOU WANT US TO... SLEEP OUT HERE?
IF I COULD JUST GET MY PHONE TO WORK, I COULD GET SOME HELP.
GIVE ME THAT. NOW THIS IS ONE THING I CAN--
AH.
NO SIGNAL
PAUL
How you holdin' up, babe?
PAUL
Been thinking about you and that black dress.
WADDAYA KNOW. NO DICE.
REALLY?
LIFE'S FULL OF SURPRISES. CAN YOU CARRY THESE OR WHAT?
$#!+.
NO SIGNAL
DAD
3 Missed Calls

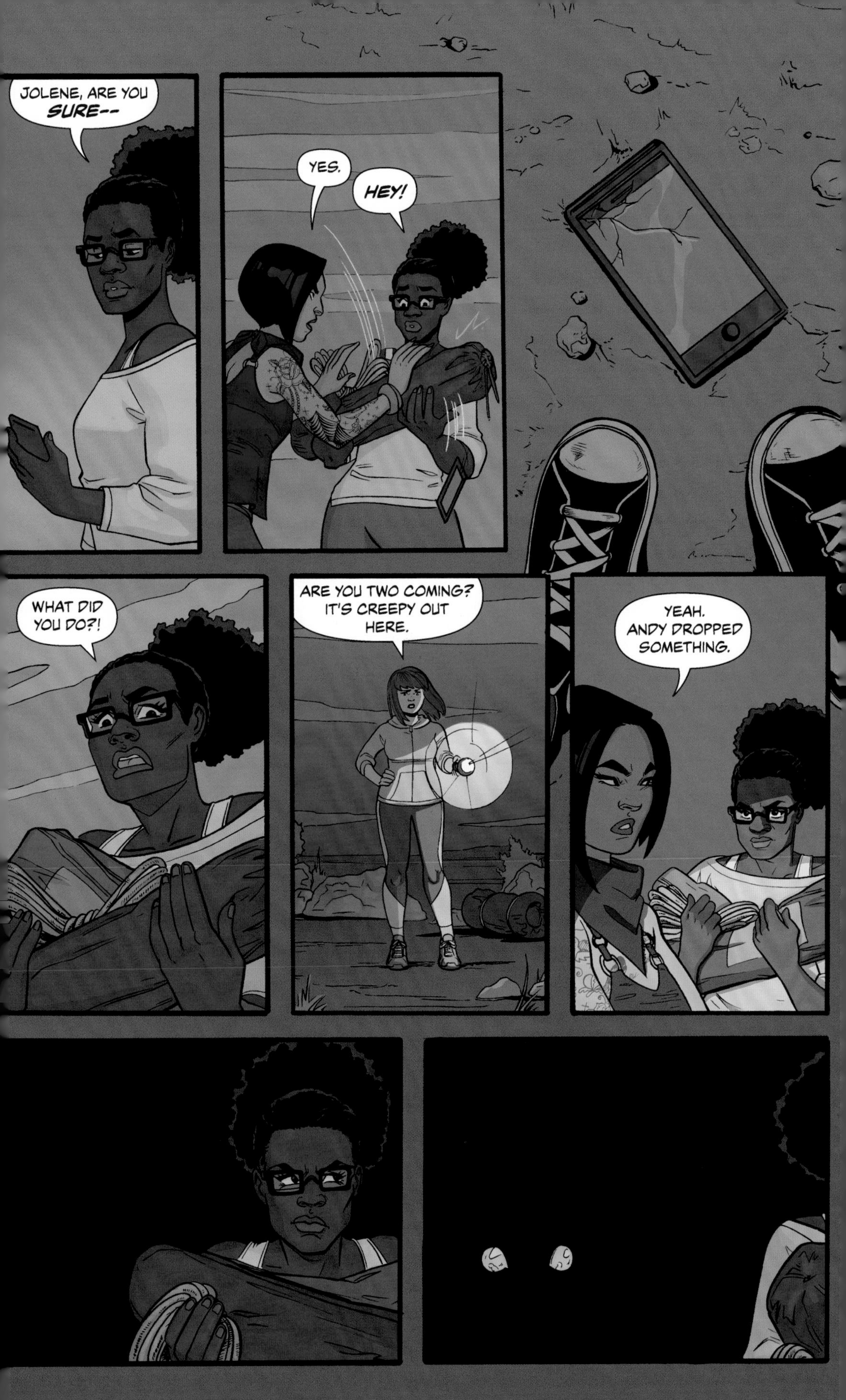
JOLENE, ARE YOU *SURE--*
YES.
HEY!
WHAT DID YOU DO?!
ARE YOU TWO COMING? IT'S CREEPY OUT HERE.
YEAH. ANDY DROPPED SOMETHING.

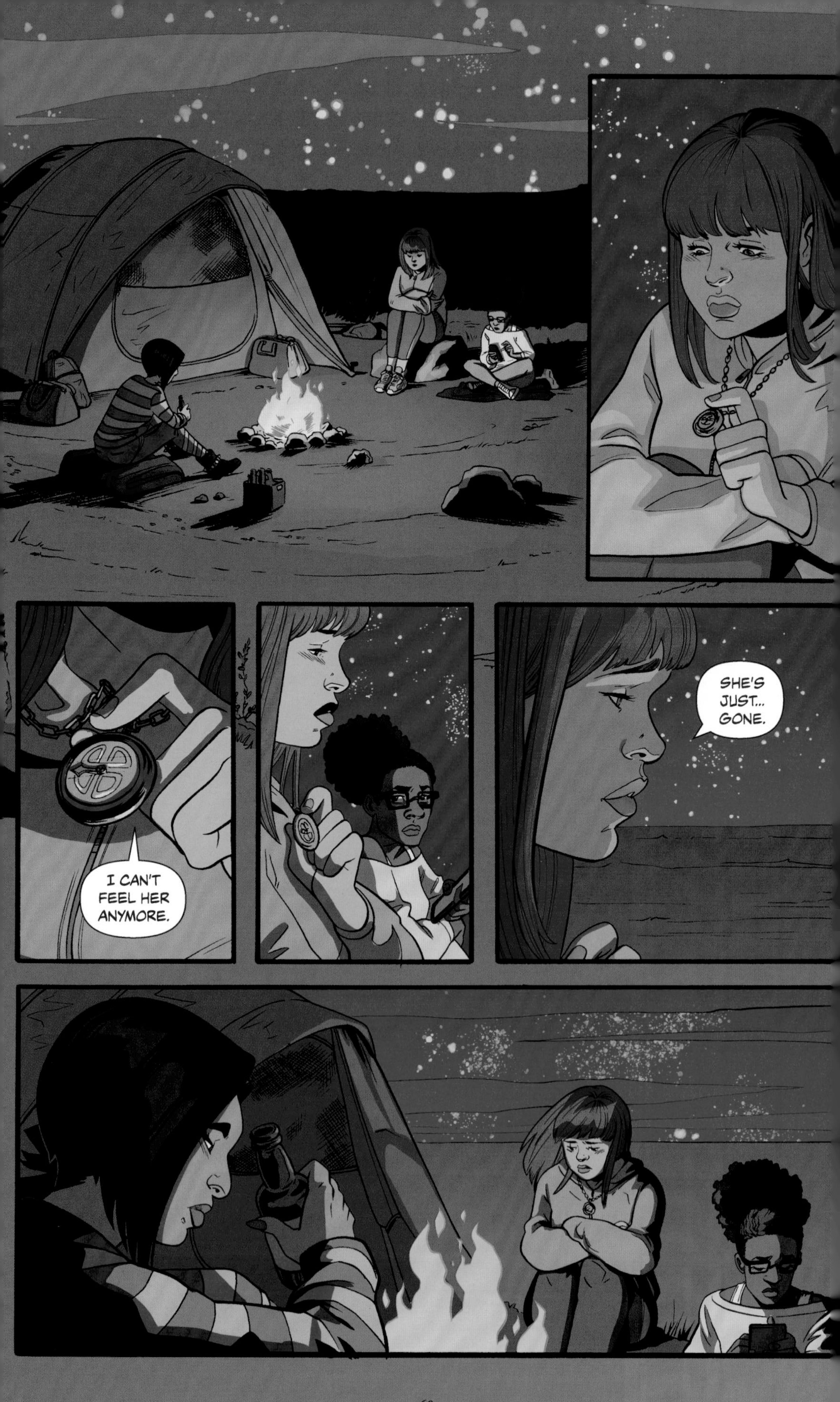
I CAN'T FEEL HER ANYMORE.
SHE'S JUST... GONE.

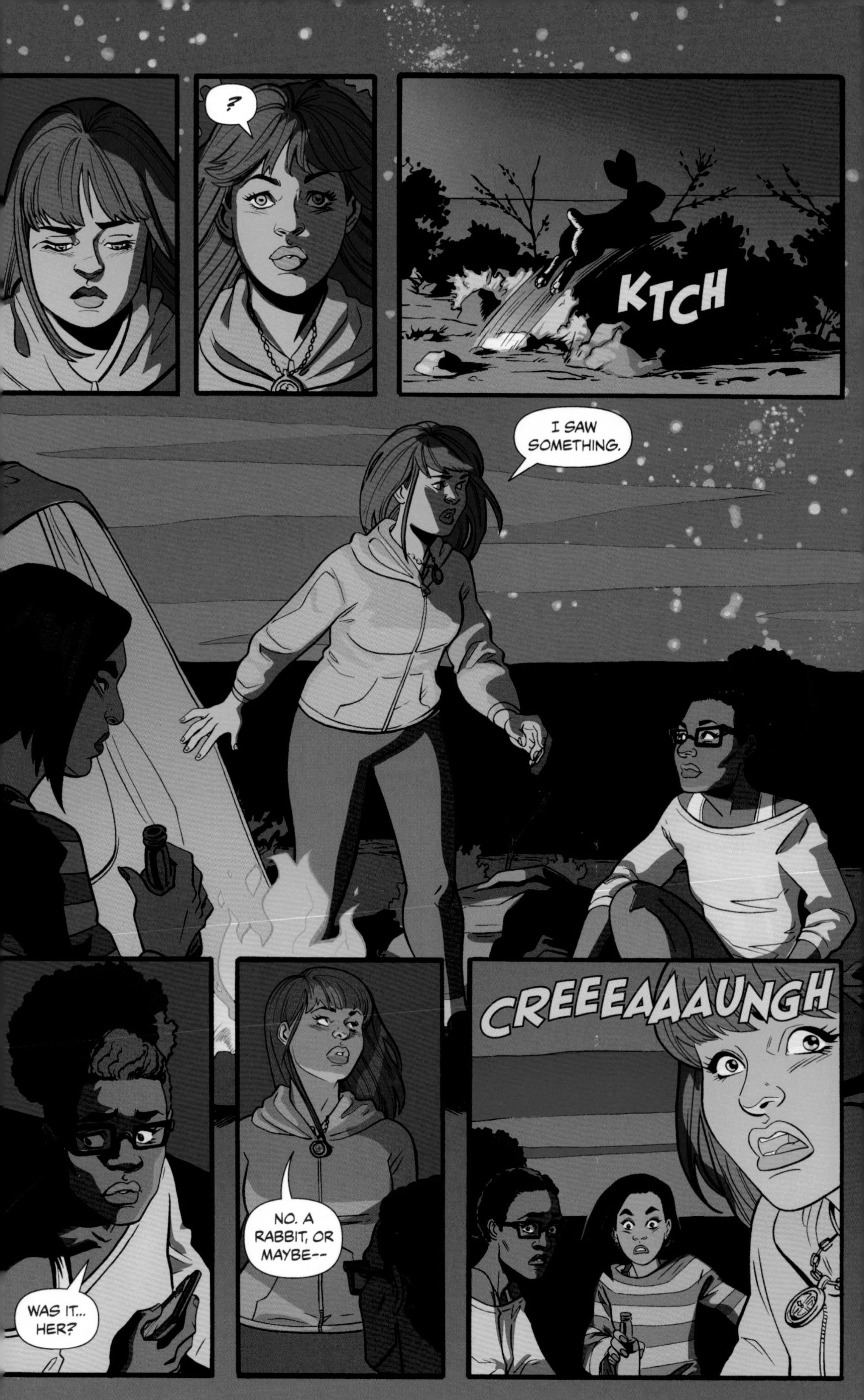
?
KTCH
I SAW SOMETHING.
WAS IT... HER?
NO. A RABBIT, OR MAYBE--
CREEEAAAAUNGH

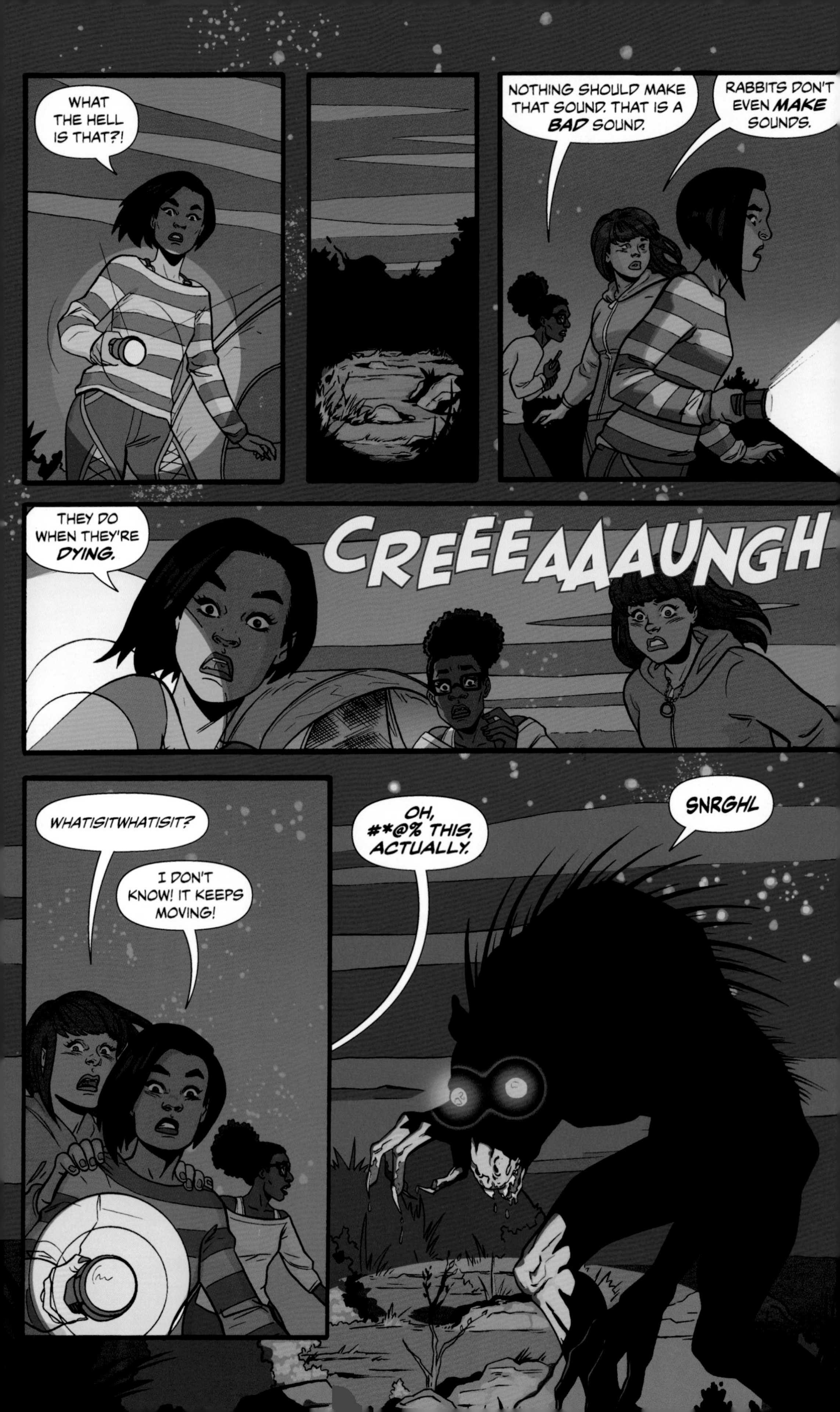
WHAT THE HELL IS THAT?!
NOTHING SHOULD MAKE THAT SOUND. THAT IS A BAD SOUND.
RABBITS DON'T EVEN MAKE SOUNDS.
THEY DO WHEN THEY'RE DYING.
CREEEAAAUNGH
WHATISITWHATISIT?
I DON'T KNOW! IT KEEPS MOVING!
OH, #*@% THIS, ACTUALLY.
SNRGHL

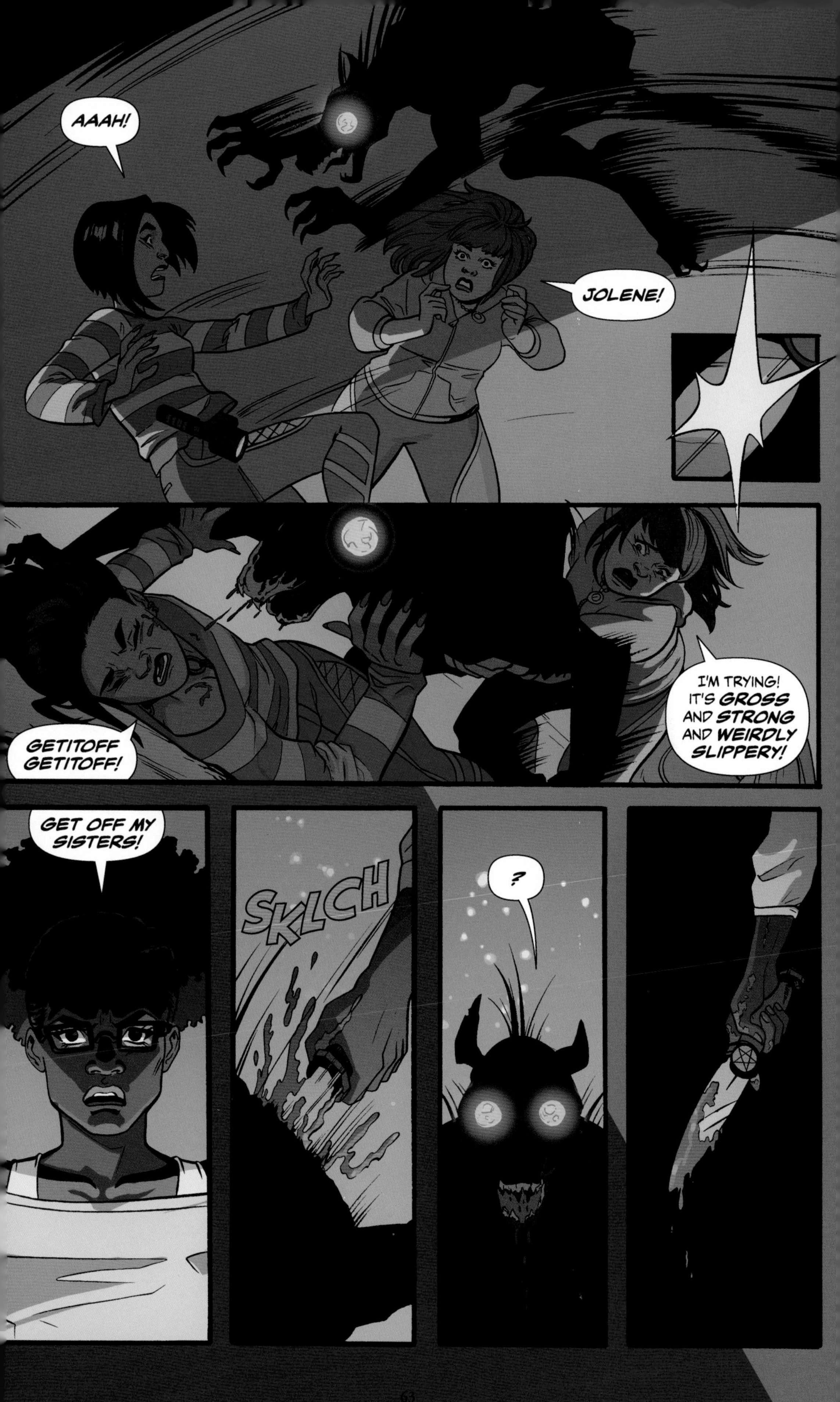

AAAH!
JOLENE!
GETITOFF GETITOFF!
I'M TRYING! IT'S GROSS AND STRONG AND WEIRDLY SLIPPERY!
GET OFF MY SISTERS!
SKLCH
?

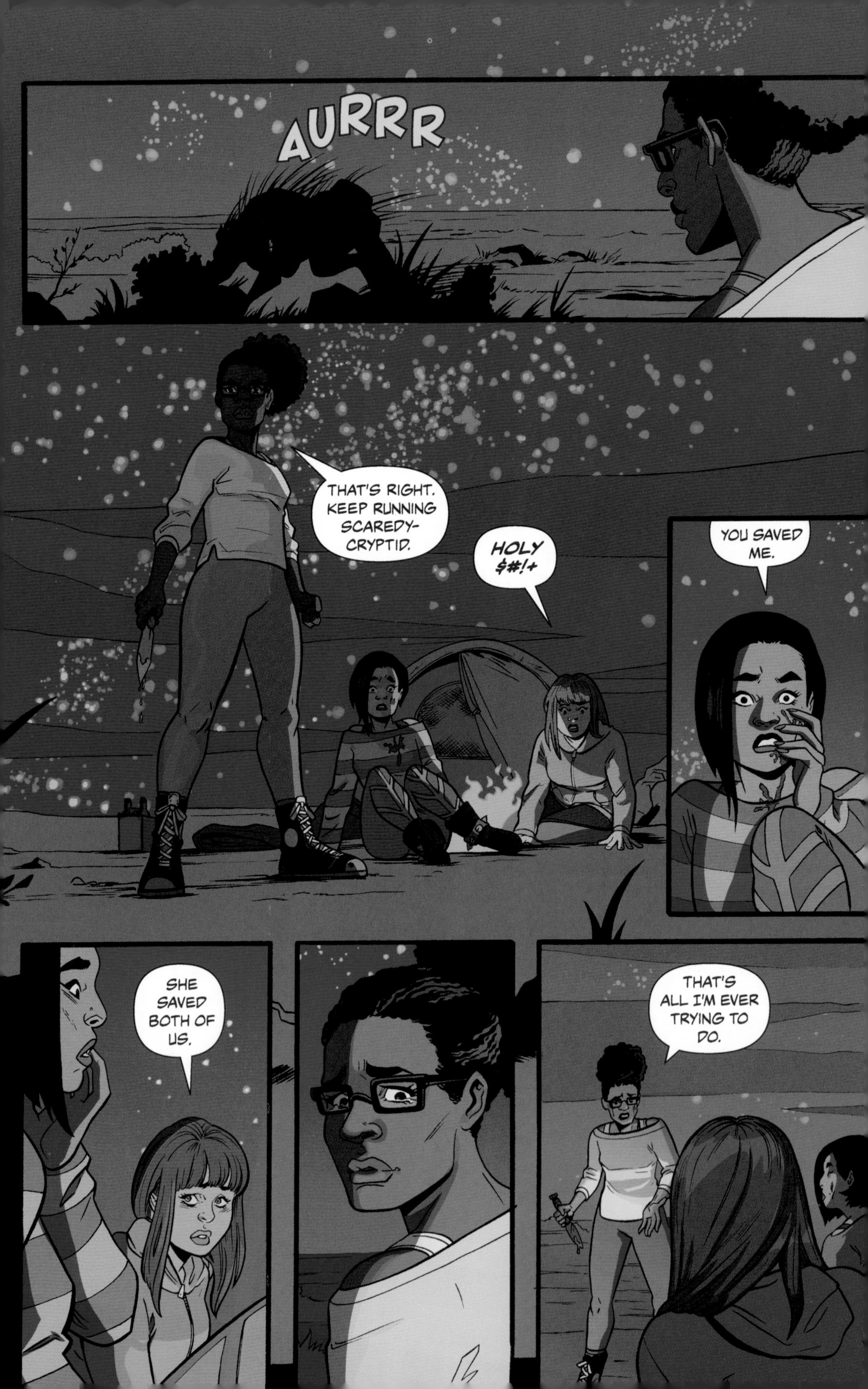
AURRR
THAT'S RIGHT. KEEP RUNNING SCAREDY-CRYPTID.
HOLY $#!+
YOU SAVED ME.
SHE SAVED BOTH OF US.
THAT'S ALL I'M EVER TRYING TO DO.

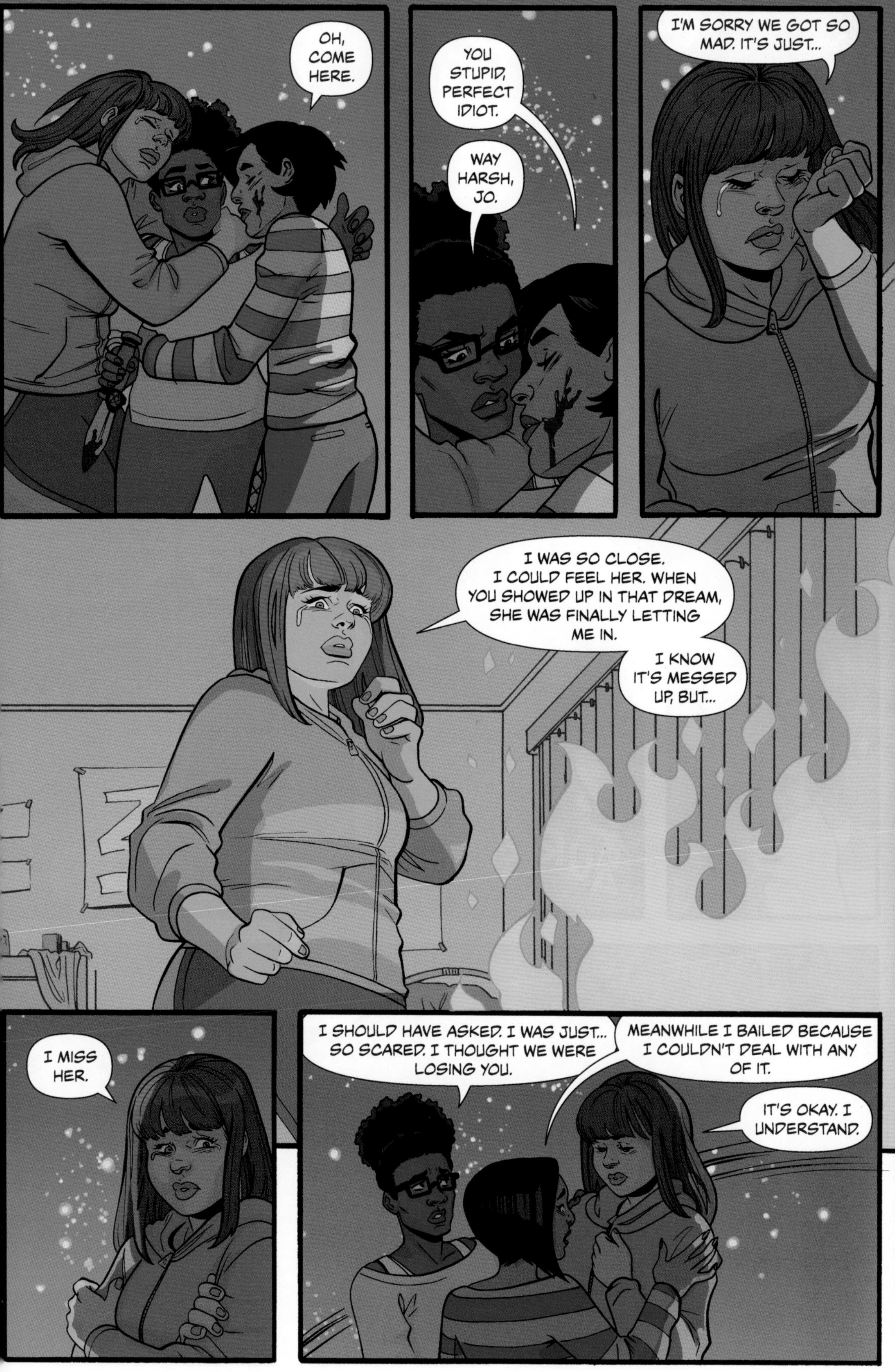
OH, COME HERE.
YOU STUPID, PERFECT IDIOT.
WAY HARSH, JO.
I'M SORRY WE GOT SO MAD. IT'S JUST...
I WAS SO CLOSE. I COULD FEEL HER. WHEN YOU SHOWED UP IN THAT DREAM, SHE WAS FINALLY LETTING ME IN.
I KNOW IT'S MESSED UP, BUT...
I MISS HER.
I SHOULD HAVE ASKED. I WAS JUST... SO SCARED. I THOUGHT WE WERE LOSING YOU.
MEANWHILE I BAILED BECAUSE I COULDN'T DEAL WITH ANY OF IT.
IT'S OKAY. I UNDERSTAND.

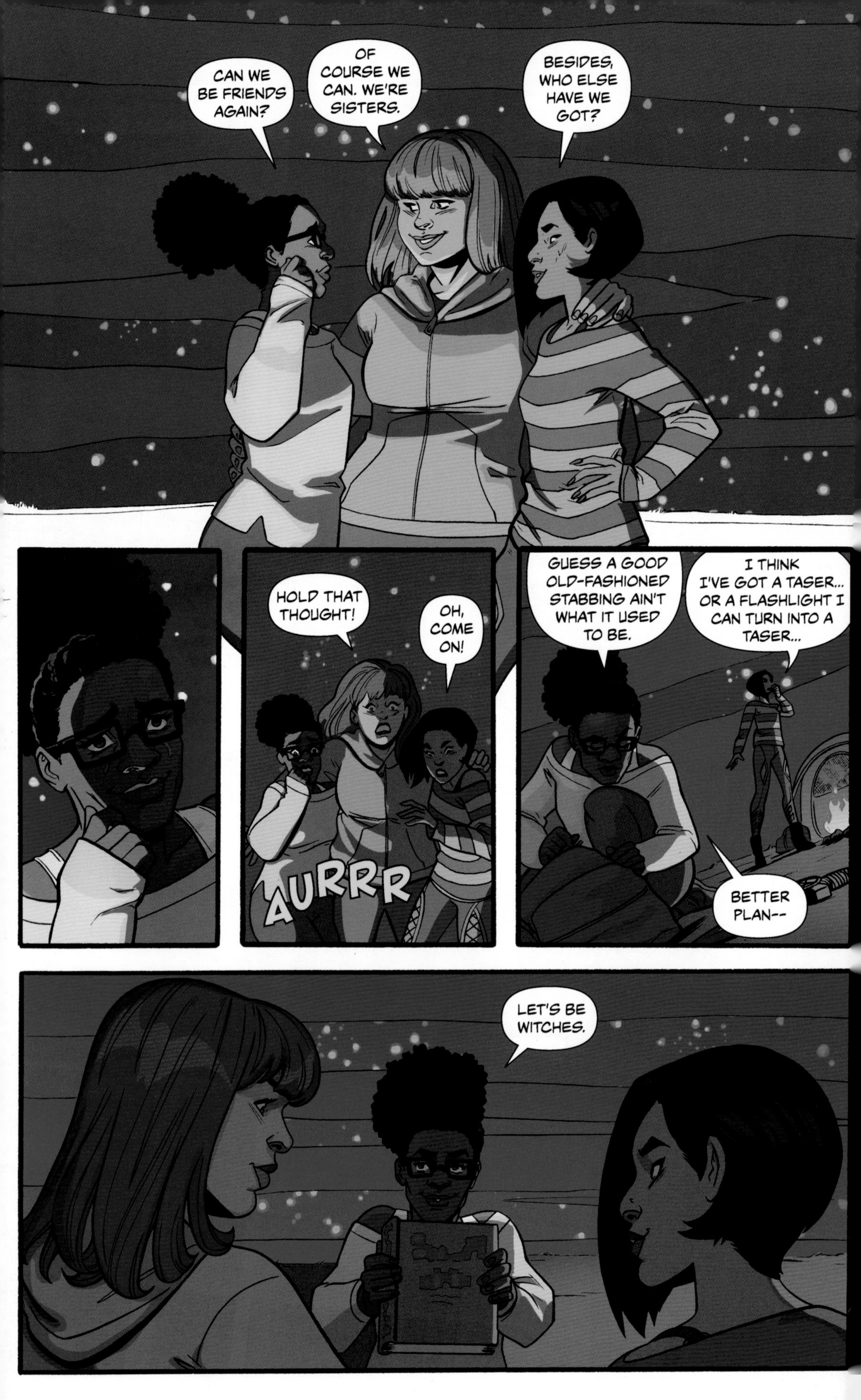
CAN WE BE FRIENDS AGAIN?
OF COURSE WE CAN. WE'RE SISTERS.
BESIDES, WHO ELSE HAVE WE GOT?
HOLD THAT THOUGHT!
OH, COME ON!
AURRR
GUESS A GOOD OLD-FASHIONED STABBING AIN'T WHAT IT USED TO BE.
I THINK I'VE GOT A TASER... OR A FLASHLIGHT I CAN TURN INTO A TASER...
BETTER PLAN--
LET'S BE WITCHES.

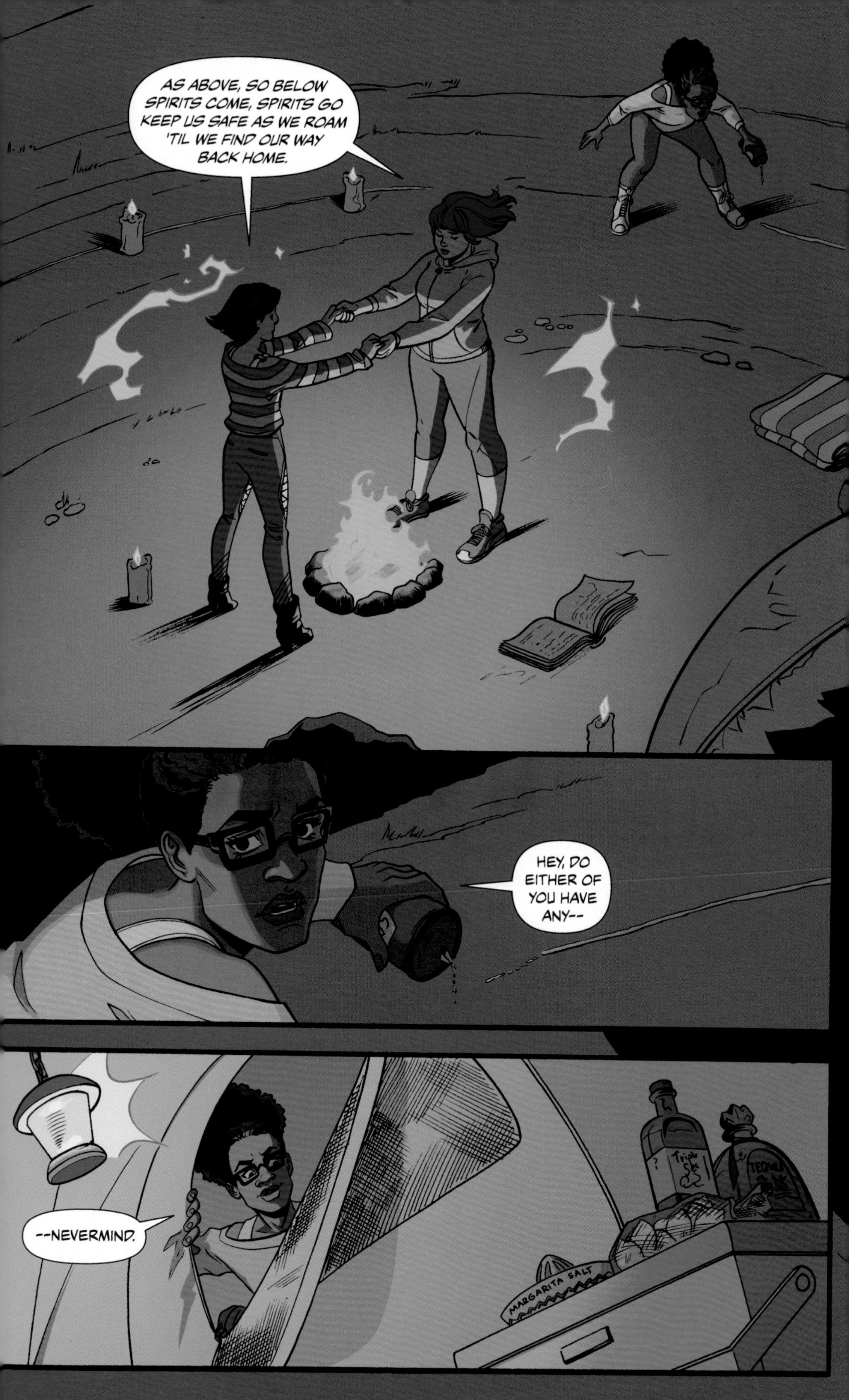
AS ABOVE, SO BELOW SPIRITS COME, SPIRITS GO KEEP US SAFE AS WE ROAM 'TIL WE FIND OUR WAY BACK HOME.
HEY, DO EITHER OF YOU HAVE ANY--
--NEVERMIND.
MARGARITA SALT
TEQUILA

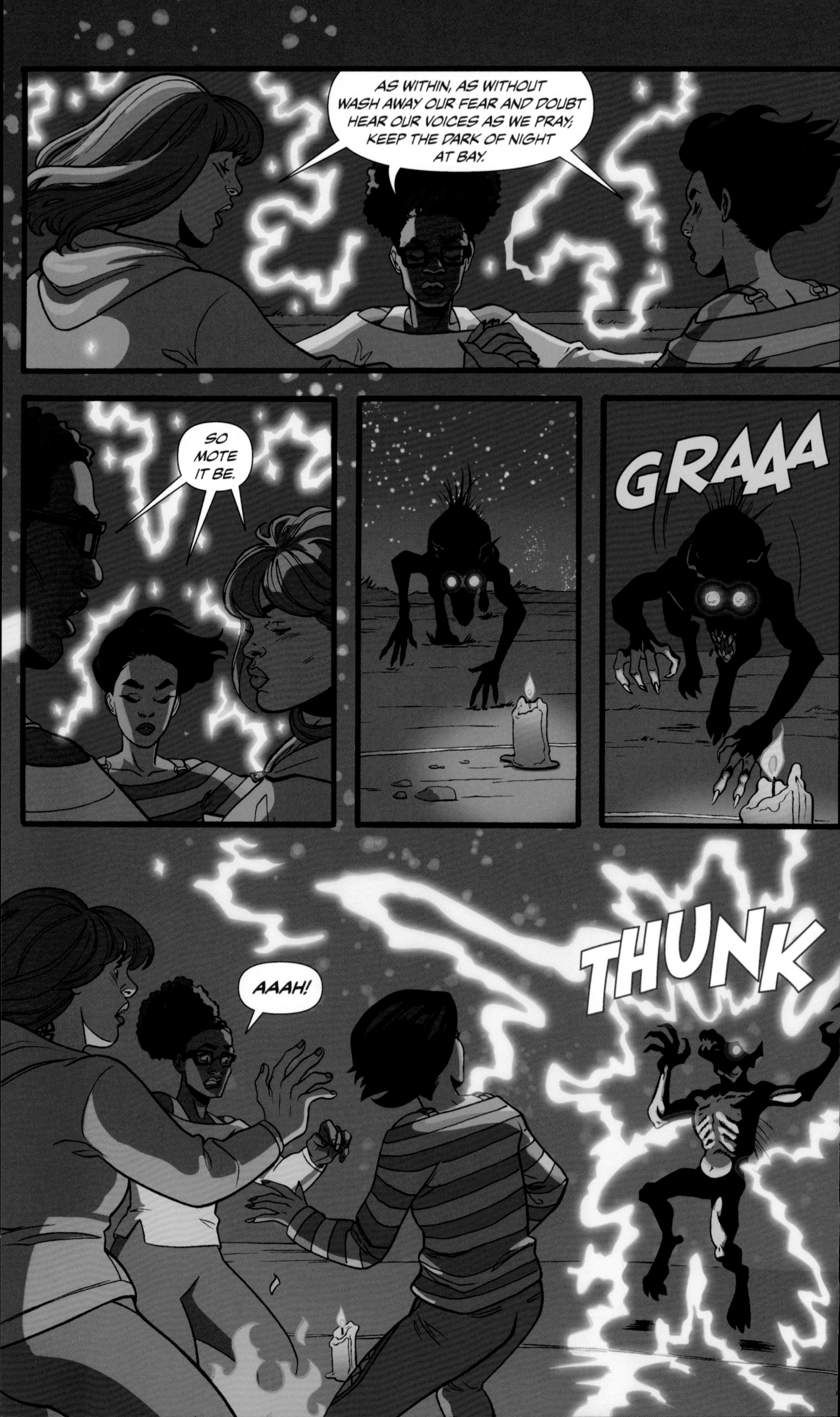
AS WITHIN, AS WITHOUT
WASH AWAY OUR FEAR AND DOUBT
HEAR OUR VOICES AS WE PRAY;
KEEP THE DARK OF NIGHT
AT BAY.
SO MOTE IT BE.
GRAAA
AAAH!
THUNK

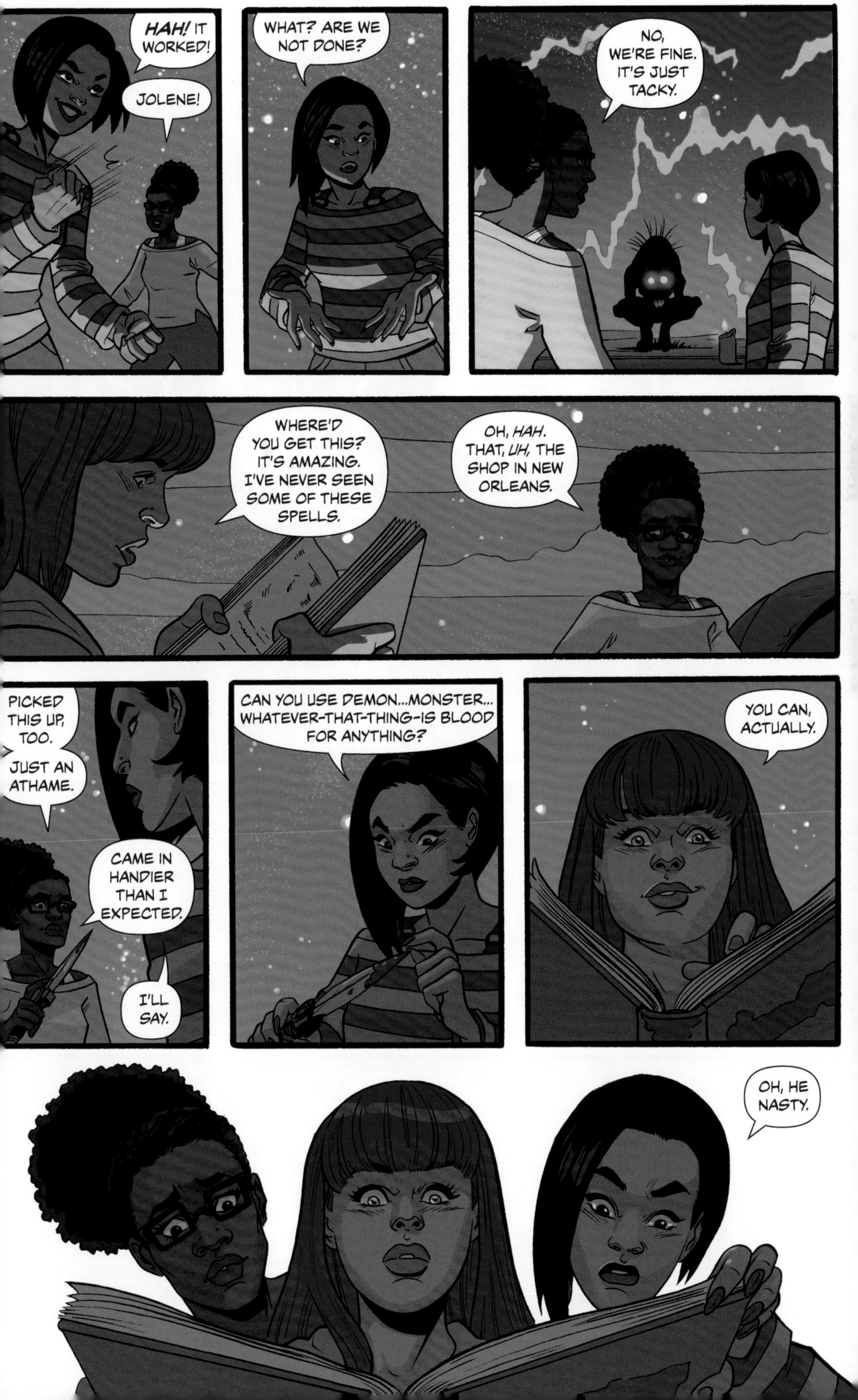
HAH! IT WORKED!
JOLENE!
WHAT? ARE WE NOT DONE?
NO, WE'RE FINE. IT'S JUST TACKY.
WHERE'D YOU GET THIS? IT'S AMAZING. I'VE NEVER SEEN SOME OF THESE SPELLS.
OH, HAH. THAT, UH, THE SHOP IN NEW ORLEANS.
PICKED THIS UP, TOO.
JUST AN ATHAME.
CAME IN HANDIER THAN I EXPECTED.
I'LL SAY.
CAN YOU USE DEMON...MONSTER... WHATEVER-THAT-THING-IS BLOOD FOR ANYTHING?
YOU CAN, ACTUALLY.
OH, HE NASTY.

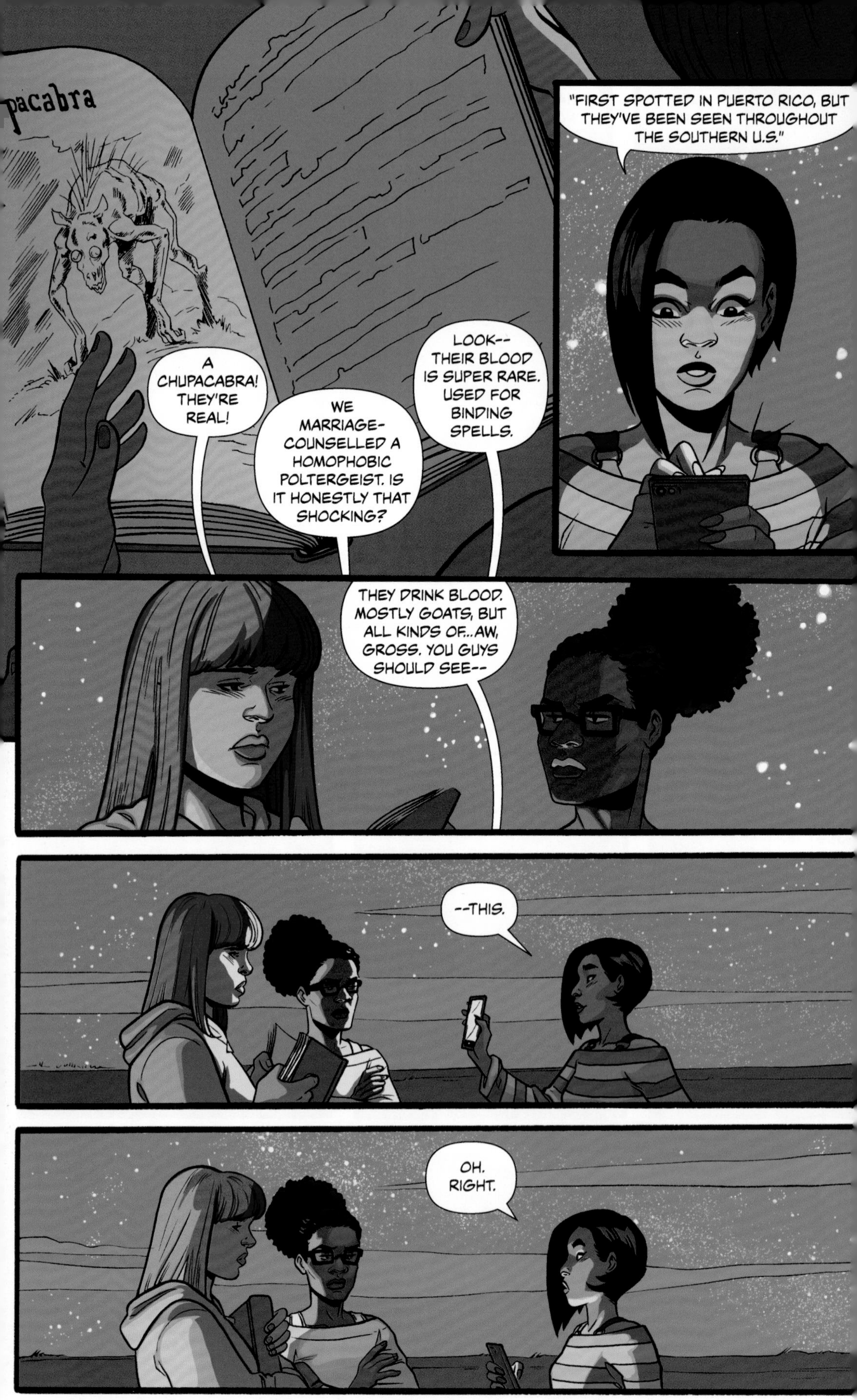
pacabra
"FIRST SPOTTED IN PUERTO RICO, BUT THEY'VE BEEN SEEN THROUGHOUT THE SOUTHERN U.S."
A CHUPACABRA! THEY'RE REAL!
WE MARRIAGE-COUNSELLED A HOMOPHOBIC POLTERGEIST. IS IT HONESTLY THAT SHOCKING?
LOOK-- THEIR BLOOD IS SUPER RARE. USED FOR BINDING SPELLS.
THEY DRINK BLOOD. MOSTLY GOATS, BUT ALL KINDS OF...AW, GROSS. YOU GUYS SHOULD SEE--
--THIS.
OH. RIGHT.

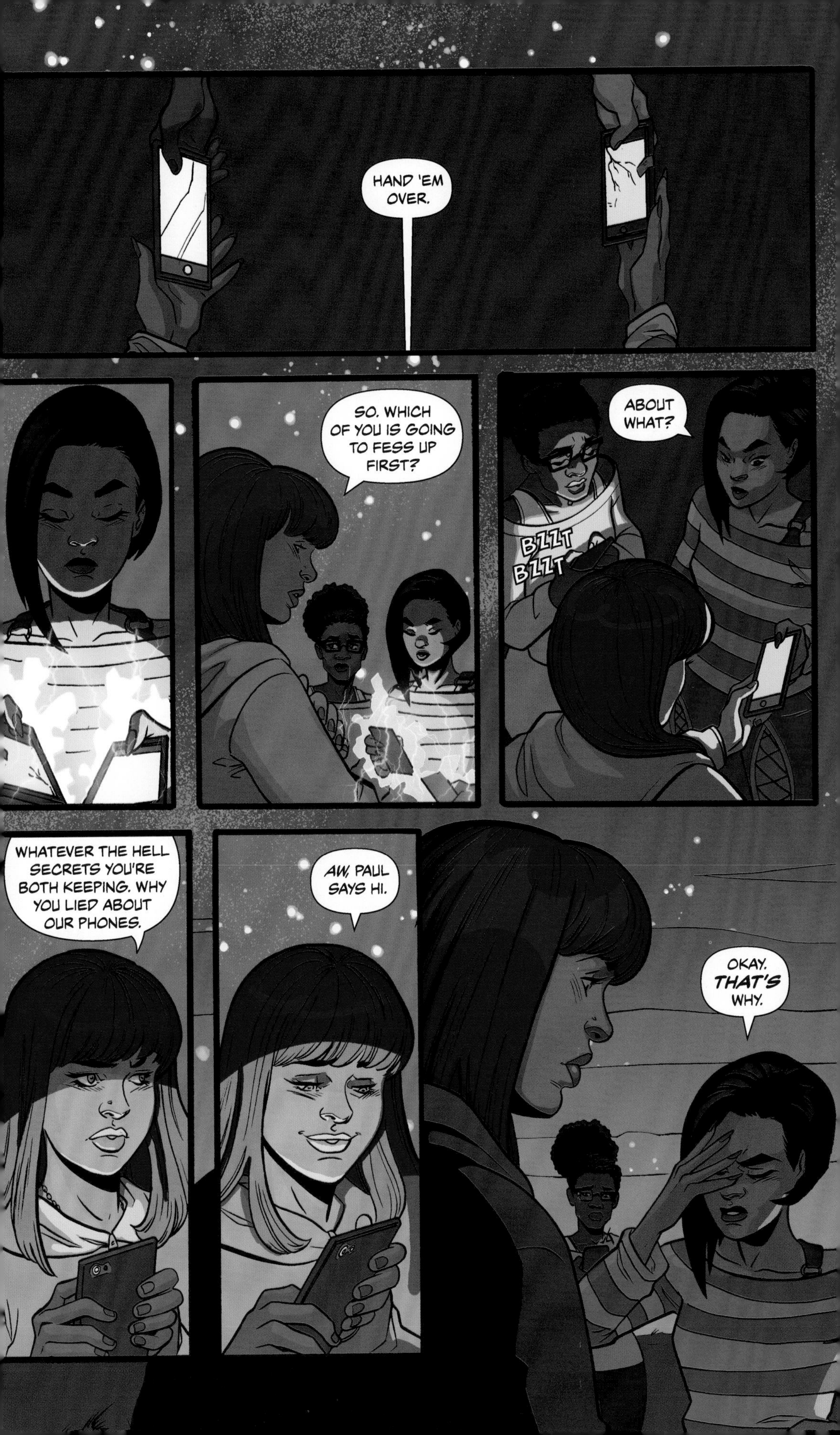
HAND 'EM OVER.
SO. WHICH OF YOU IS GOING TO FESS UP FIRST?
BZZT BZZT
ABOUT WHAT?
WHATEVER THE HELL SECRETS YOU'RE BOTH KEEPING. WHY YOU LIED ABOUT OUR PHONES.
AW, PAUL SAYS HI.
OKAY. *THAT'S* WHY.

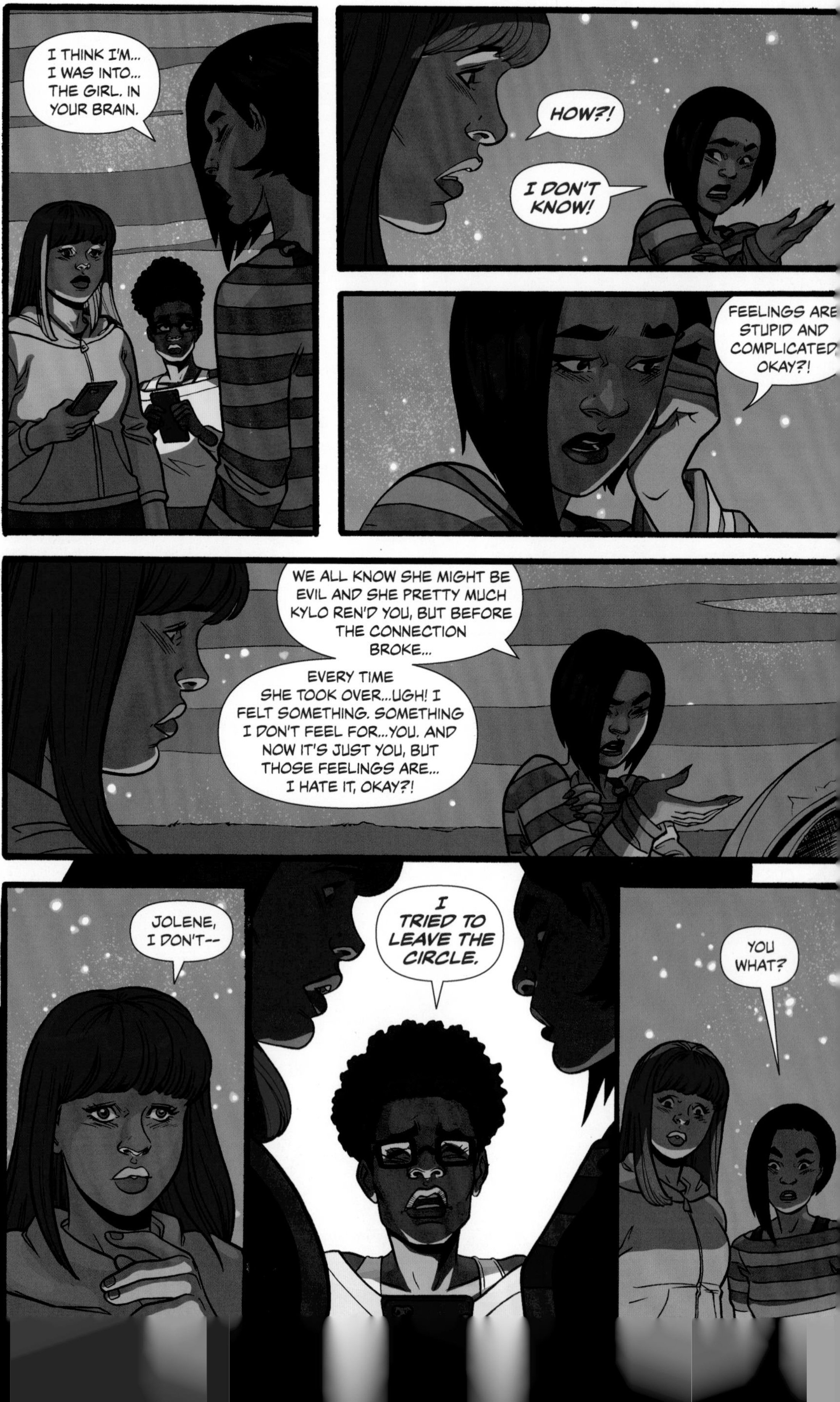
I THINK I'M... I WAS INTO... THE GIRL. IN YOUR BRAIN.
HOW?!
I DON'T KNOW!
FEELINGS ARE STUPID AND COMPLICATED OKAY?!
WE ALL KNOW SHE MIGHT BE EVIL AND SHE PRETTY MUCH KYLO REN'D YOU, BUT BEFORE THE CONNECTION BROKE...
EVERY TIME SHE TOOK OVER...UGH! I FELT SOMETHING. SOMETHING I DON'T FEEL FOR...YOU. AND NOW IT'S JUST YOU, BUT THOSE FEELINGS ARE... I HATE IT, OKAY?!
JOLENE, I DON'T--
I TRIED TO LEAVE THE CIRCLE.
YOU WHAT?

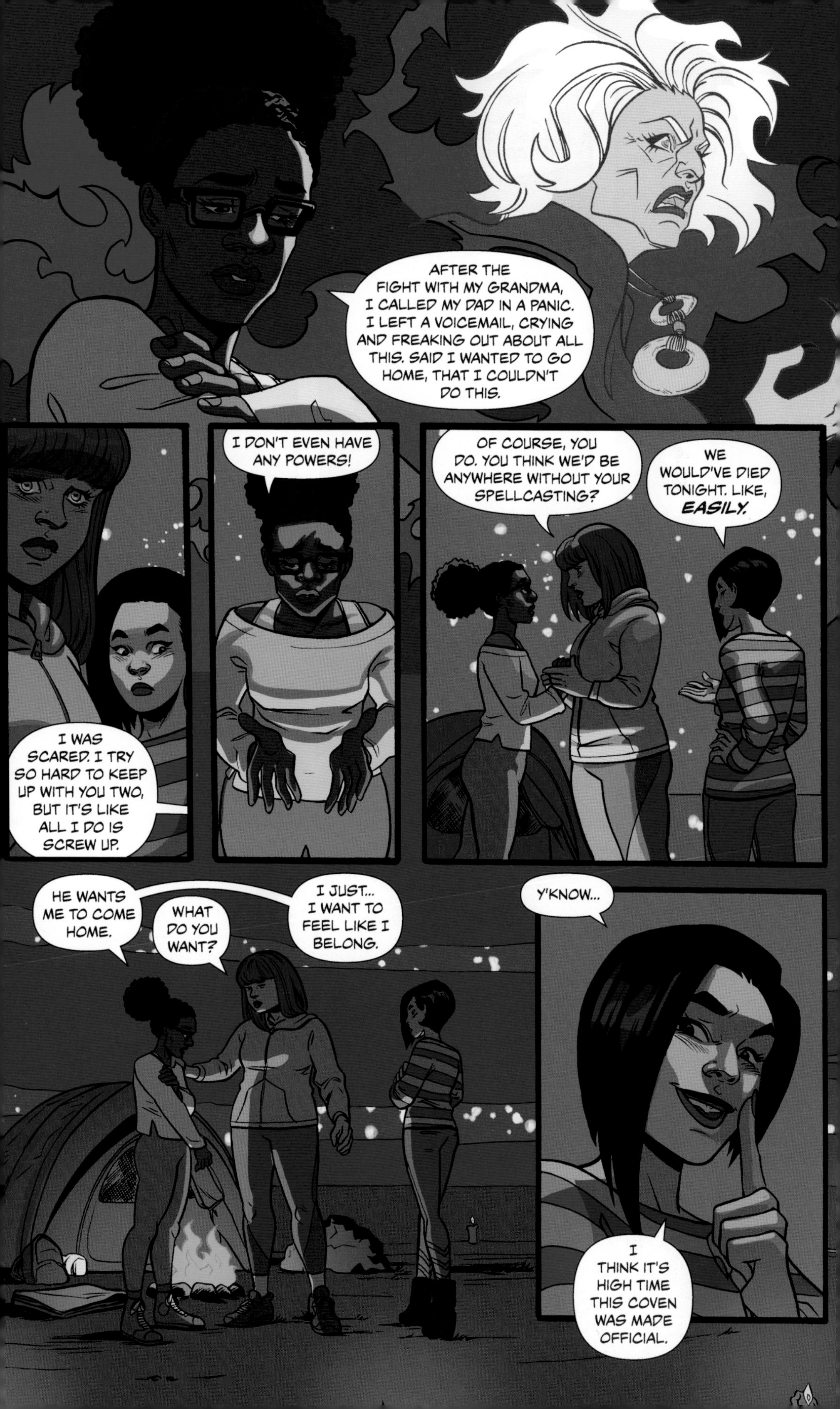
AFTER THE FIGHT WITH MY GRANDMA, I CALLED MY DAD IN A PANIC. I LEFT A VOICEMAIL, CRYING AND FREAKING OUT ABOUT ALL THIS. SAID I WANTED TO GO HOME, THAT I COULDN'T DO THIS.
I WAS SCARED. I TRY SO HARD TO KEEP UP WITH YOU TWO, BUT IT'S LIKE ALL I DO IS SCREW UP.
I DON'T EVEN HAVE ANY POWERS!
OF COURSE, YOU DO. YOU THINK WE'D BE ANYWHERE WITHOUT YOUR SPELLCASTING?
WE WOULD'VE DIED TONIGHT. LIKE, *EASILY.*
HE WANTS ME TO COME HOME.
WHAT DO YOU WANT?
I JUST... I WANT TO FEEL LIKE I BELONG.
Y'KNOW...
I THINK IT'S HIGH TIME THIS COVEN WAS MADE OFFICIAL.

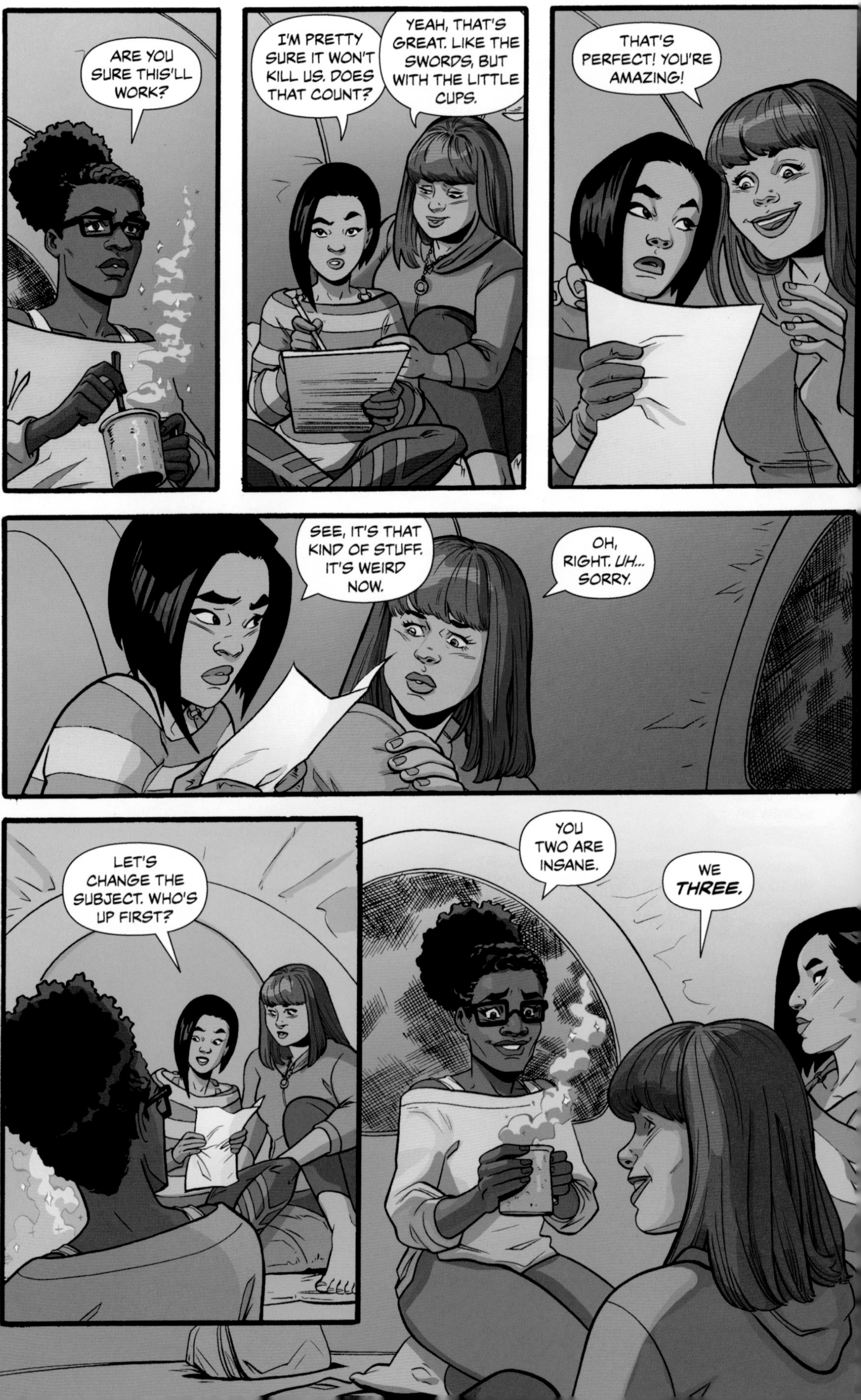
ARE YOU SURE THIS'LL WORK?
I'M PRETTY SURE IT WON'T KILL US. DOES THAT COUNT?
YEAH, THAT'S GREAT. LIKE THE SWORDS, BUT WITH THE LITTLE CUPS.
THAT'S PERFECT! YOU'RE AMAZING!
SEE, IT'S THAT KIND OF STUFF. IT'S WEIRD NOW.
OH, RIGHT. *UH...* SORRY.
LET'S CHANGE THE SUBJECT. WHO'S UP FIRST?
YOU TWO ARE INSANE.
WE ***THREE.***

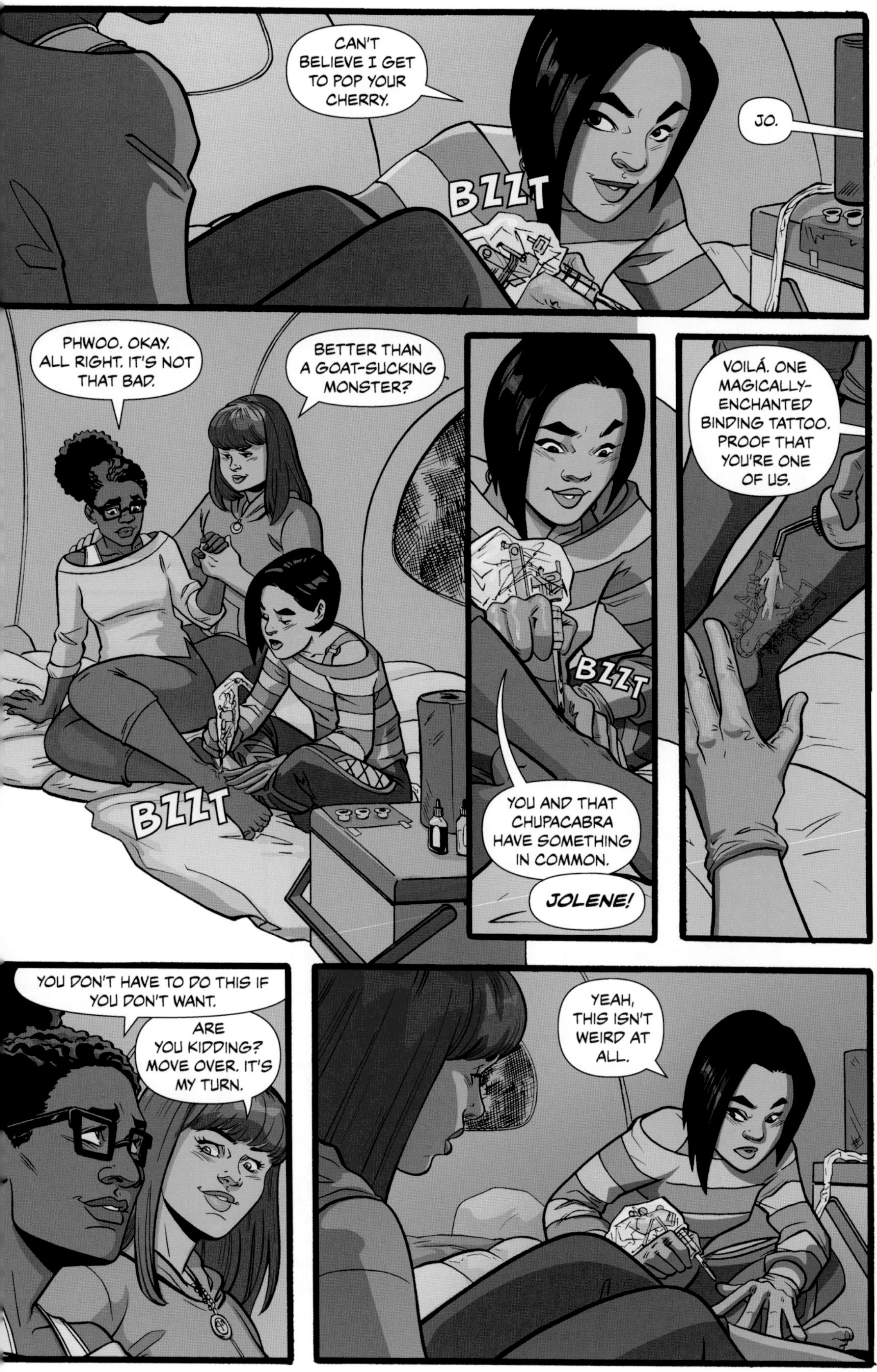
CAN'T BELIEVE I GET TO POP YOUR CHERRY.
JO.
BZZT
PHWOO. OKAY. ALL RIGHT. IT'S NOT THAT BAD.
BETTER THAN A GOAT-SUCKING MONSTER?
BZZT
BZZT
YOU AND THAT CHUPACABRA HAVE SOMETHING IN COMMON.
JOLENE!
VOILÁ. ONE MAGICALLY-ENCHANTED BINDING TATTOO. PROOF THAT YOU'RE ONE OF US.
YOU DON'T HAVE TO DO THIS IF YOU DON'T WANT.
ARE YOU KIDDING? MOVE OVER. IT'S MY TURN.
YEAH, THIS ISN'T WEIRD AT ALL.

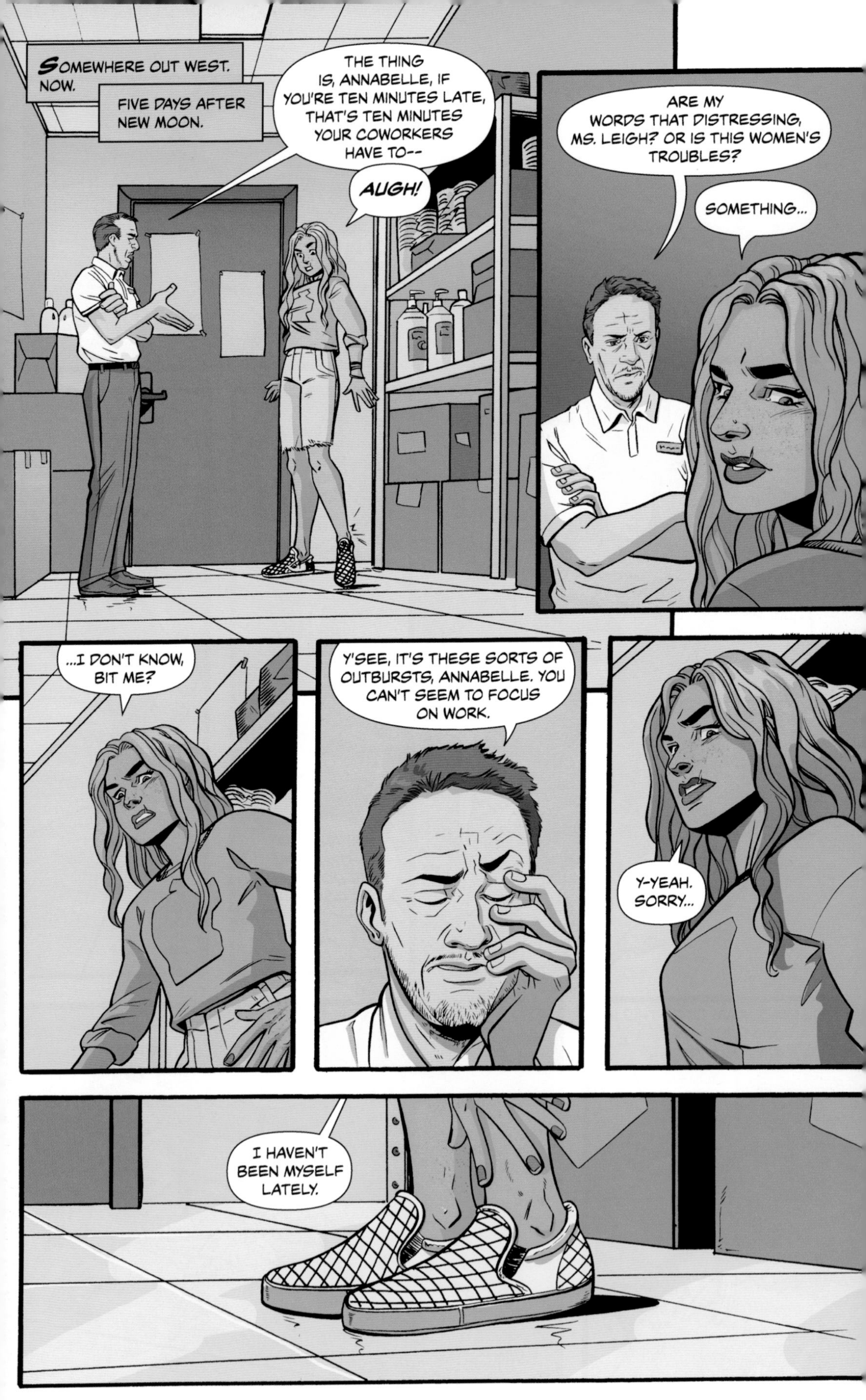
SOMEWHERE OUT WEST. NOW.
FIVE DAYS AFTER NEW MOON.
THE THING IS, ANNABELLE, IF YOU'RE TEN MINUTES LATE, THAT'S TEN MINUTES YOUR COWORKERS HAVE TO--
AUGH!
ARE MY WORDS THAT DISTRESSING, MS. LEIGH? OR IS THIS WOMEN'S TROUBLES?
SOMETHING...
...I DON'T KNOW, BIT ME?
Y'SEE, IT'S THESE SORTS OF OUTBURSTS, ANNABELLE. YOU CAN'T SEEM TO FOCUS ON WORK.
Y-YEAH. SORRY...
I HAVEN'T BEEN MYSELF LATELY.

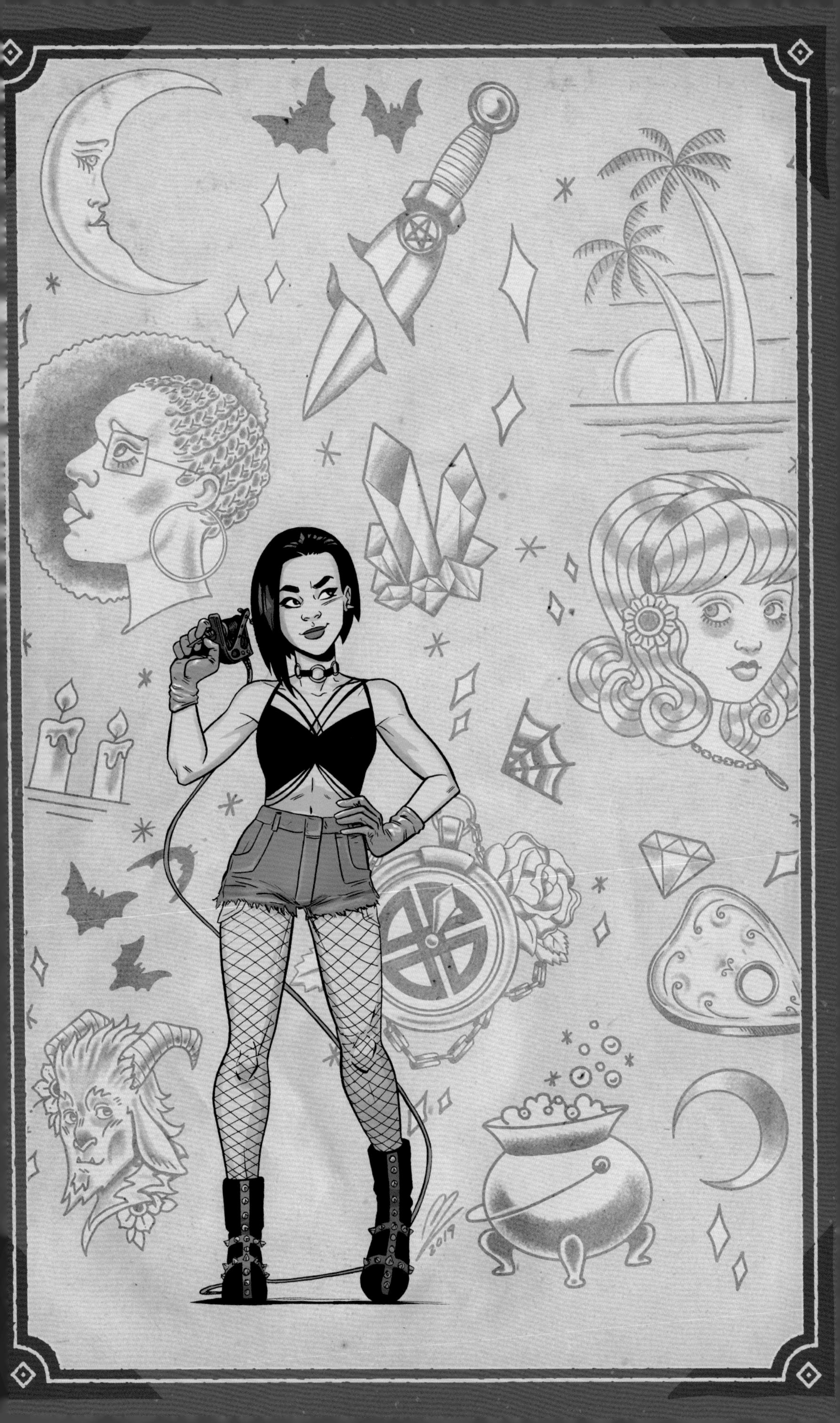

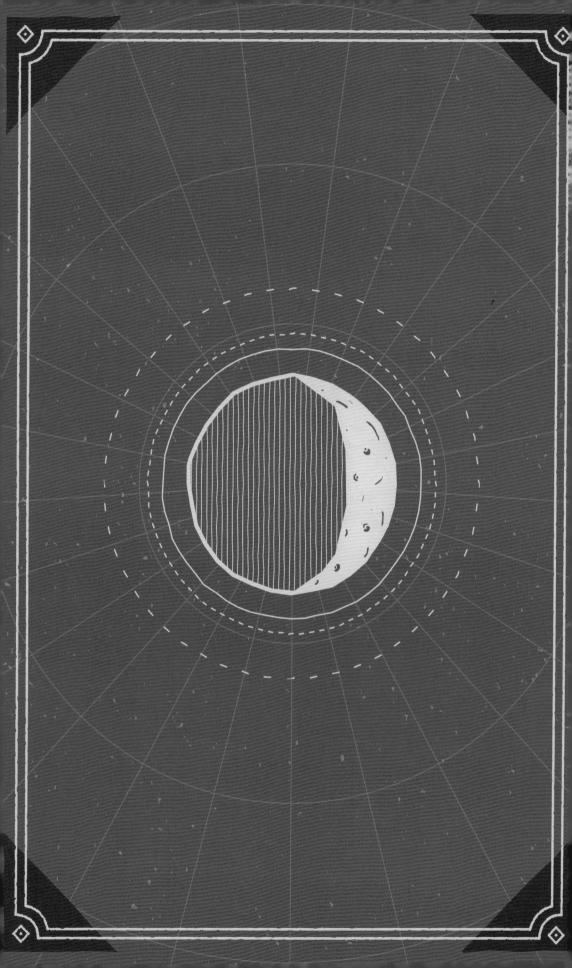

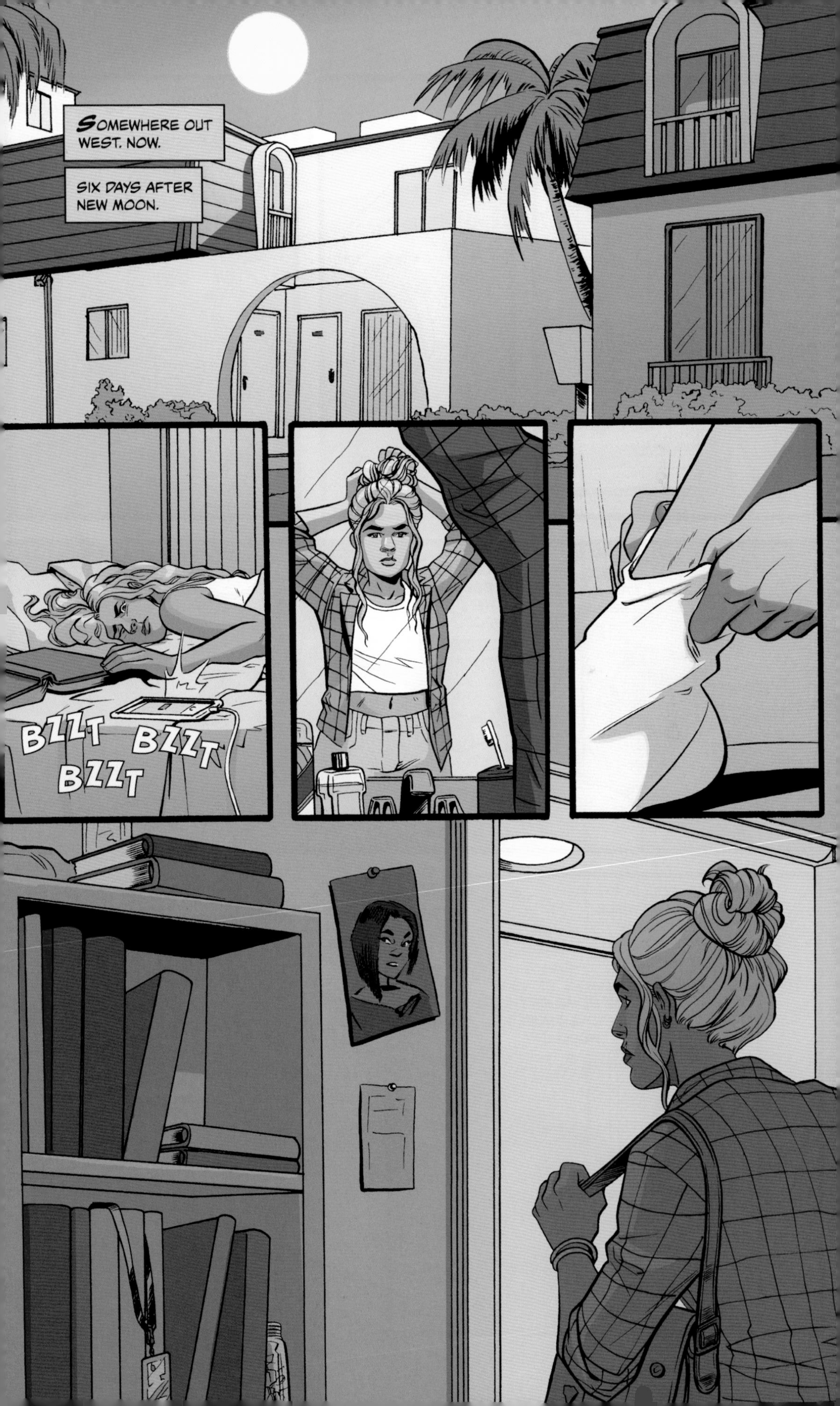
SOMEWHERE OUT WEST. NOW.
SIX DAYS AFTER NEW MOON.
BZZT
BZZT
BZZT

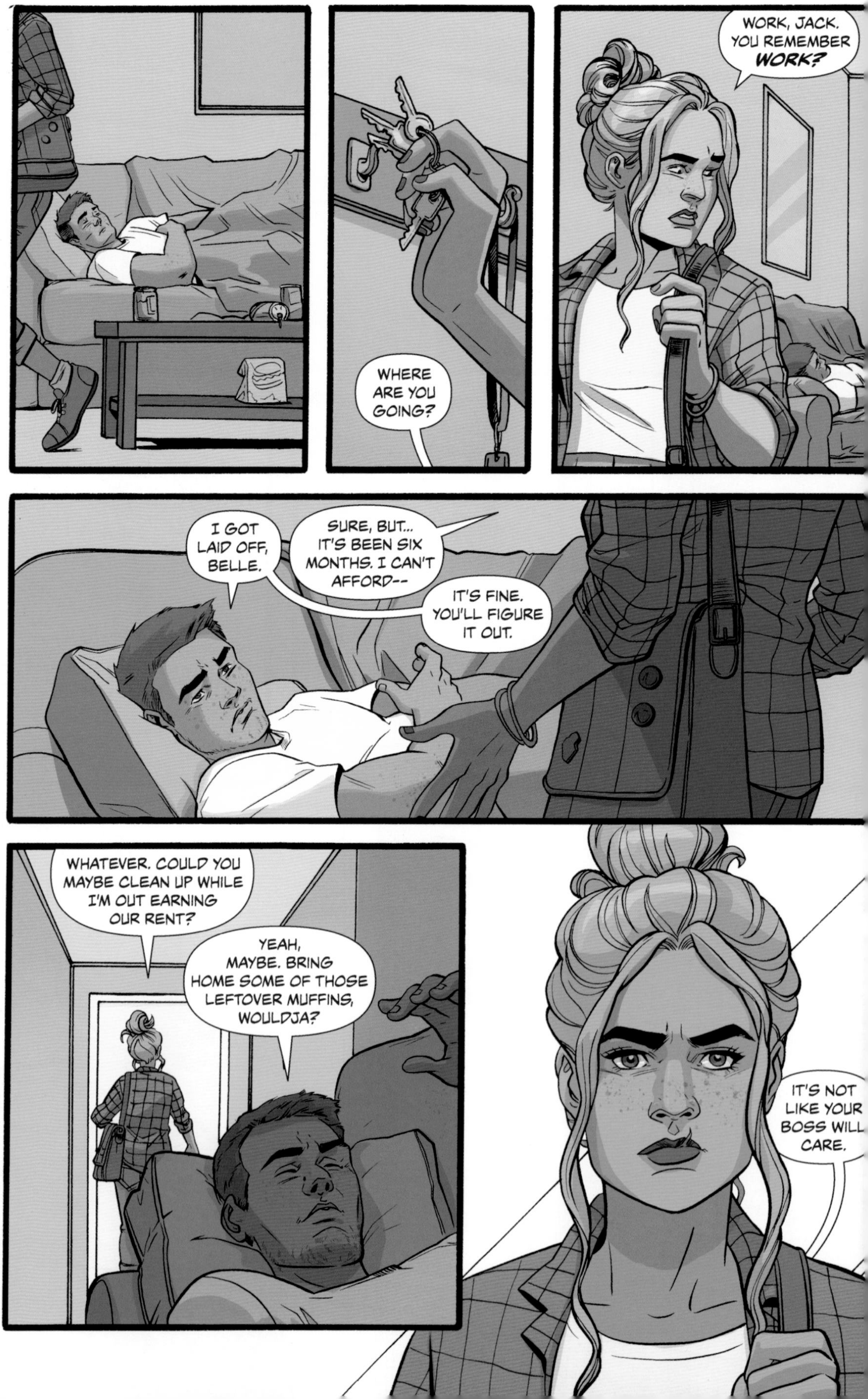

WHERE ARE YOU GOING?
WORK, JACK. YOU REMEMBER WORK?
I GOT LAID OFF, BELLE.
SURE, BUT... IT'S BEEN SIX MONTHS. I CAN'T AFFORD--
IT'S FINE. YOU'LL FIGURE IT OUT.
WHATEVER. COULD YOU MAYBE CLEAN UP WHILE I'M OUT EARNING OUR RENT?
YEAH, MAYBE. BRING HOME SOME OF THOSE LEFTOVER MUFFINS, WOULDJA?
IT'S NOT LIKE YOUR BOSS WILL CARE.

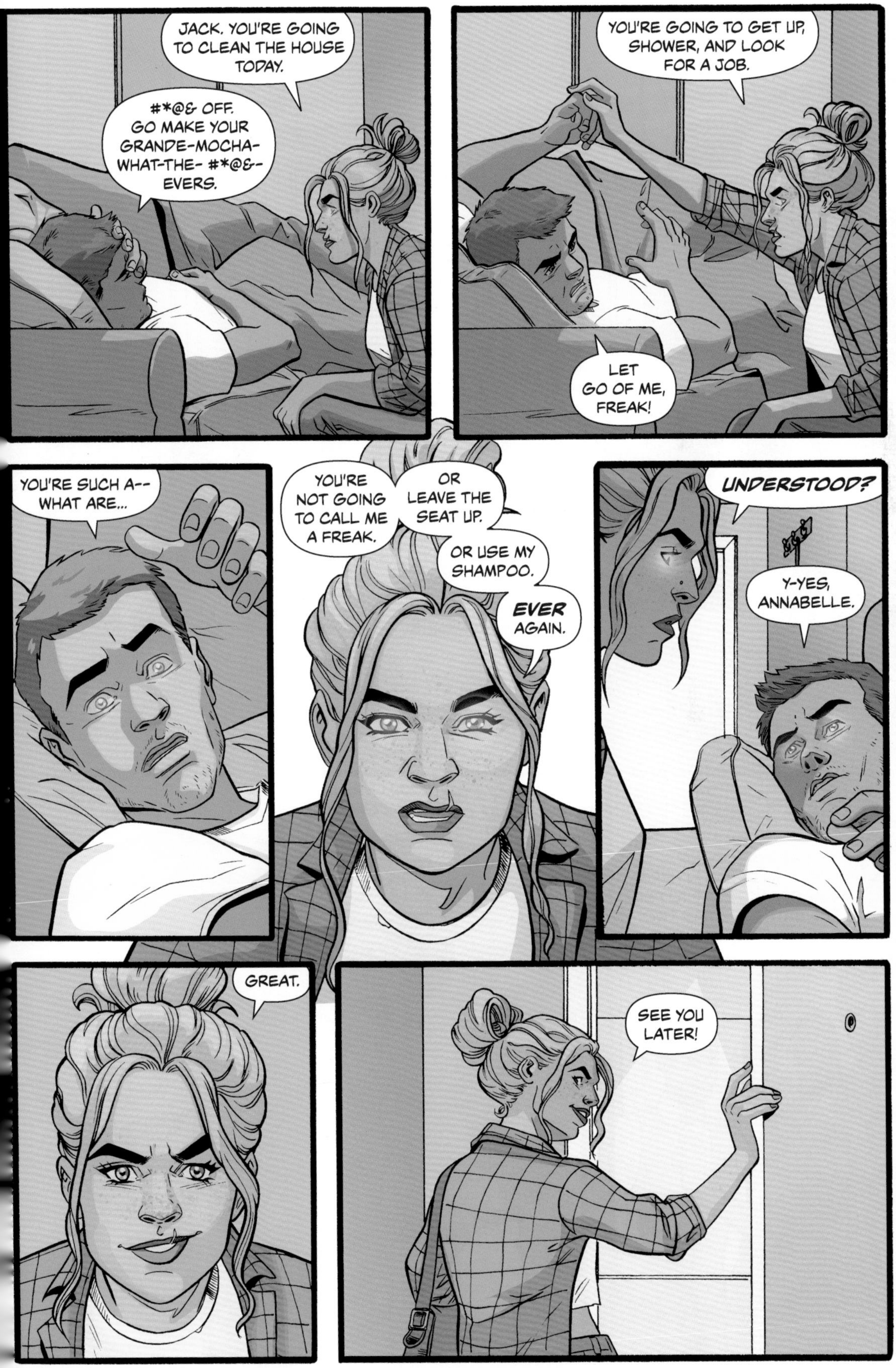
JACK. YOU'RE GOING TO CLEAN THE HOUSE TODAY.
#*@& OFF. GO MAKE YOUR GRANDE-MOCHA-WHAT-THE- #*@&-EVERS.
YOU'RE GOING TO GET UP, SHOWER, AND LOOK FOR A JOB.
LET GO OF ME, FREAK!
YOU'RE SUCH A--WHAT ARE...
YOU'RE NOT GOING TO CALL ME A FREAK.
OR LEAVE THE SEAT UP.
OR USE MY SHAMPOO.
EVER AGAIN.
UNDERSTOOD?
Y-YES, ANNABELLE.
GREAT.
SEE YOU LATER!

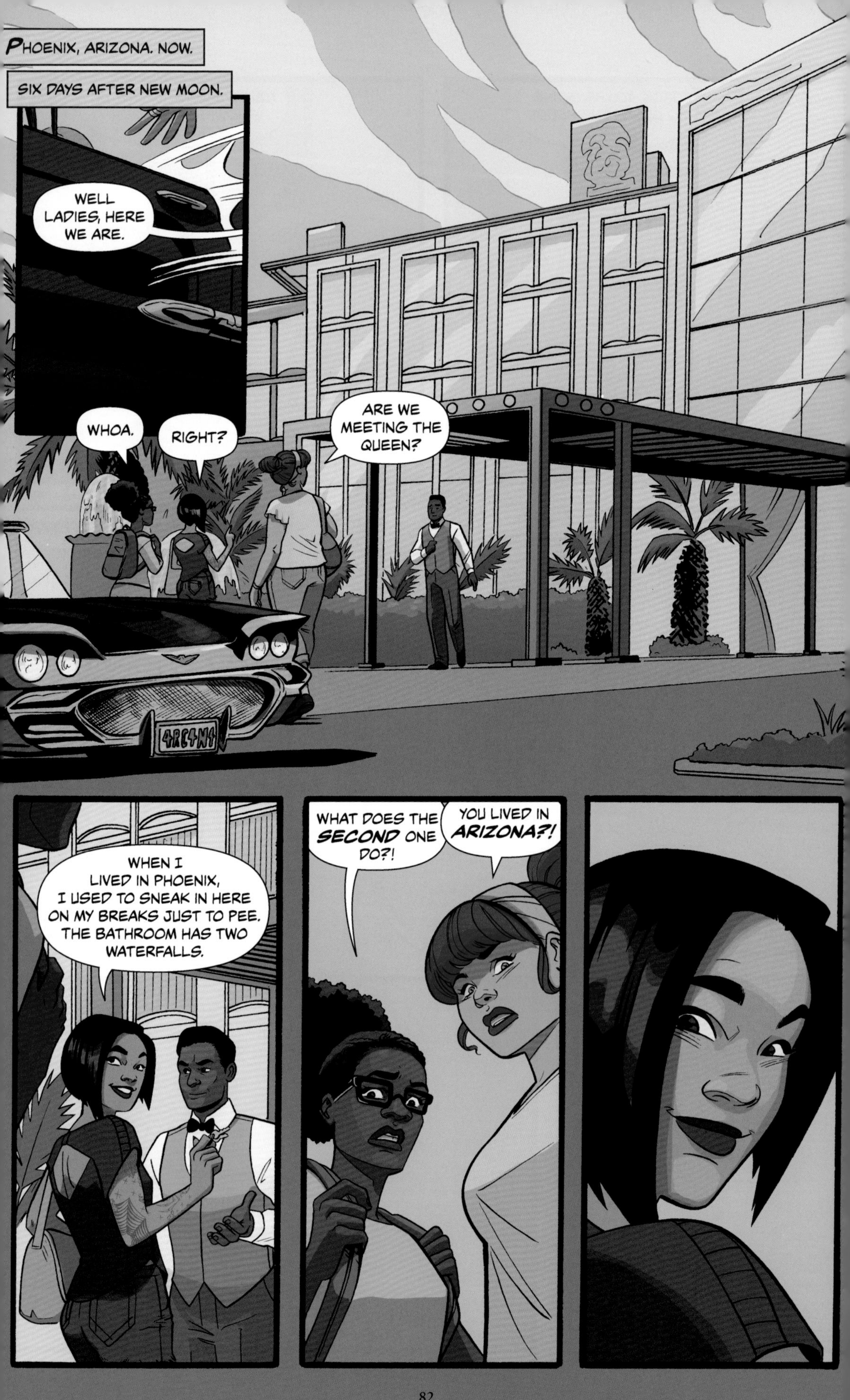
PHOENIX, ARIZONA. NOW.
SIX DAYS AFTER NEW MOON.
WELL LADIES, HERE WE ARE.
WHOA.
RIGHT?
ARE WE MEETING THE QUEEN?
WHEN I LIVED IN PHOENIX, I USED TO SNEAK IN HERE ON MY BREAKS JUST TO PEE. THE BATHROOM HAS TWO WATERFALLS.
WHAT DOES THE SECOND ONE DO?!
YOU LIVED IN ARIZONA?!

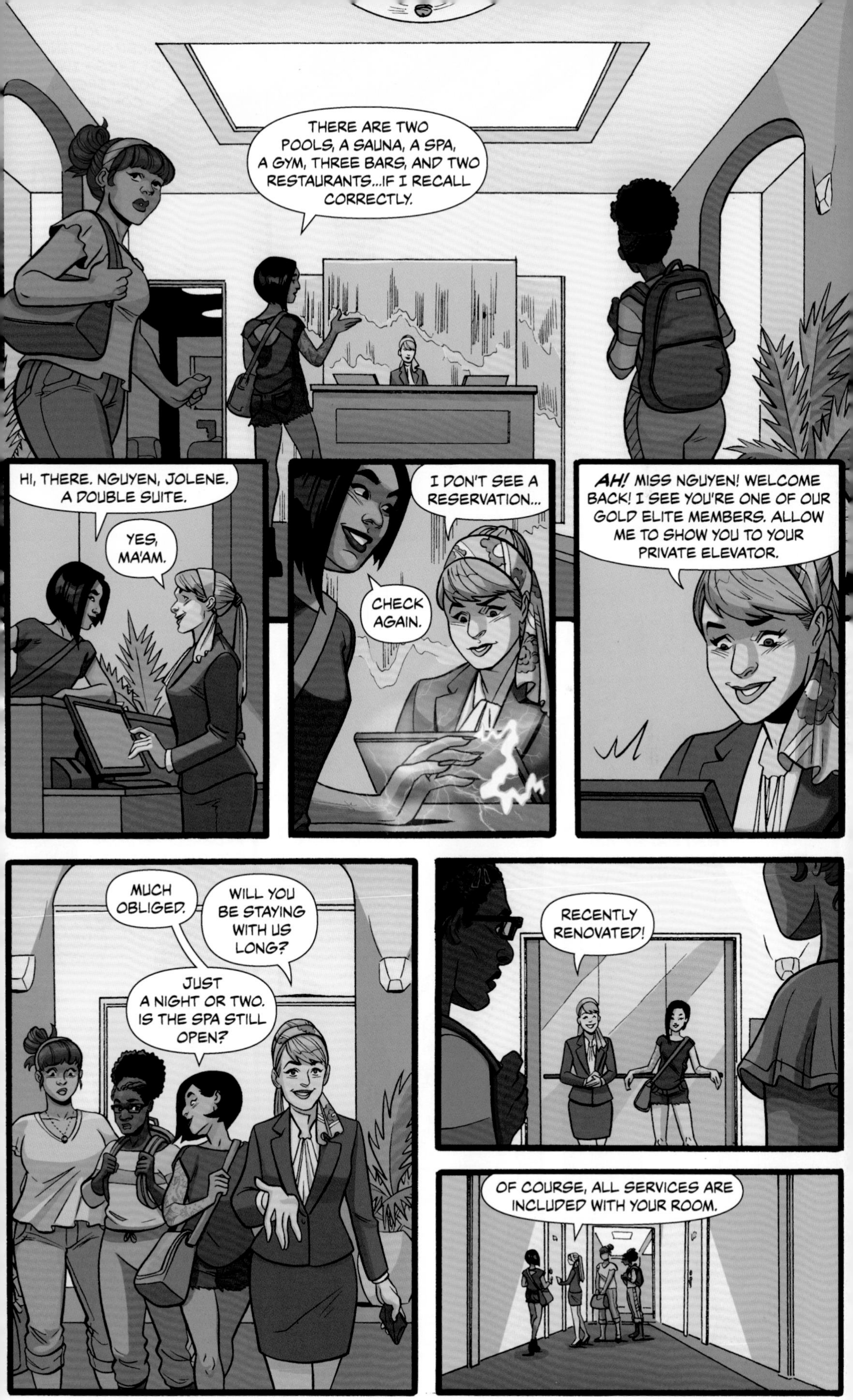
THERE ARE TWO POOLS, A SAUNA, A SPA, A GYM, THREE BARS, AND TWO RESTAURANTS...IF I RECALL CORRECTLY.
HI, THERE. NGUYEN, JOLENE. A DOUBLE SUITE.
YES, MA'AM.
I DON'T SEE A RESERVATION...
CHECK AGAIN.
AH! MISS NGUYEN! WELCOME BACK! I SEE YOU'RE ONE OF OUR GOLD ELITE MEMBERS. ALLOW ME TO SHOW YOU TO YOUR PRIVATE ELEVATOR.
MUCH OBLIGED.
WILL YOU BE STAYING WITH US LONG?
JUST A NIGHT OR TWO. IS THE SPA STILL OPEN?
RECENTLY RENOVATED!
OF COURSE, ALL SERVICES ARE INCLUDED WITH YOUR ROOM.

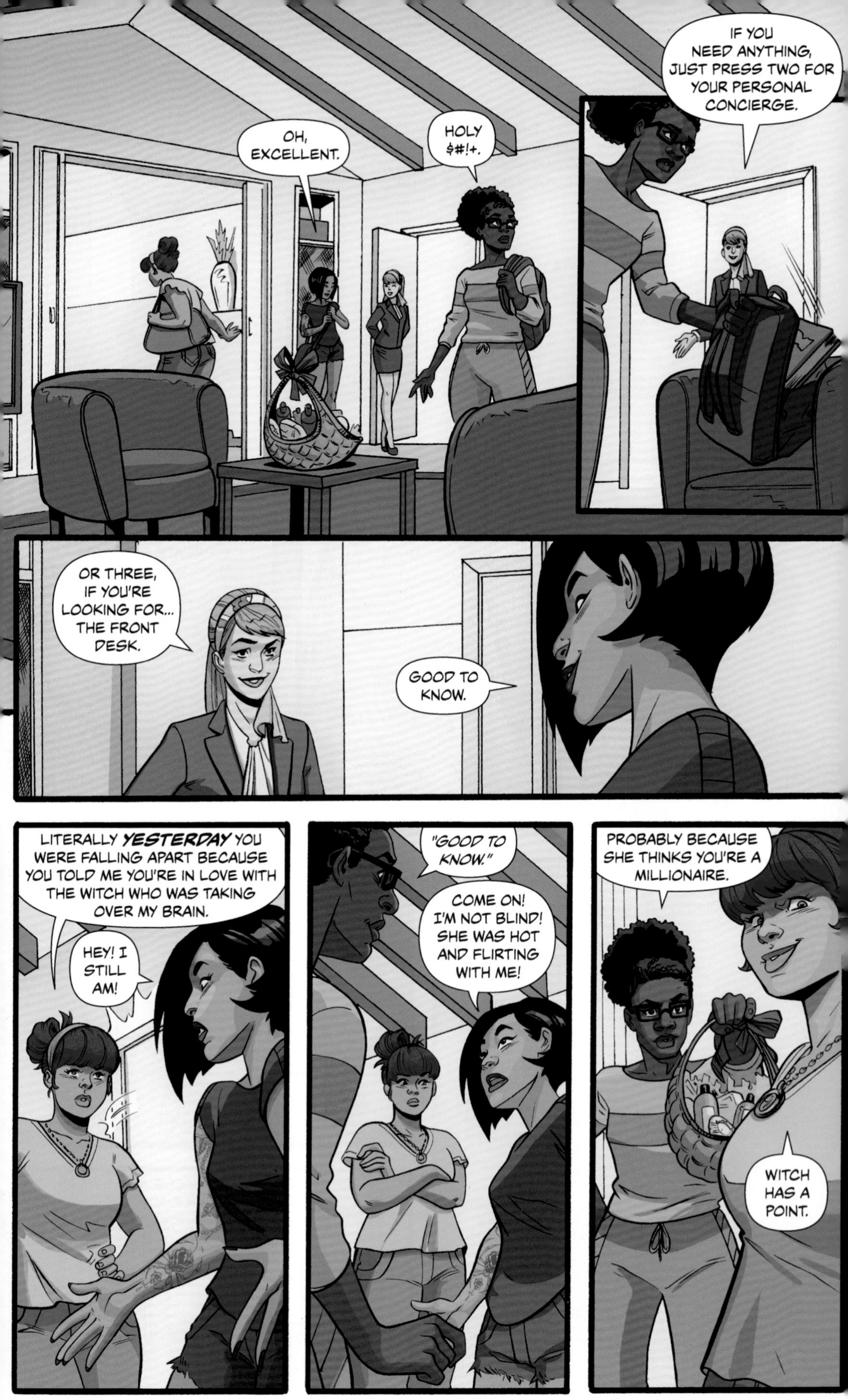
OH, EXCELLENT.
HOLY $#!+.
IF YOU NEED ANYTHING, JUST PRESS TWO FOR YOUR PERSONAL CONCIERGE.
OR THREE, IF YOU'RE LOOKING FOR... THE FRONT DESK.
GOOD TO KNOW.
LITERALLY YESTERDAY YOU WERE FALLING APART BECAUSE YOU TOLD ME YOU'RE IN LOVE WITH THE WITCH WHO WAS TAKING OVER MY BRAIN.
HEY! I STILL AM!
"GOOD TO KNOW."
COME ON! I'M NOT BLIND! SHE WAS HOT AND FLIRTING WITH ME!
PROBABLY BECAUSE SHE THINKS YOU'RE A MILLIONAIRE.
WITCH HAS A POINT.

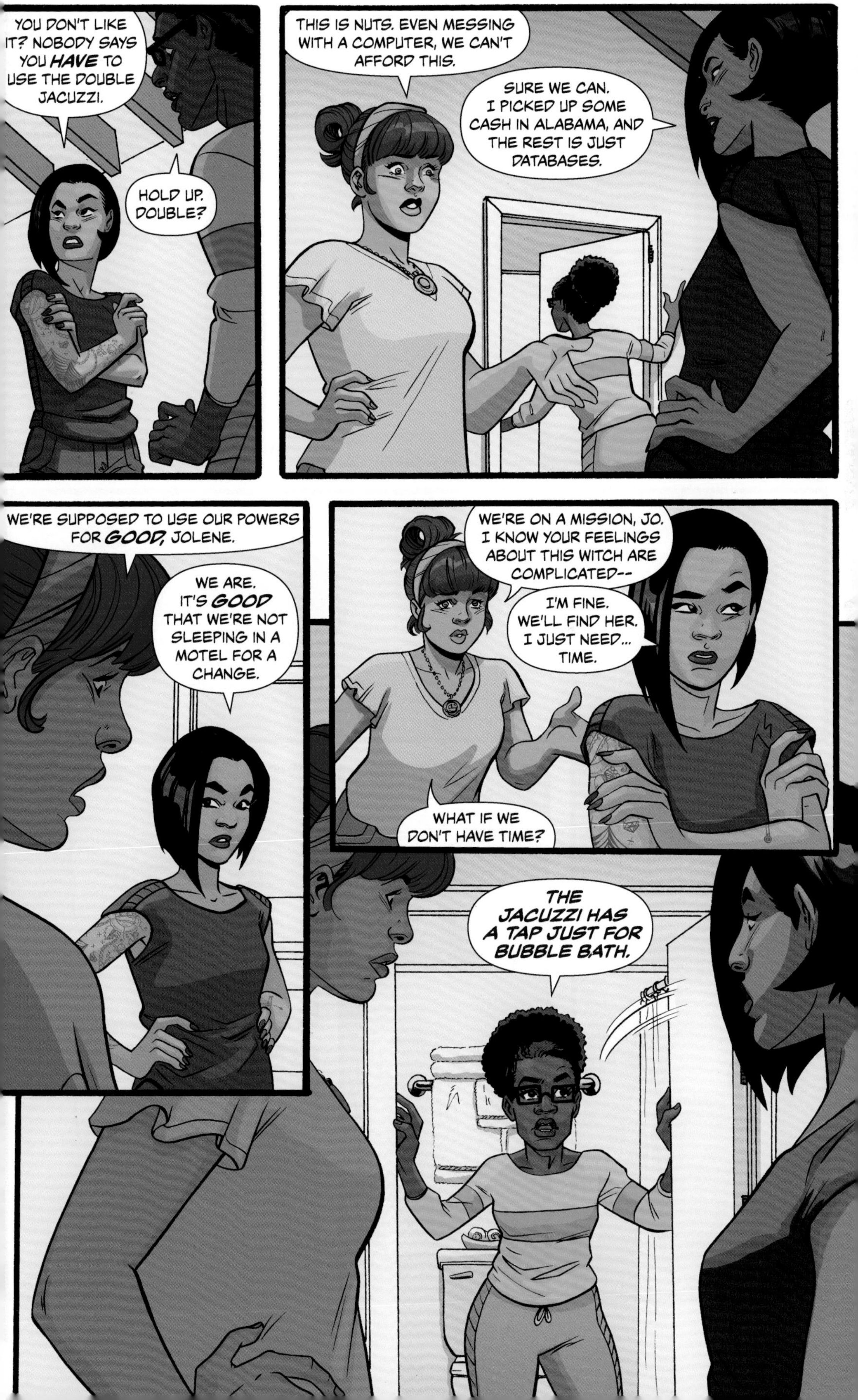

YOU DON'T LIKE IT? NOBODY SAYS YOU HAVE TO USE THE DOUBLE JACUZZI.
HOLD UP. DOUBLE?
THIS IS NUTS. EVEN MESSING WITH A COMPUTER, WE CAN'T AFFORD THIS.
SURE WE CAN. I PICKED UP SOME CASH IN ALABAMA, AND THE REST IS JUST DATABASES.
WE'RE SUPPOSED TO USE OUR POWERS FOR GOOD, JOLENE.
WE ARE. IT'S GOOD THAT WE'RE NOT SLEEPING IN A MOTEL FOR A CHANGE.
WE'RE ON A MISSION, JO. I KNOW YOUR FEELINGS ABOUT THIS WITCH ARE COMPLICATED--
I'M FINE. WE'LL FIND HER. I JUST NEED... TIME.
WHAT IF WE DON'T HAVE TIME?
THE JACUZZI HAS A TAP JUST FOR BUBBLE BATH.

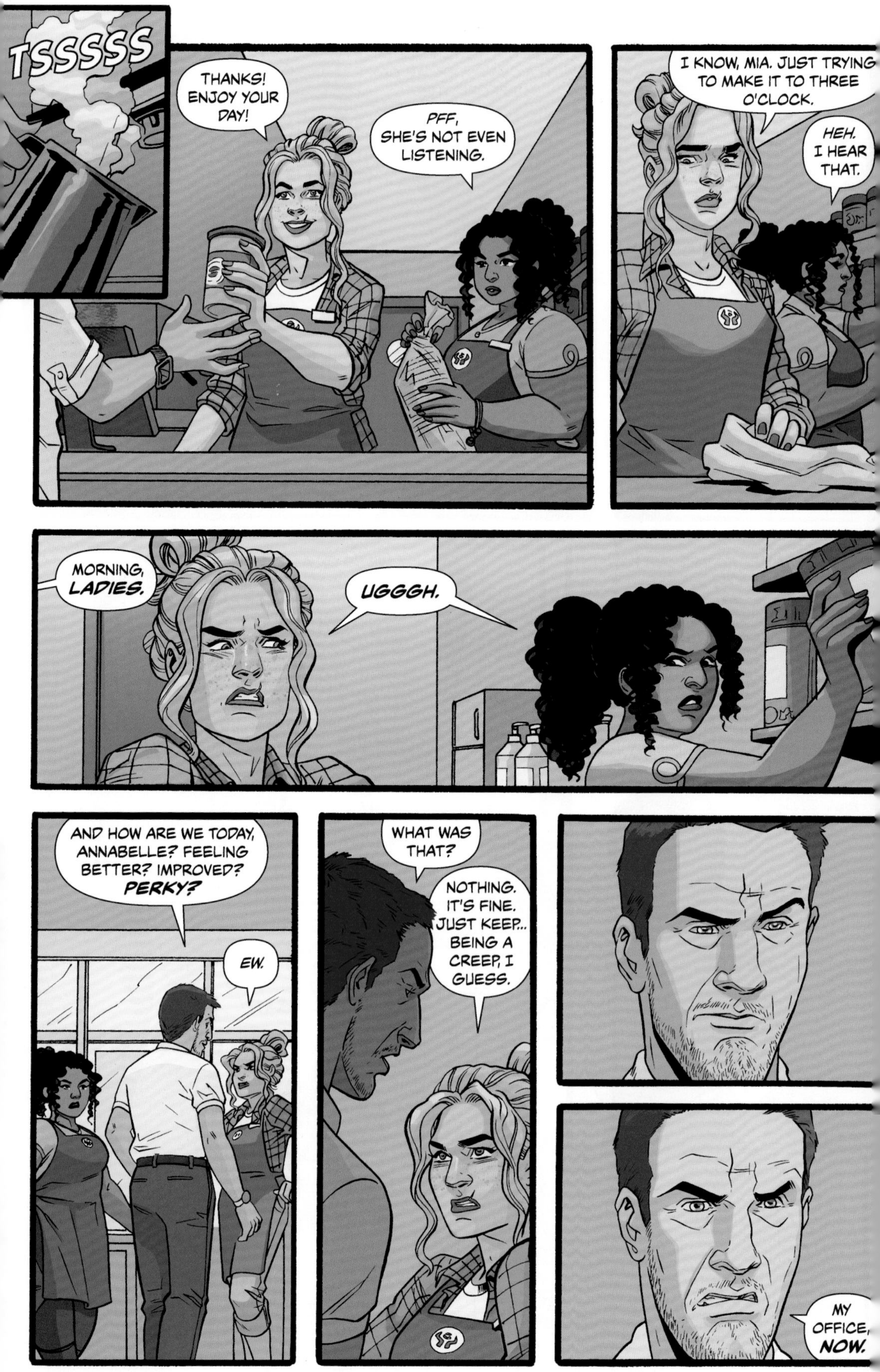
TSSSSS
THANKS! ENJOY YOUR DAY!
PFF, SHE'S NOT EVEN LISTENING.
I KNOW, MIA. JUST TRYING TO MAKE IT TO THREE O'CLOCK.
HEH. I HEAR THAT.
MORNING, LADIES.
UGGGH.
AND HOW ARE WE TODAY, ANNABELLE? FEELING BETTER? IMPROVED? PERKY?
EW.
WHAT WAS THAT?
NOTHING. IT'S FINE. JUST KEEP... BEING A CREEP, I GUESS.
MY OFFICE, NOW.

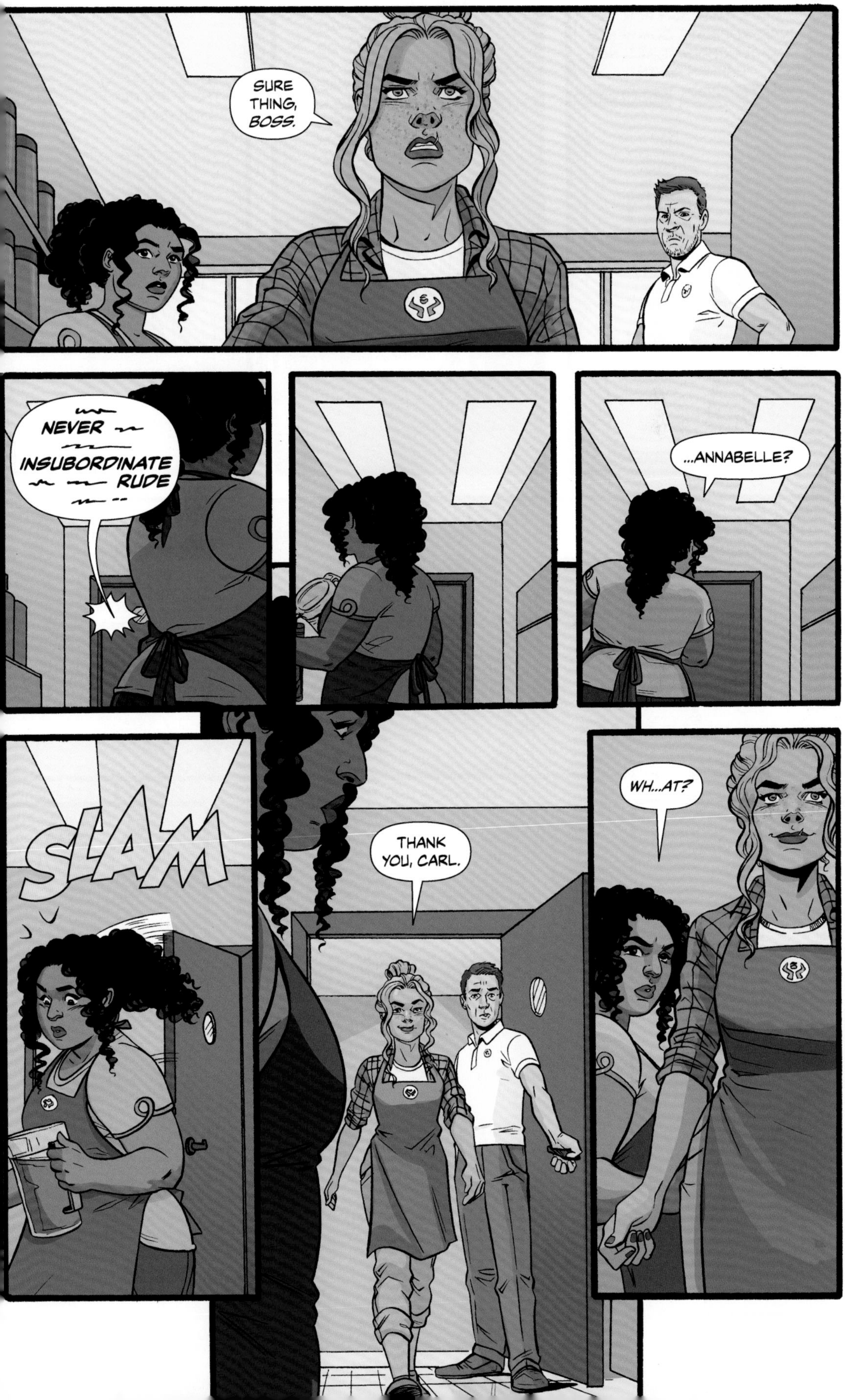
SURE THING, BOSS.
NEVER
INSUBORDINATE
RUDE
...ANNABELLE?
SLAM
THANK YOU, CARL.
WH...AT?

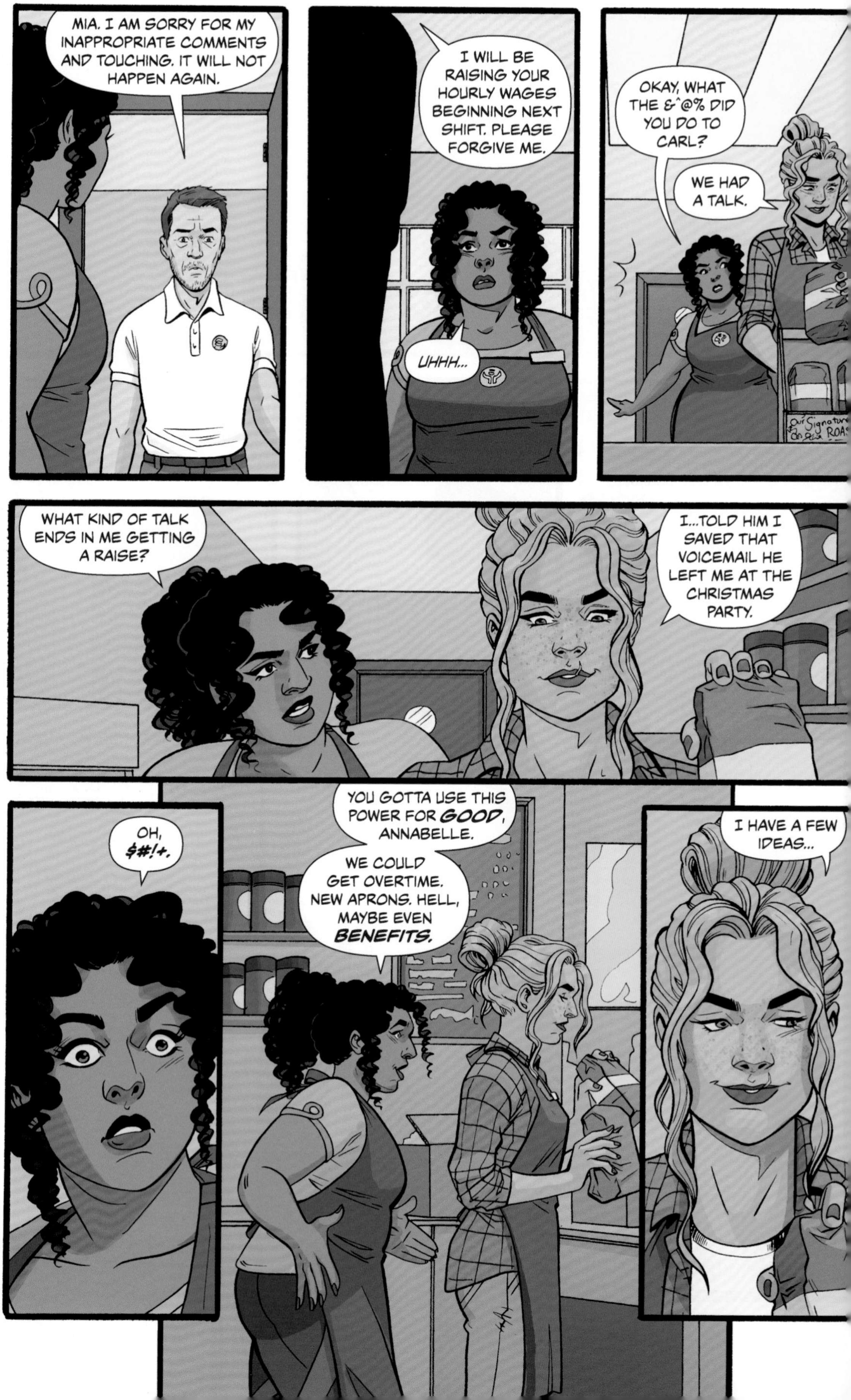
MIA. I AM SORRY FOR MY INAPPROPRIATE COMMENTS AND TOUCHING. IT WILL NOT HAPPEN AGAIN.
I WILL BE RAISING YOUR HOURLY WAGES BEGINNING NEXT SHIFT. PLEASE FORGIVE ME.
UHHH...
OKAY, WHAT THE &^@% DID YOU DO TO CARL?
WE HAD A TALK.
WHAT KIND OF TALK ENDS IN ME GETTING A RAISE?
I...TOLD HIM I SAVED THAT VOICEMAIL HE LEFT ME AT THE CHRISTMAS PARTY.
OH, $#!+.
YOU GOTTA USE THIS POWER FOR GOOD, ANNABELLE.
WE COULD GET OVERTIME. NEW APRONS. HELL, MAYBE EVEN BENEFITS.
I HAVE A FEW IDEAS...

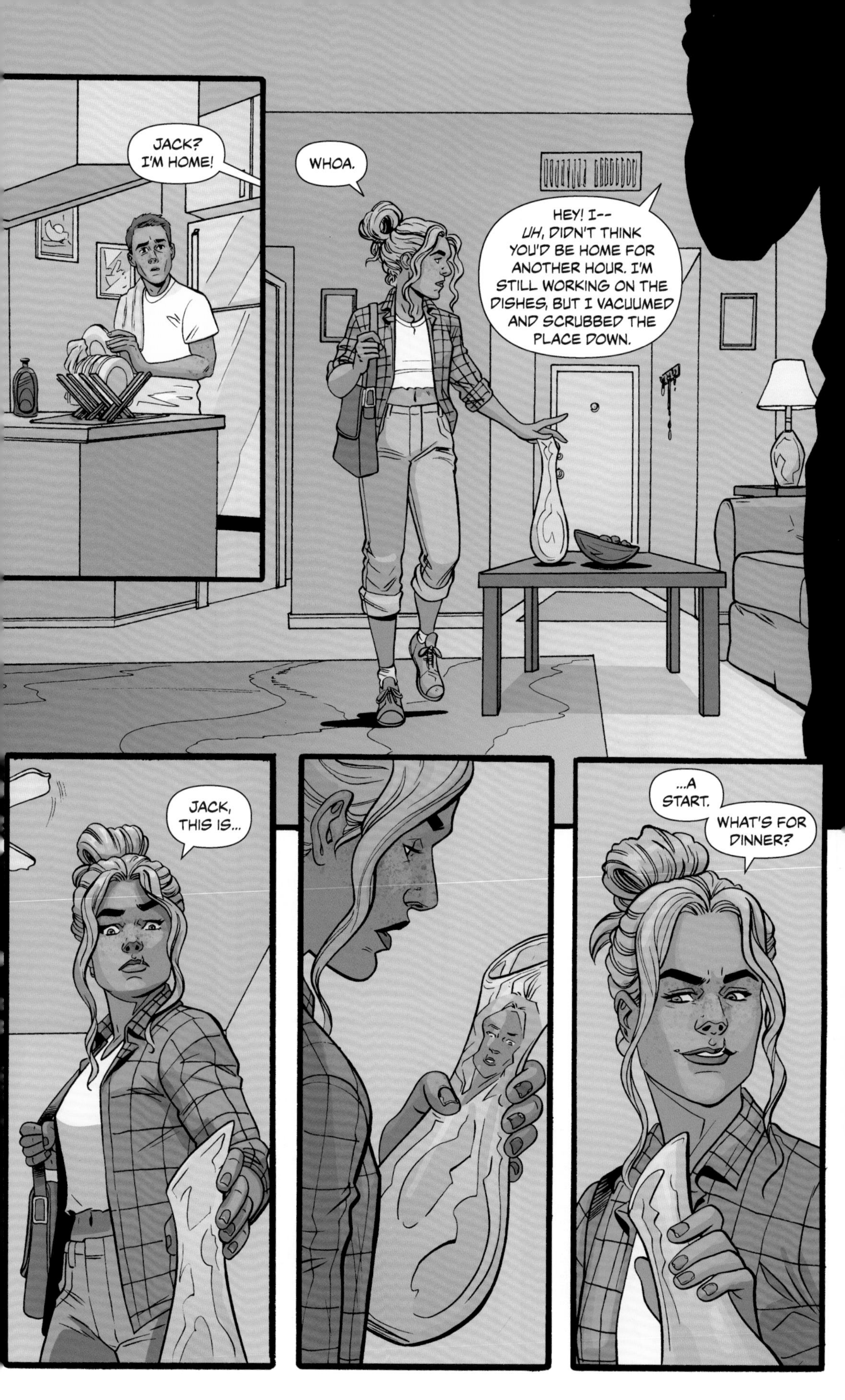
JACK? I'M HOME!
WHOA.
HEY! I-- UH, DIDN'T THINK YOU'D BE HOME FOR ANOTHER HOUR. I'M STILL WORKING ON THE DISHES, BUT I VACUUMED AND SCRUBBED THE PLACE DOWN.
JACK, THIS IS...
...A START.
WHAT'S FOR DINNER?

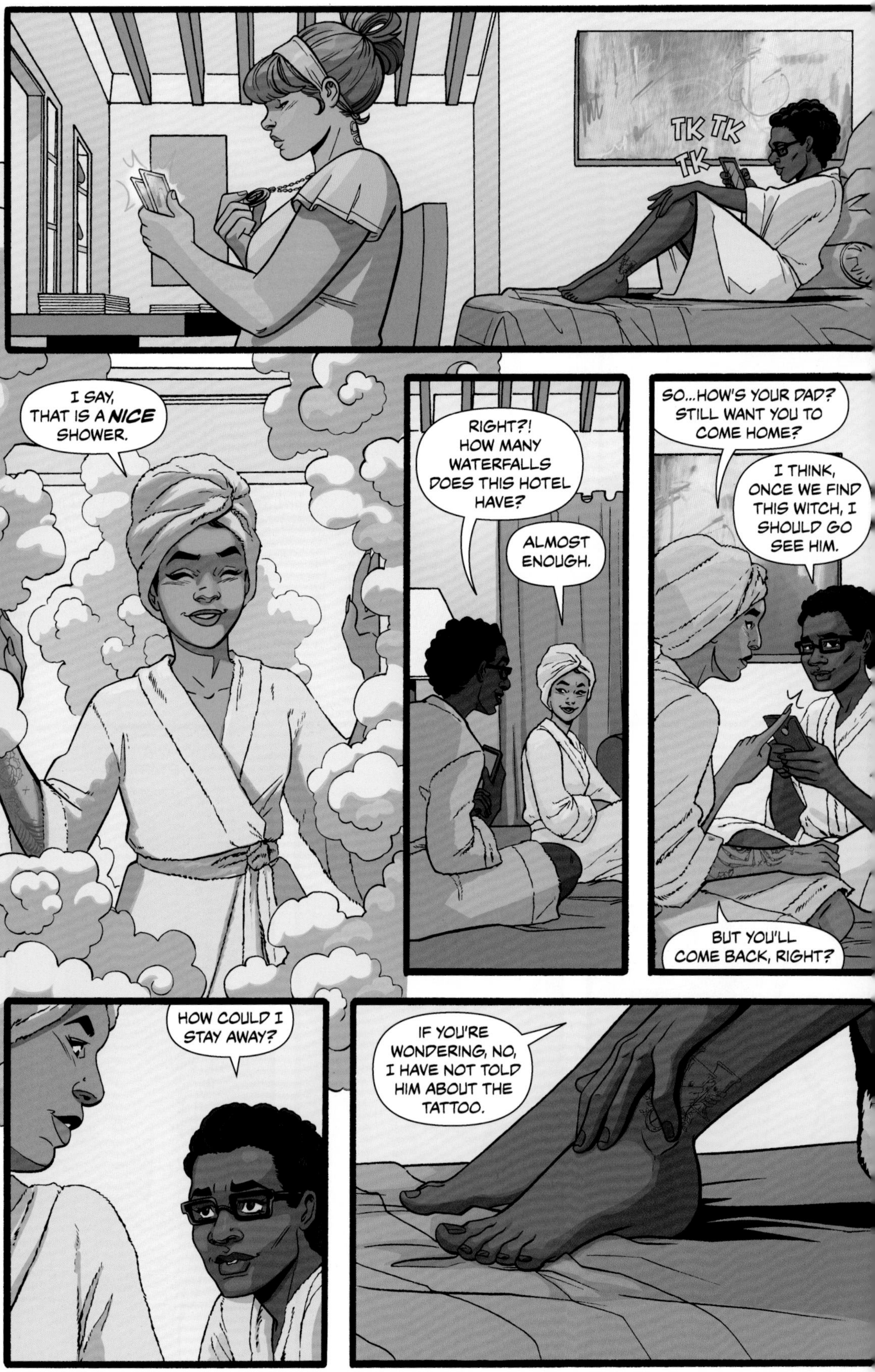
TK TK
TK
I SAY, THAT IS A NICE SHOWER.
RIGHT?! HOW MANY WATERFALLS DOES THIS HOTEL HAVE?
ALMOST ENOUGH.
SO...HOW'S YOUR DAD? STILL WANT YOU TO COME HOME?
I THINK, ONCE WE FIND THIS WITCH, I SHOULD GO SEE HIM.
BUT YOU'LL COME BACK, RIGHT?
HOW COULD I STAY AWAY?
IF YOU'RE WONDERING, NO, I HAVE NOT TOLD HIM ABOUT THE TATTOO.

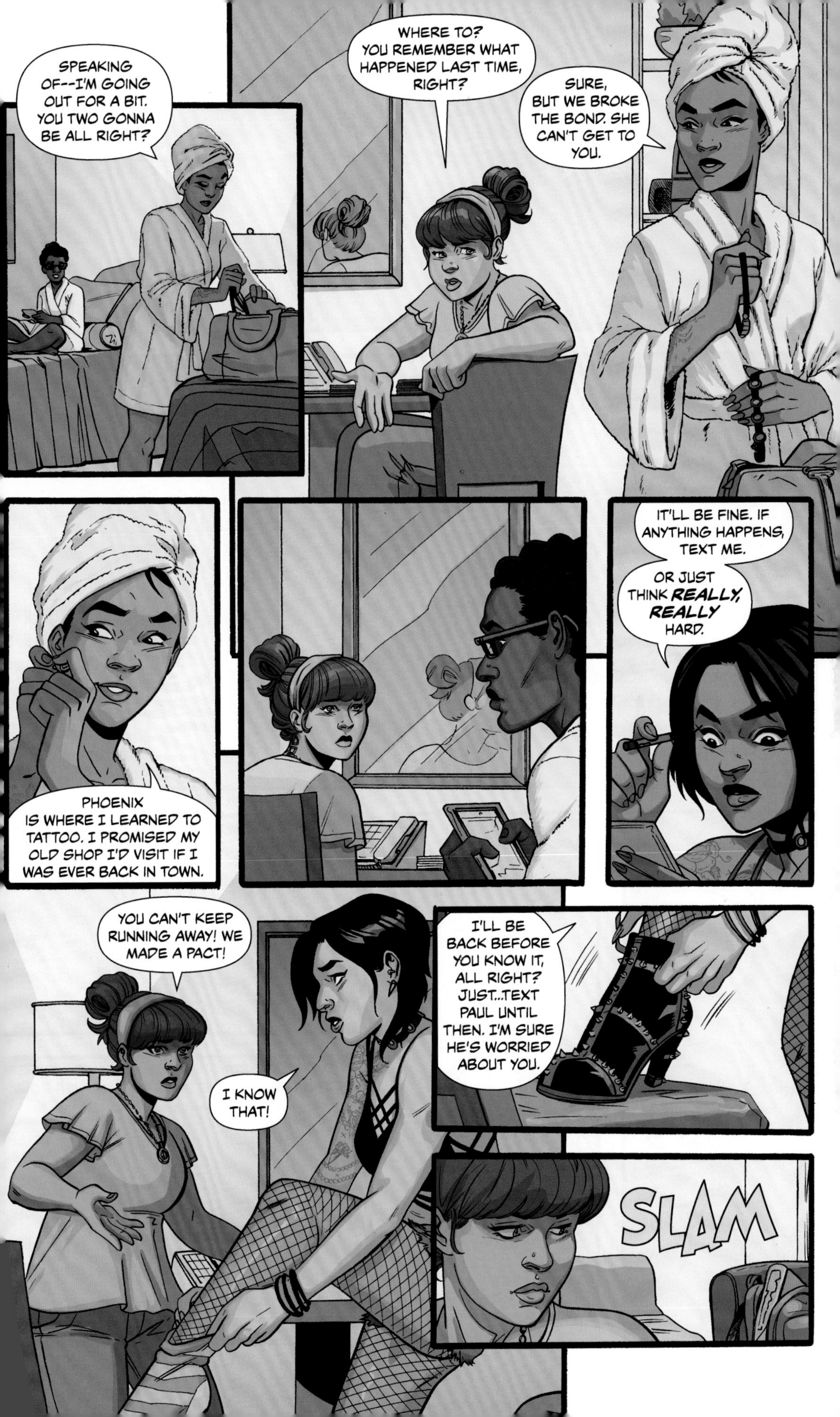
SPEAKING OF--I'M GOING OUT FOR A BIT. YOU TWO GONNA BE ALL RIGHT?
WHERE TO? YOU REMEMBER WHAT HAPPENED LAST TIME, RIGHT?
SURE, BUT WE BROKE THE BOND. SHE CAN'T GET TO YOU.
PHOENIX IS WHERE I LEARNED TO TATTOO. I PROMISED MY OLD SHOP I'D VISIT IF I WAS EVER BACK IN TOWN.
IT'LL BE FINE. IF ANYTHING HAPPENS, TEXT ME.
OR JUST THINK ***REALLY, REALLY*** HARD.
YOU CAN'T KEEP RUNNING AWAY! WE MADE A PACT!
I KNOW THAT!
I'LL BE BACK BEFORE YOU KNOW IT, ALL RIGHT? JUST...TEXT PAUL UNTIL THEN. I'M SURE HE'S WORRIED ABOUT YOU.
SLAM

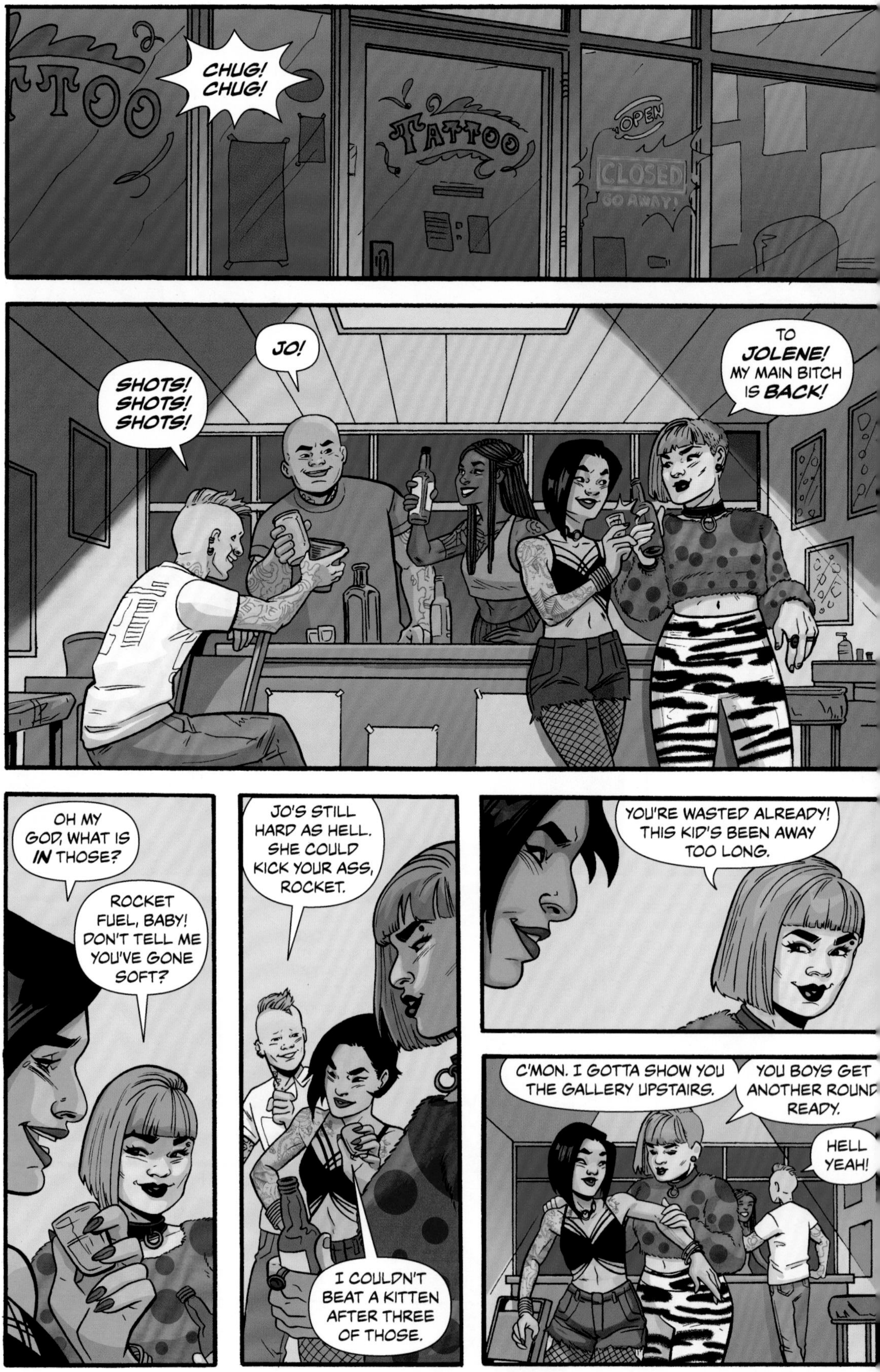
TTOO
CHUG! CHUG!
TATTOO
OPEN
CLOSED GO AWAY!
SHOTS! SHOTS! SHOTS!
JO!
TO JOLENE! MY MAIN BITCH IS BACK!
OH MY GOD, WHAT IS IN THOSE?
ROCKET FUEL, BABY! DON'T TELL ME YOU'VE GONE SOFT?
JO'S STILL HARD AS HELL. SHE COULD KICK YOUR ASS, ROCKET.
I COULDN'T BEAT A KITTEN AFTER THREE OF THOSE.
YOU'RE WASTED ALREADY! THIS KID'S BEEN AWAY TOO LONG.
C'MON. I GOTTA SHOW YOU THE GALLERY UPSTAIRS.
YOU BOYS GET ANOTHER ROUND READY.
HELL YEAH!

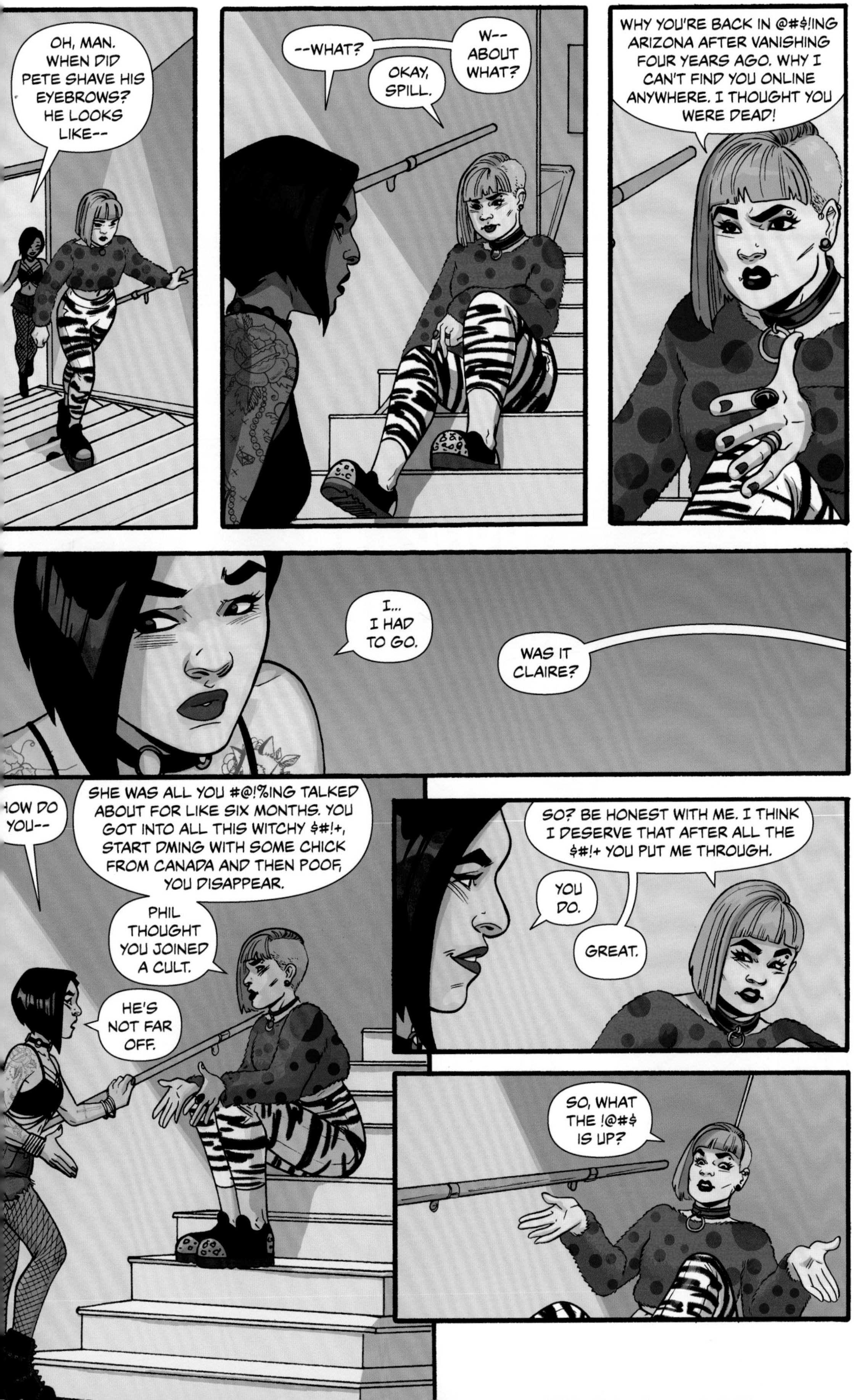
OH, MAN. WHEN DID PETE SHAVE HIS EYEBROWS? HE LOOKS LIKE--
--WHAT?
W-- ABOUT WHAT?
OKAY, SPILL.
WHY YOU'RE BACK IN @#$!ING ARIZONA AFTER VANISHING FOUR YEARS AGO. WHY I CAN'T FIND YOU ONLINE ANYWHERE. I THOUGHT YOU WERE DEAD!
I... I HAD TO GO.
WAS IT CLAIRE?
HOW DO YOU--
SHE WAS ALL YOU #@!%ING TALKED ABOUT FOR LIKE SIX MONTHS. YOU GOT INTO ALL THIS WITCHY $#!+, START DMING WITH SOME CHICK FROM CANADA AND THEN POOF, YOU DISAPPEAR.
PHIL THOUGHT YOU JOINED A CULT.
HE'S NOT FAR OFF.
SO? BE HONEST WITH ME. I THINK I DESERVE THAT AFTER ALL THE $#!+ YOU PUT ME THROUGH.
YOU DO.
GREAT.
SO, WHAT THE !@#$ IS UP?

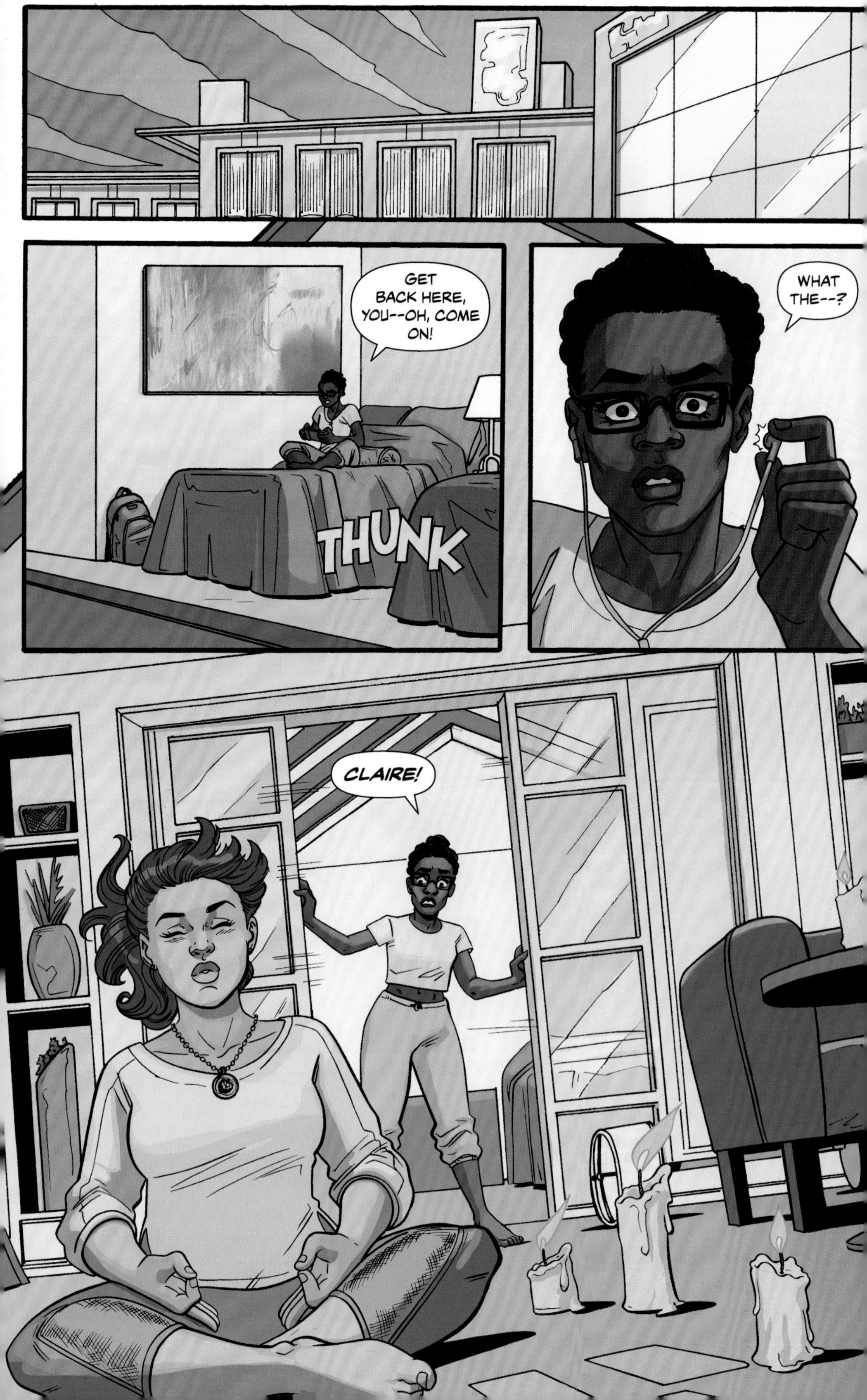
GET BACK HERE, YOU--OH, COME ON!
THUNK
WHAT THE--?
CLAIRE!

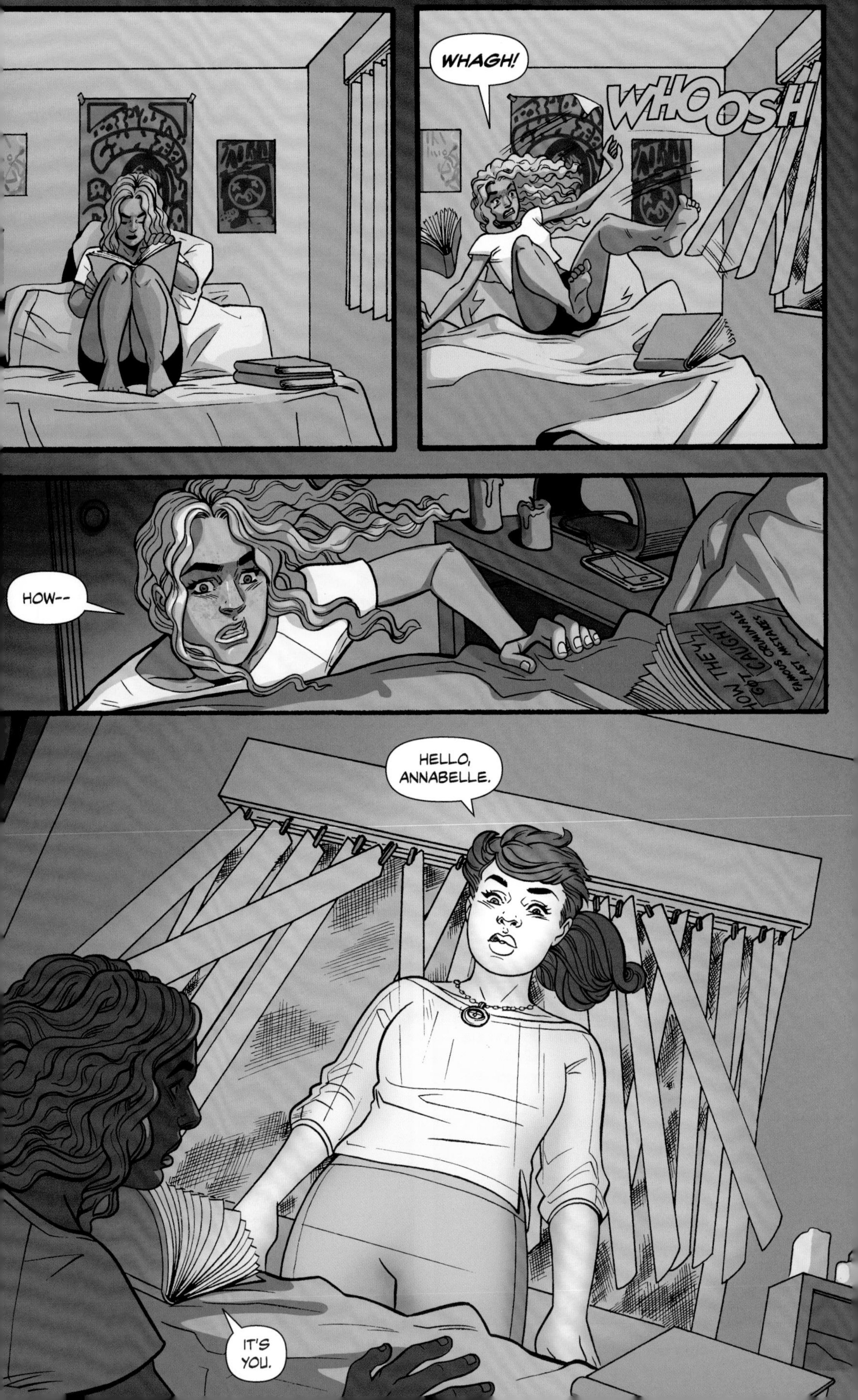
WHAGH!
WHOOSH
HOW--
HOW THEY GOT CAUGHT
FAMOUS CRIMINALS LAST MISTAKES
HELLO, ANNABELLE.
IT'S YOU.

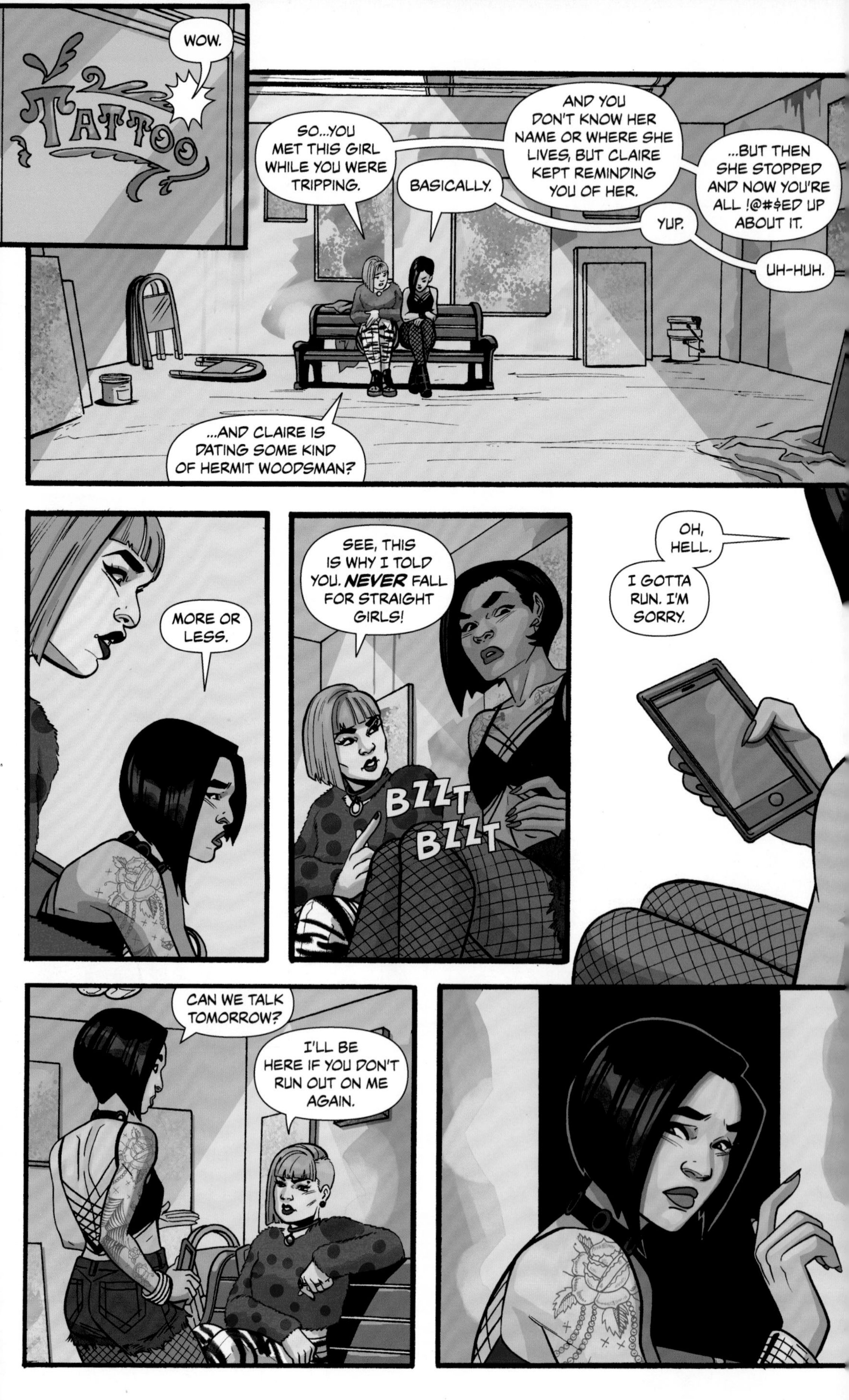
TATTOO
WOW.
SO...YOU MET THIS GIRL WHILE YOU WERE TRIPPING.
BASICALLY.
AND YOU DON'T KNOW HER NAME OR WHERE SHE LIVES, BUT CLAIRE KEPT REMINDING YOU OF HER.
YUP.
...BUT THEN SHE STOPPED AND NOW YOU'RE ALL !@#$ED UP ABOUT IT.
UH-HUH.
...AND CLAIRE IS DATING SOME KIND OF HERMIT WOODSMAN?
MORE OR LESS.
SEE, THIS IS WHY I TOLD YOU. NEVER FALL FOR STRAIGHT GIRLS!
BZZT BZZT
OH, HELL.
I GOTTA RUN. I'M SORRY.
CAN WE TALK TOMORROW?
I'LL BE HERE IF YOU DON'T RUN OUT ON ME AGAIN.

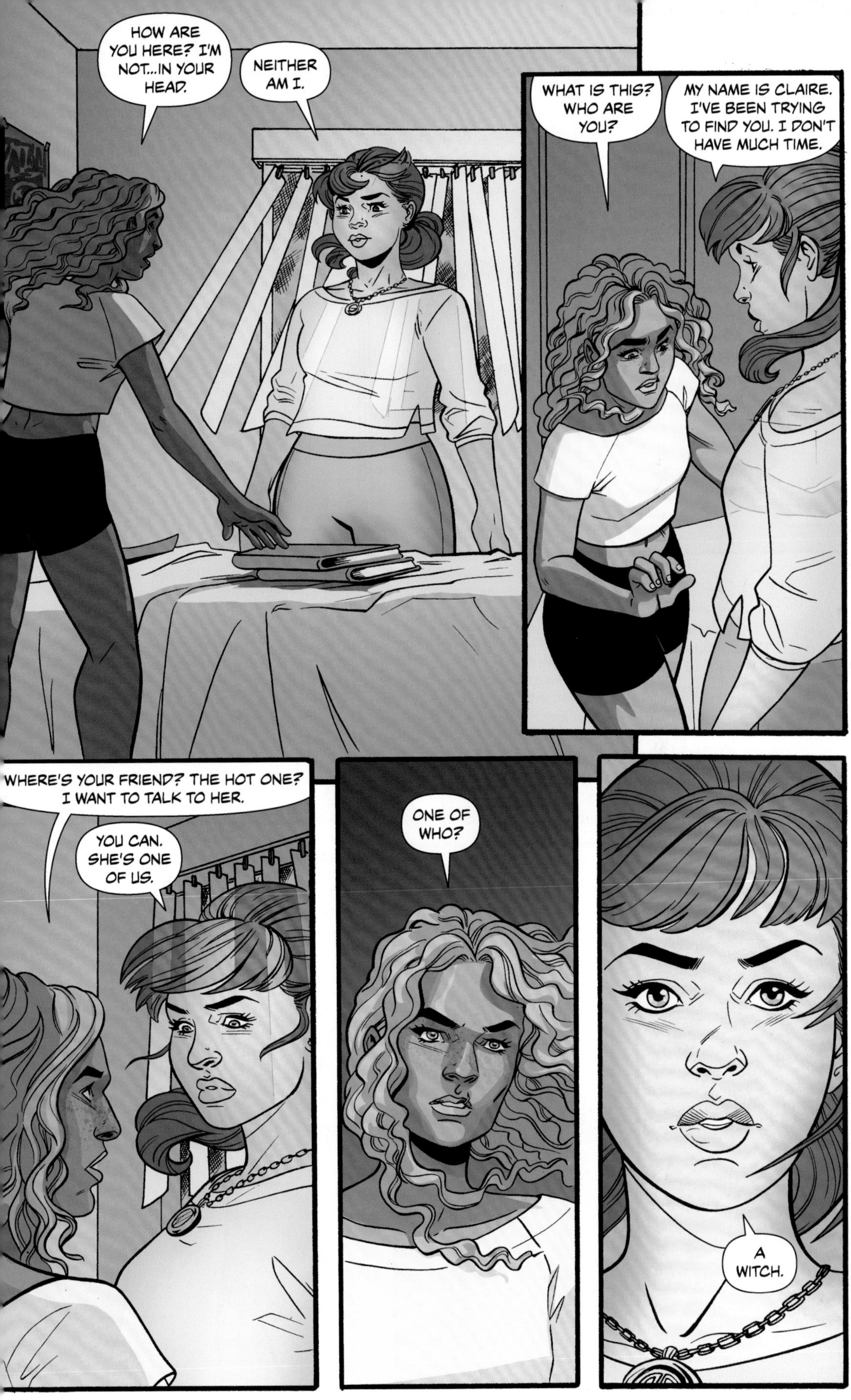
HOW ARE YOU HERE? I'M NOT...IN YOUR HEAD.
NEITHER AM I.
WHAT IS THIS? WHO ARE YOU?
MY NAME IS CLAIRE. I'VE BEEN TRYING TO FIND YOU. I DON'T HAVE MUCH TIME.
WHERE'S YOUR FRIEND? THE HOT ONE? I WANT TO TALK TO HER.
YOU CAN. SHE'S ONE OF US.
ONE OF WHO?
A WITCH.

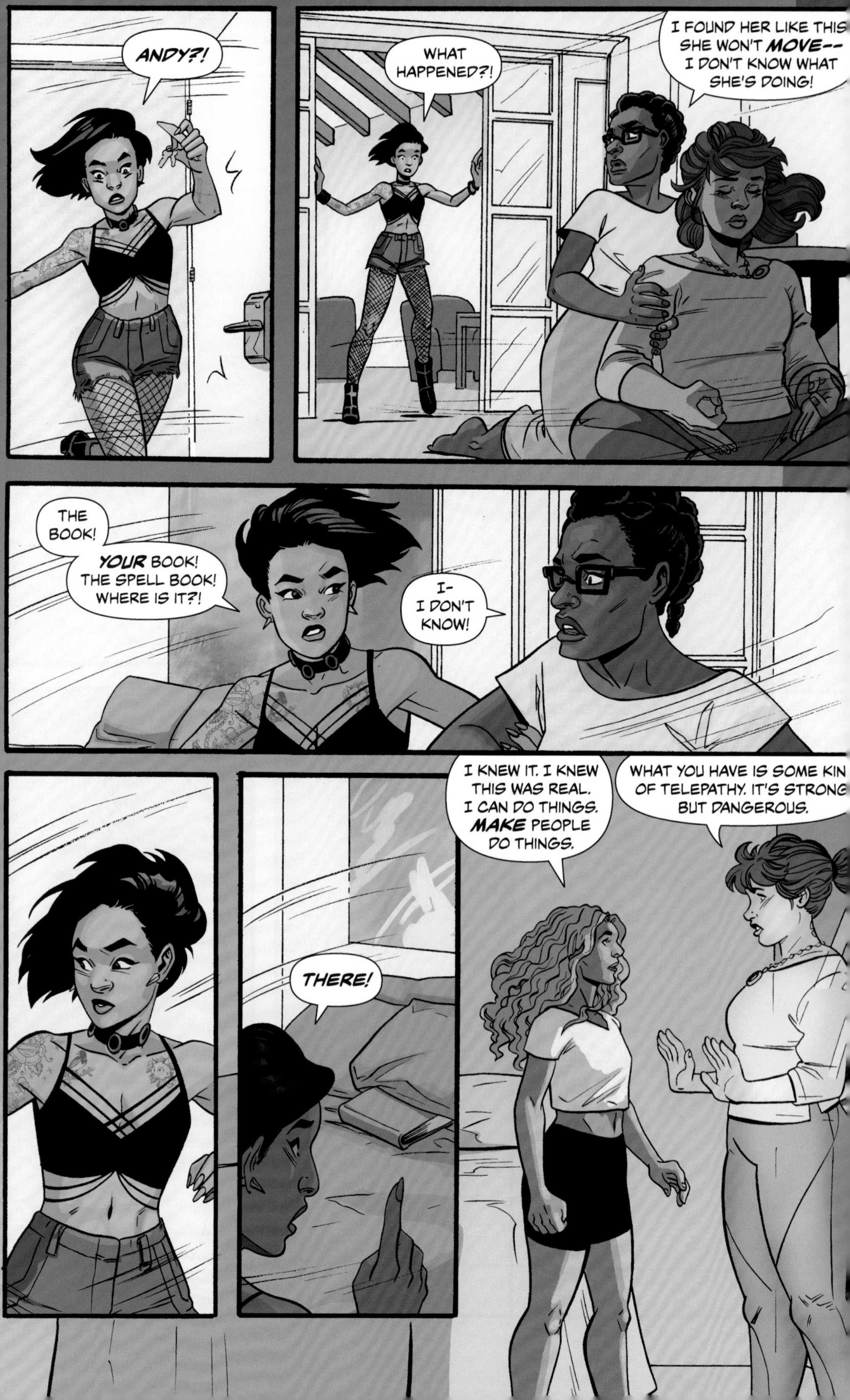
ANDY?!
WHAT HAPPENED?!
I FOUND HER LIKE THIS SHE WON'T MOVE-- I DON'T KNOW WHAT SHE'S DOING!
THE BOOK!
YOUR BOOK! THE SPELL BOOK! WHERE IS IT?!
I- I DON'T KNOW!
THERE!
I KNEW IT. I KNEW THIS WAS REAL. I CAN DO THINGS. MAKE PEOPLE DO THINGS.
WHAT YOU HAVE IS SOME KIN OF TELEPATHY. IT'S STRONG BUT DANGEROUS.

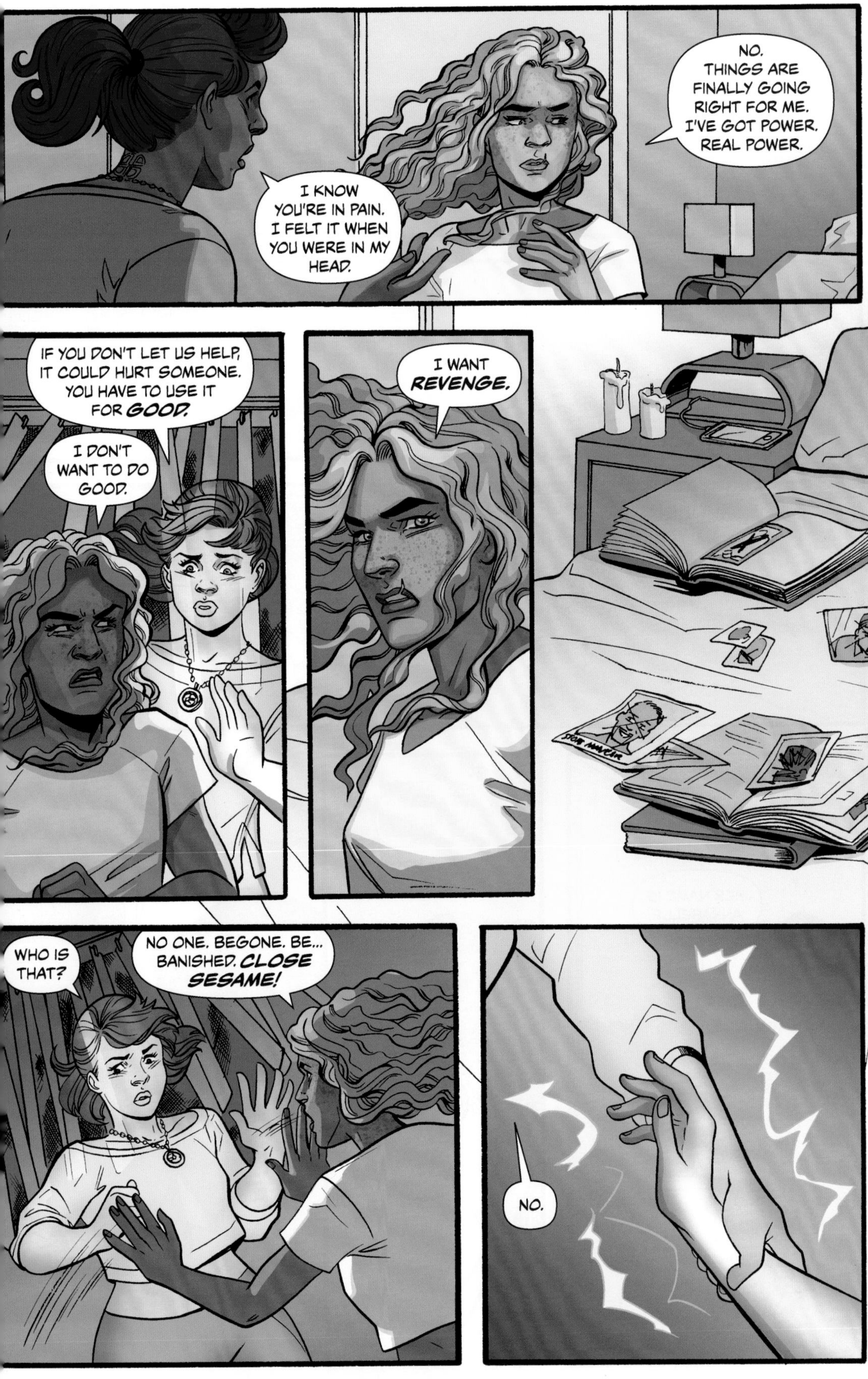
I KNOW YOU'RE IN PAIN. I FELT IT WHEN YOU WERE IN MY HEAD.
NO. THINGS ARE FINALLY GOING RIGHT FOR ME. I'VE GOT POWER. REAL POWER.
IF YOU DON'T LET US HELP, IT COULD HURT SOMEONE. YOU HAVE TO USE IT FOR GOOD.
I DON'T WANT TO DO GOOD.
I WANT REVENGE.
WHO IS THAT?
NO ONE. BEGONE. BE... BANISHED. CLOSE SESAME!
NO.

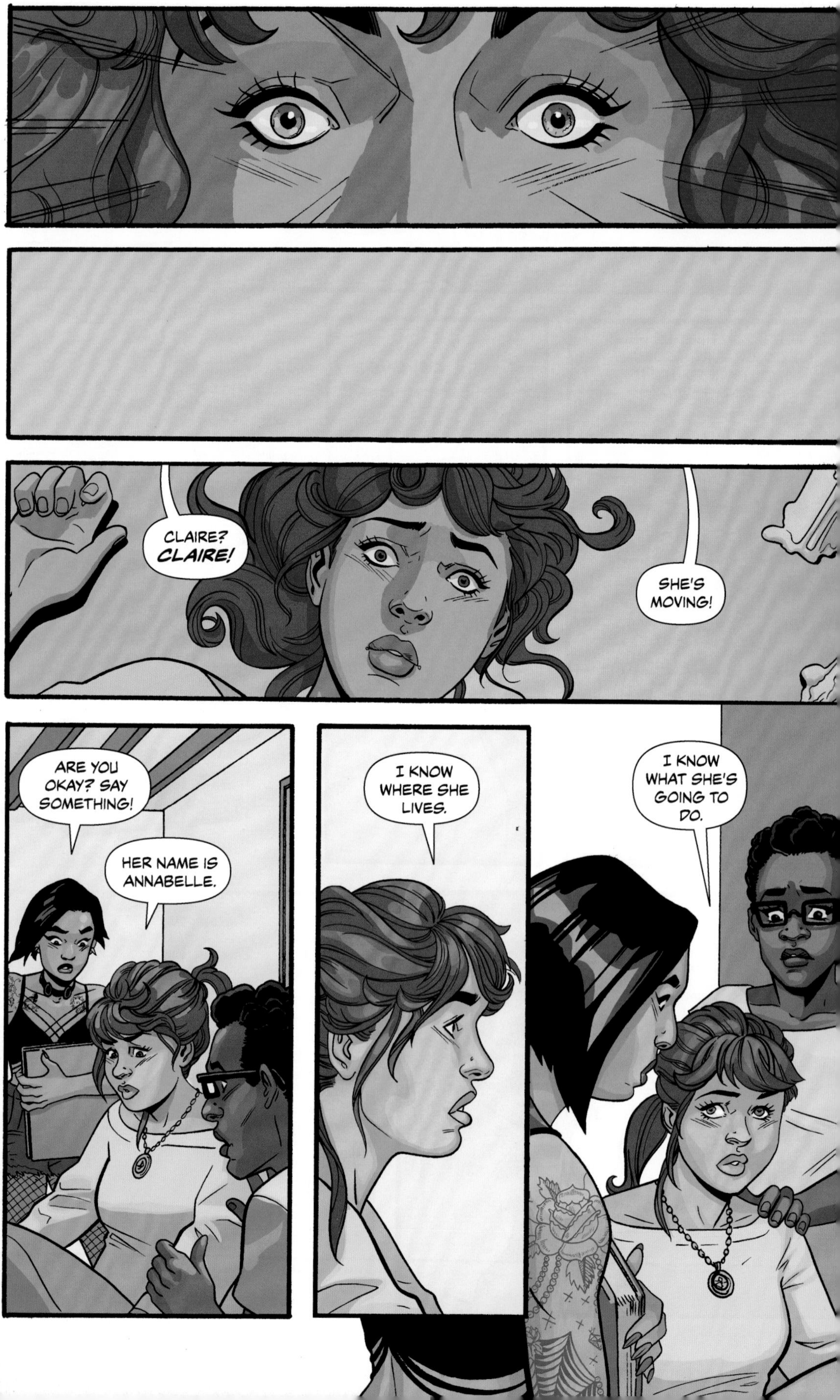
CLAIRE? CLAIRE!
SHE'S MOVING!
ARE YOU OKAY? SAY SOMETHING!
HER NAME IS ANNABELLE.
I KNOW WHERE SHE LIVES.
I KNOW WHAT SHE'S GOING TO DO.

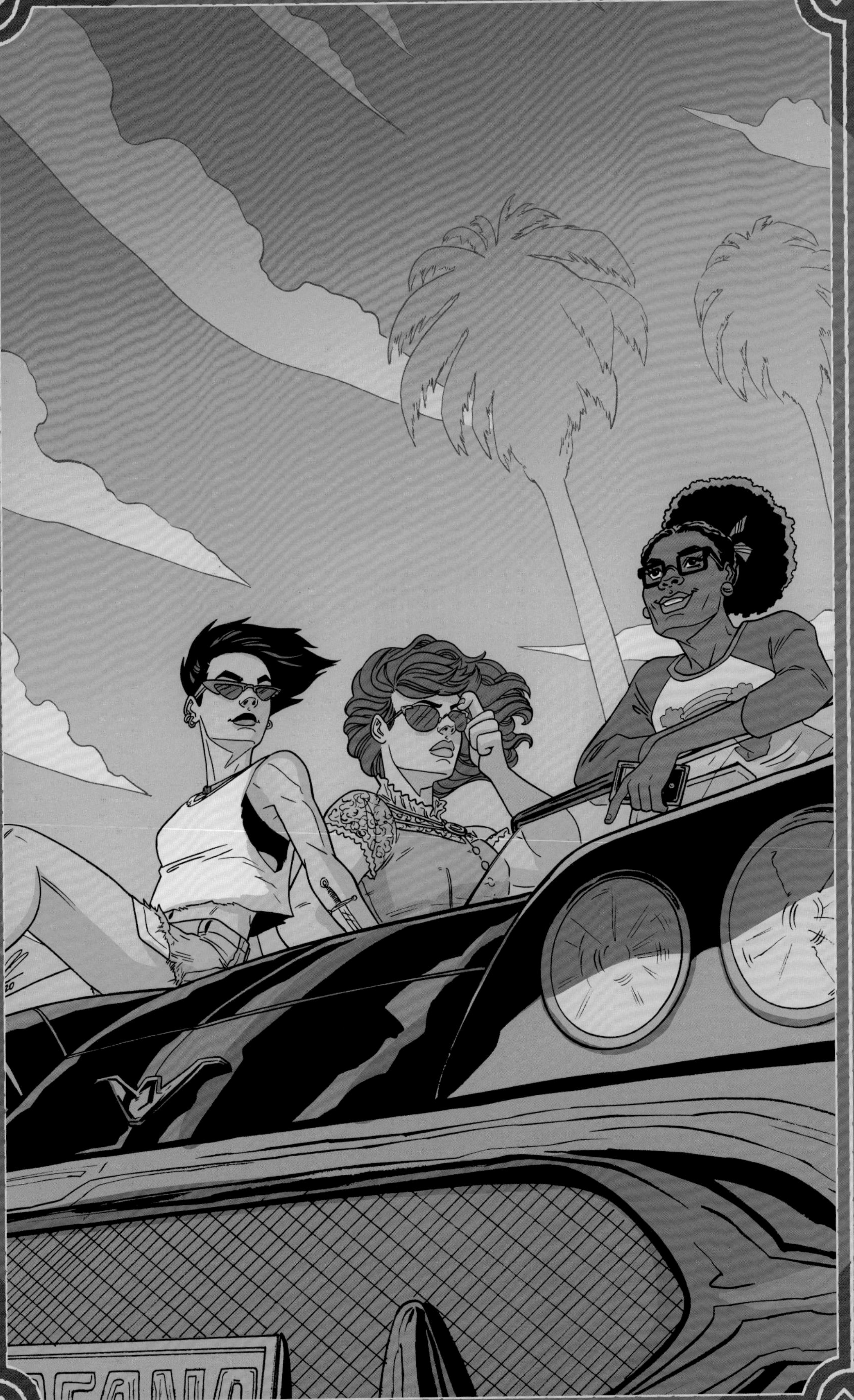

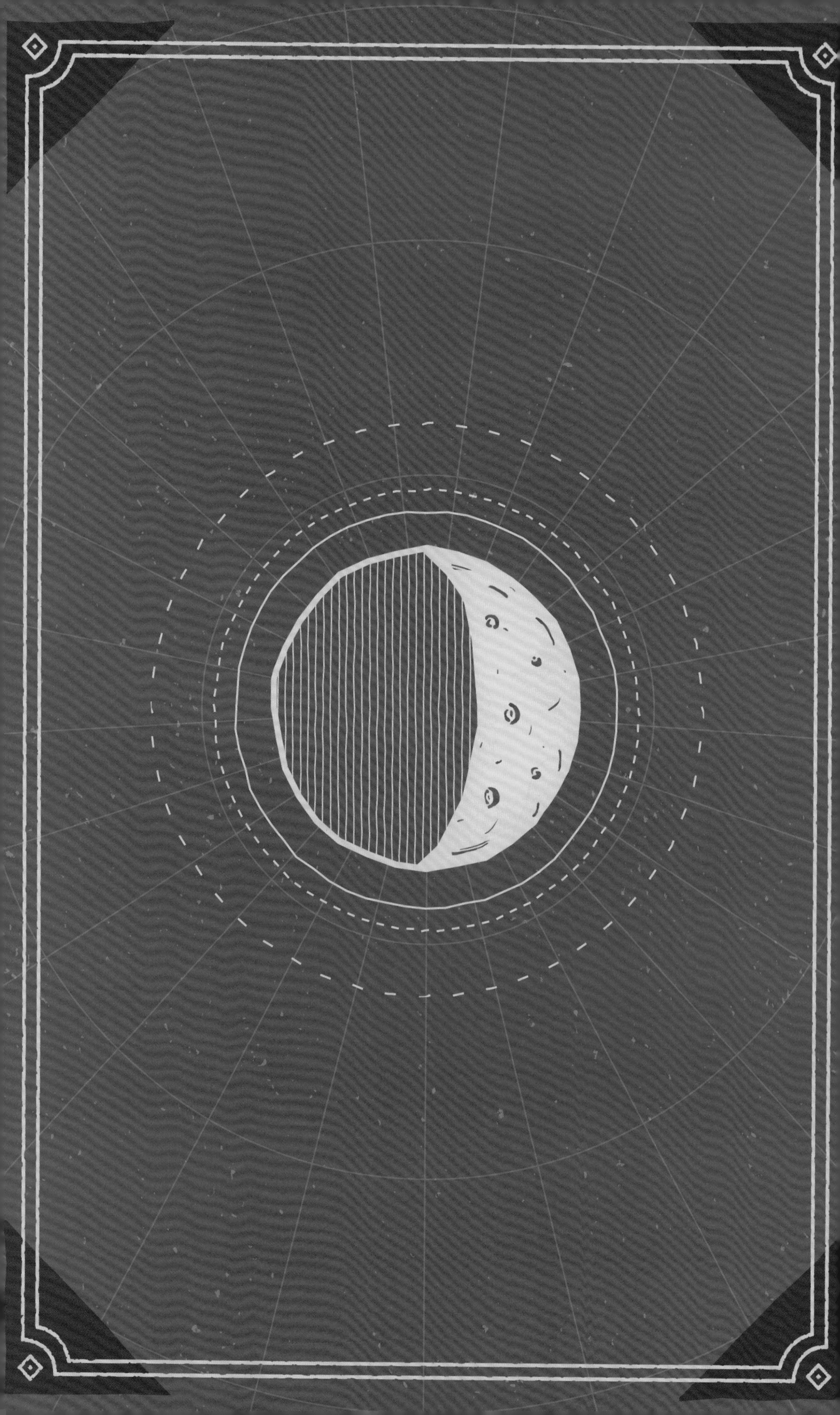

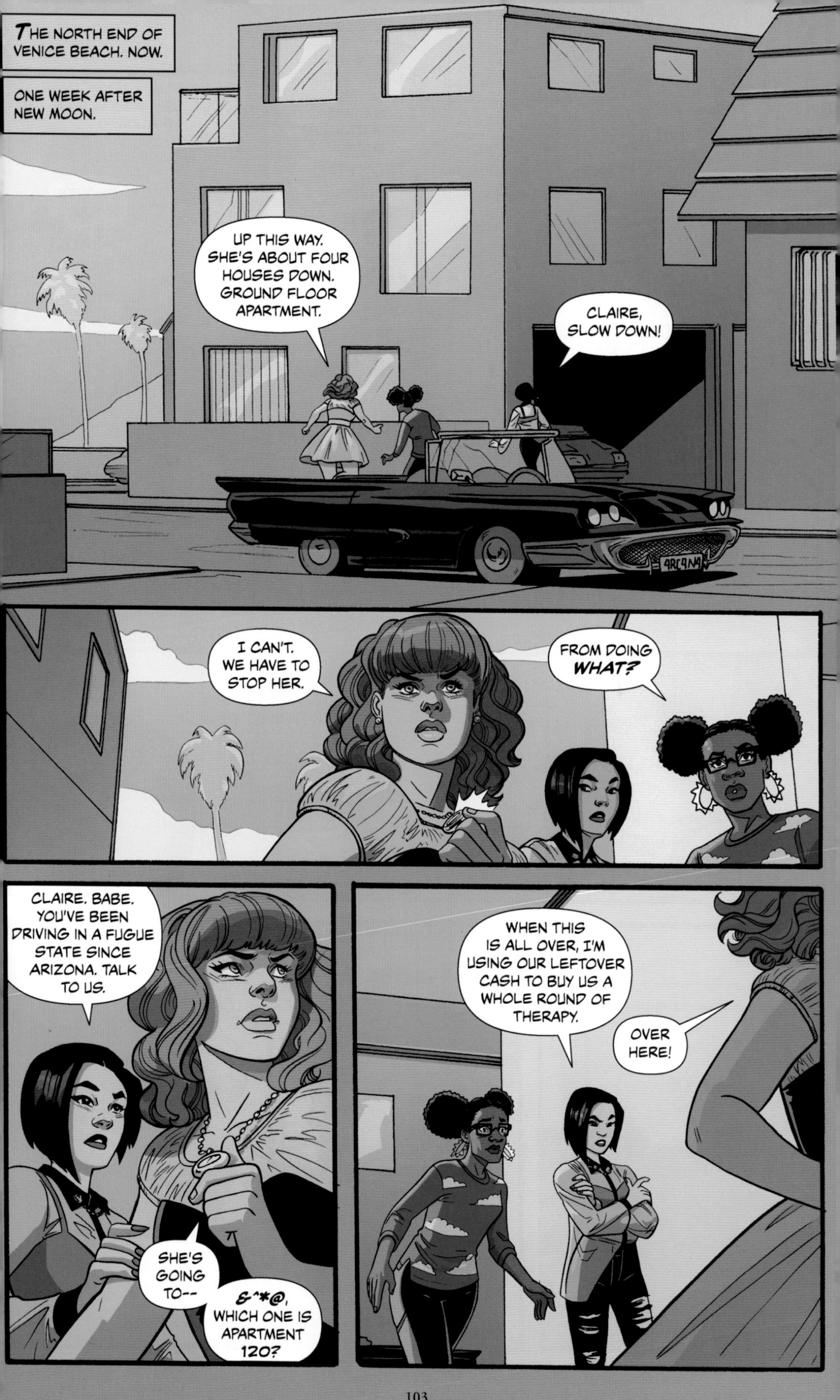
THE NORTH END OF VENICE BEACH. NOW.
ONE WEEK AFTER NEW MOON.
UP THIS WAY. SHE'S ABOUT FOUR HOUSES DOWN. GROUND FLOOR APARTMENT.
CLAIRE, SLOW DOWN!
4RC9NA
I CAN'T. WE HAVE TO STOP HER.
FROM DOING *WHAT?*
CLAIRE. BABE. YOU'VE BEEN DRIVING IN A FUGUE STATE SINCE ARIZONA. TALK TO US.
SHE'S GOING TO--
&^*@, WHICH ONE IS APARTMENT 120?
WHEN THIS IS ALL OVER, I'M USING OUR LEFTOVER CASH TO BUY US A WHOLE ROUND OF THERAPY.
OVER HERE!

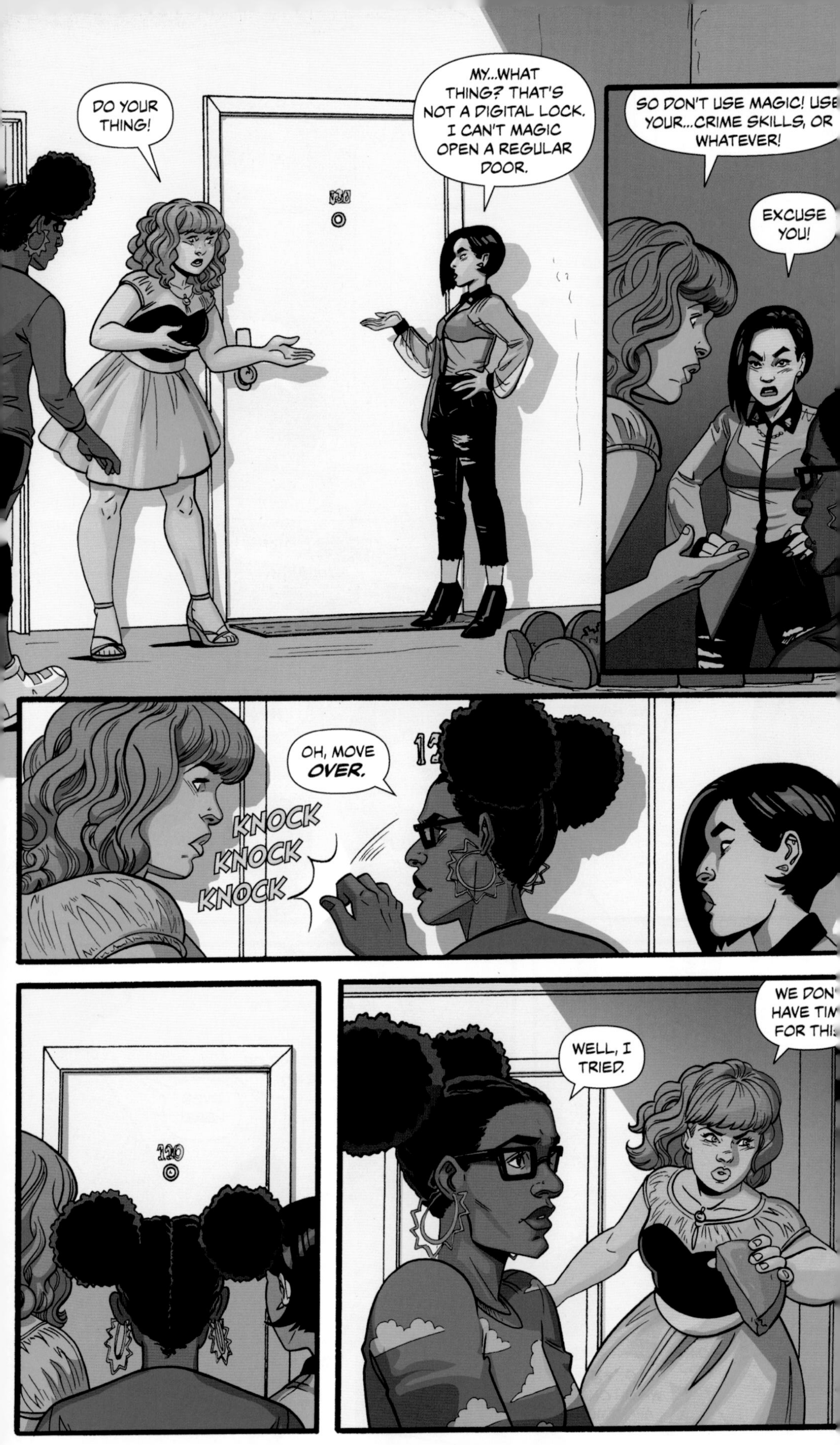
DO YOUR THING!
MY...WHAT THING? THAT'S NOT A DIGITAL LOCK. I CAN'T MAGIC OPEN A REGULAR DOOR.
SO DON'T USE MAGIC! USE YOUR...CRIME SKILLS, OR WHATEVER!
EXCUSE YOU!
OH, MOVE OVER.
KNOCK KNOCK KNOCK
WELL, I TRIED.
WE DON' HAVE TIM FOR THI

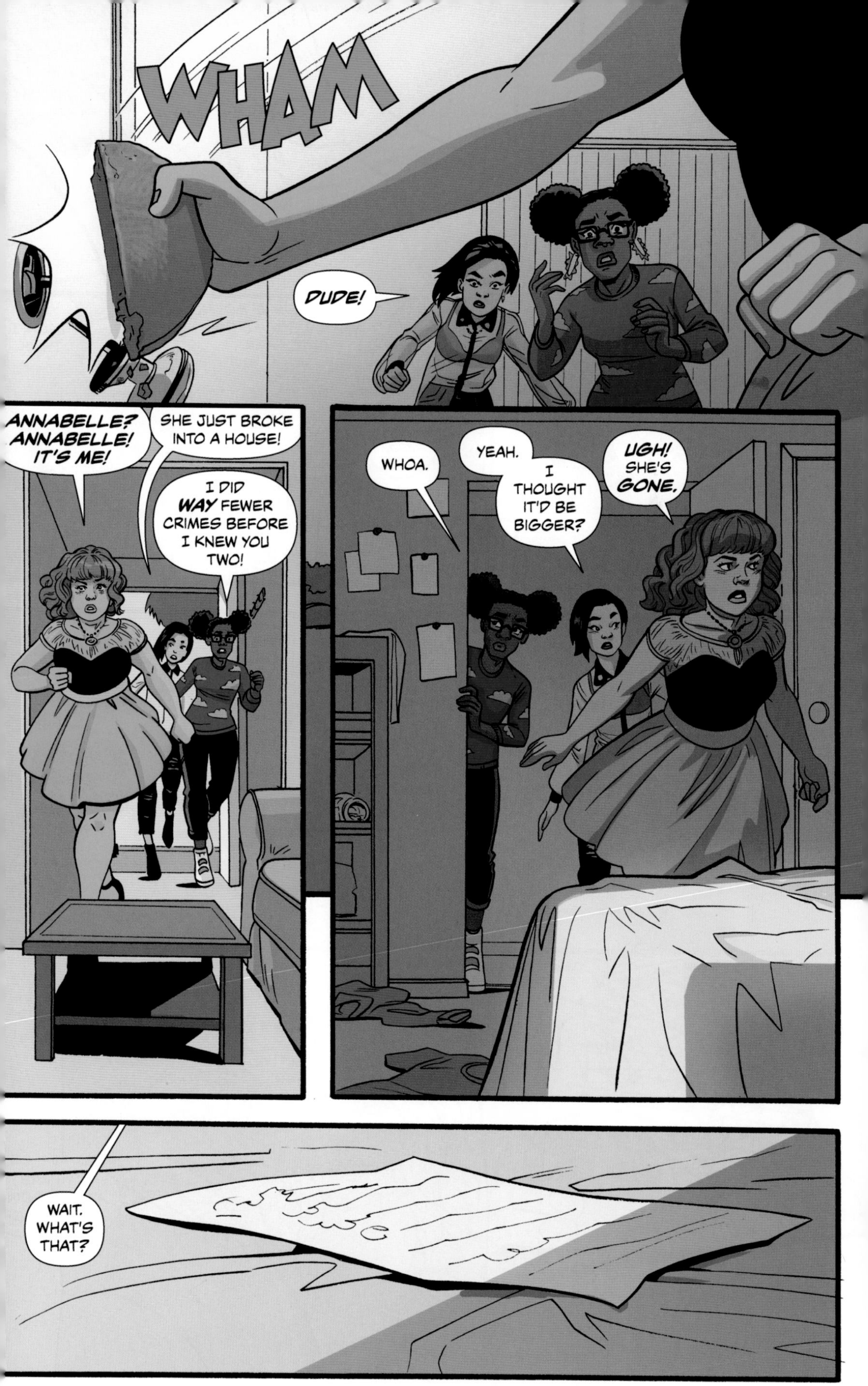
WHAM
DUDE!
ANNABELLE? ANNABELLE! IT'S ME!
SHE JUST BROKE INTO A HOUSE!
I DID WAY FEWER CRIMES BEFORE I KNEW YOU TWO!
WHOA.
YEAH.
I THOUGHT IT'D BE BIGGER?
UGH! SHE'S GONE.
WAIT. WHAT'S THAT?

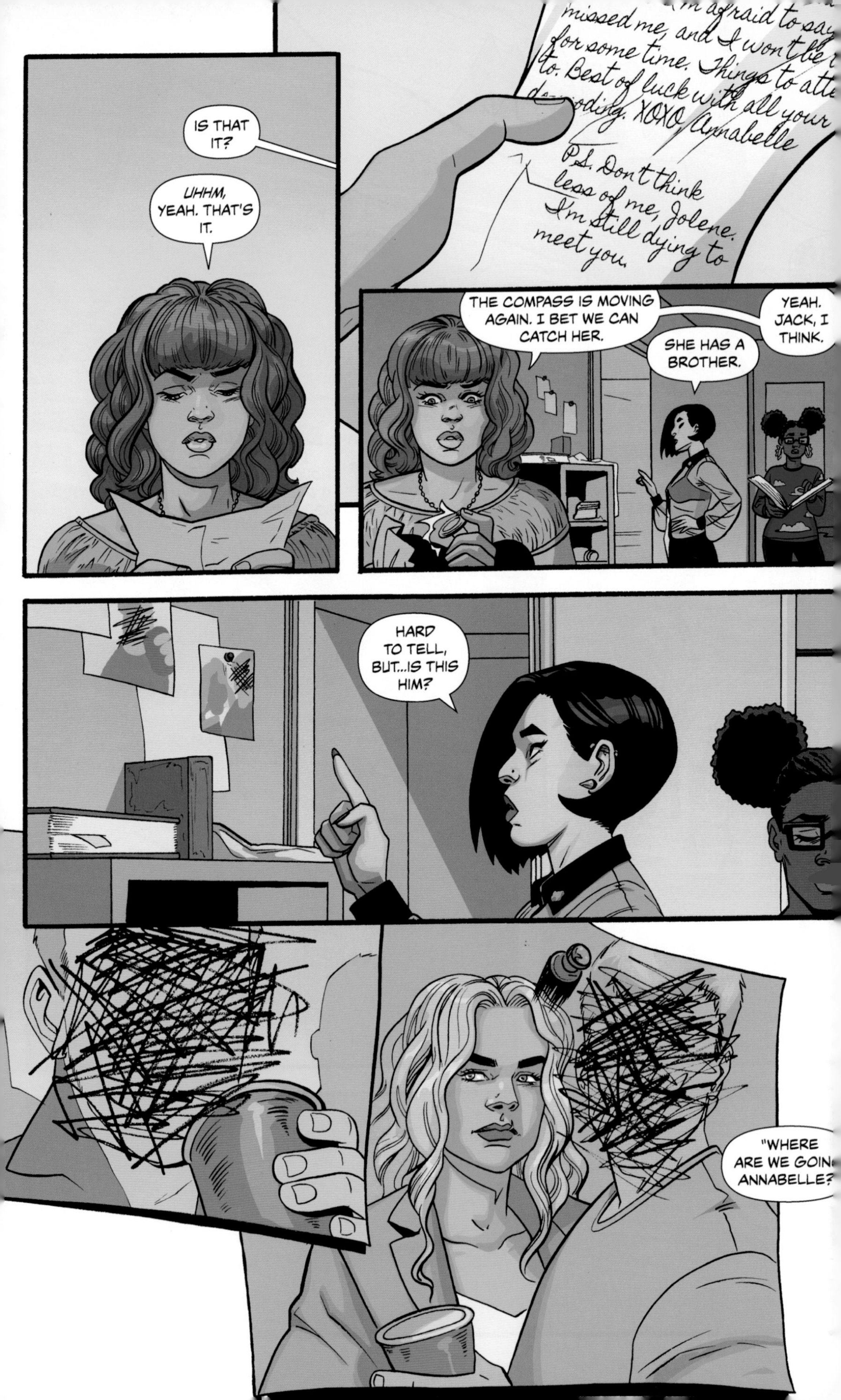
missed me, and I won't be
for some time. Things to atte
to. Best of luck with all your
decoding. XOXO, Annabelle
P.S. Don't think
less of me, Jolene.
I'm still dying to
meet you.
IS THAT IT?
UHHM, YEAH. THAT'S IT.
THE COMPASS IS MOVING AGAIN. I BET WE CAN CATCH HER.
YEAH. JACK, I THINK.
SHE HAS A BROTHER.
HARD TO TELL, BUT...IS THIS HIM?
"WHERE ARE WE GOIN
ANNABELLE?

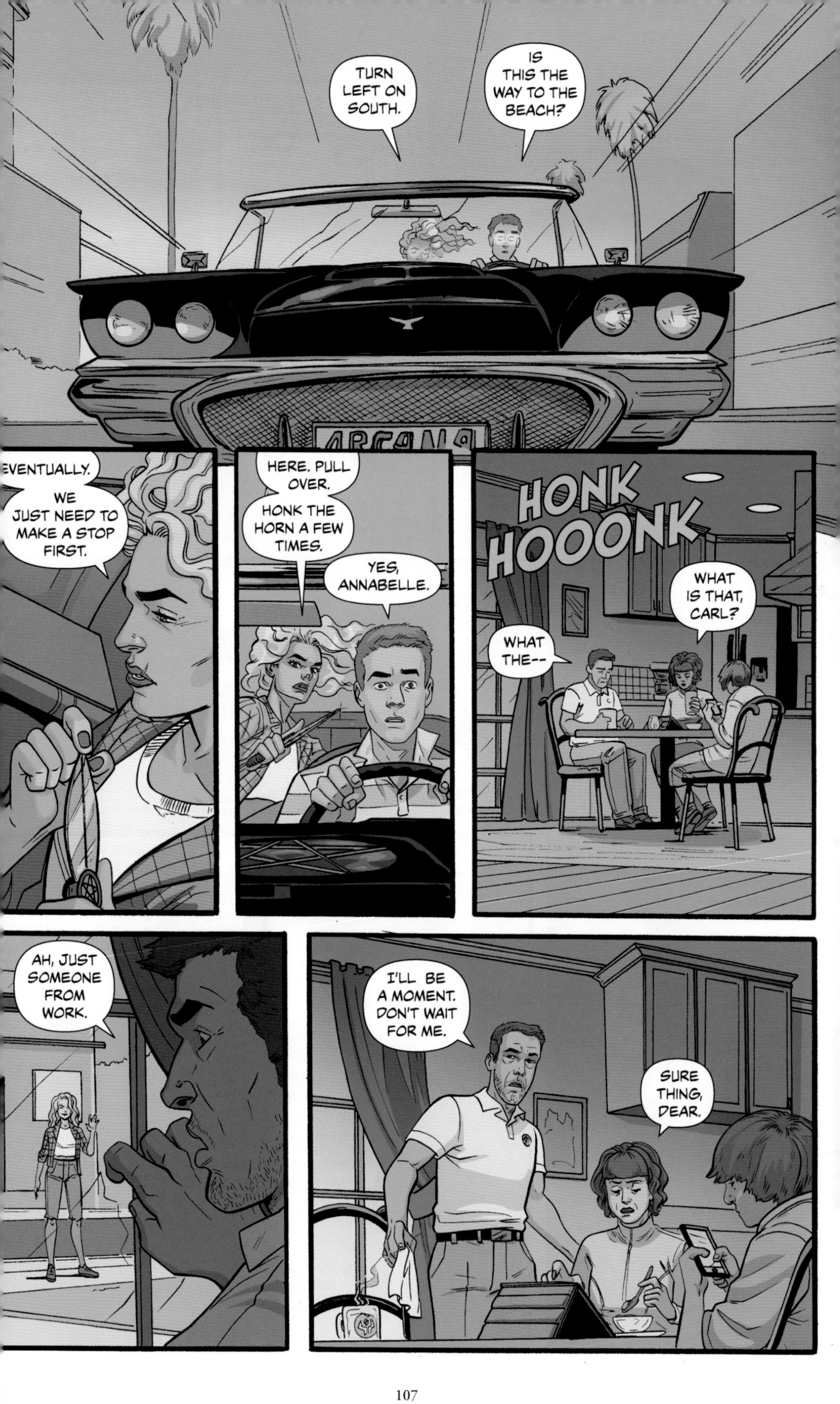
TURN LEFT ON SOUTH.
IS THIS THE WAY TO THE BEACH?
EVENTUALLY.
WE JUST NEED TO MAKE A STOP FIRST.
HERE. PULL OVER.
HONK THE HORN A FEW TIMES.
YES, ANNABELLE.
HONK
HOOONK
WHAT IS THAT, CARL?
WHAT THE--
AH, JUST SOMEONE FROM WORK.
I'LL BE A MOMENT. DON'T WAIT FOR ME.
SURE THING, DEAR.

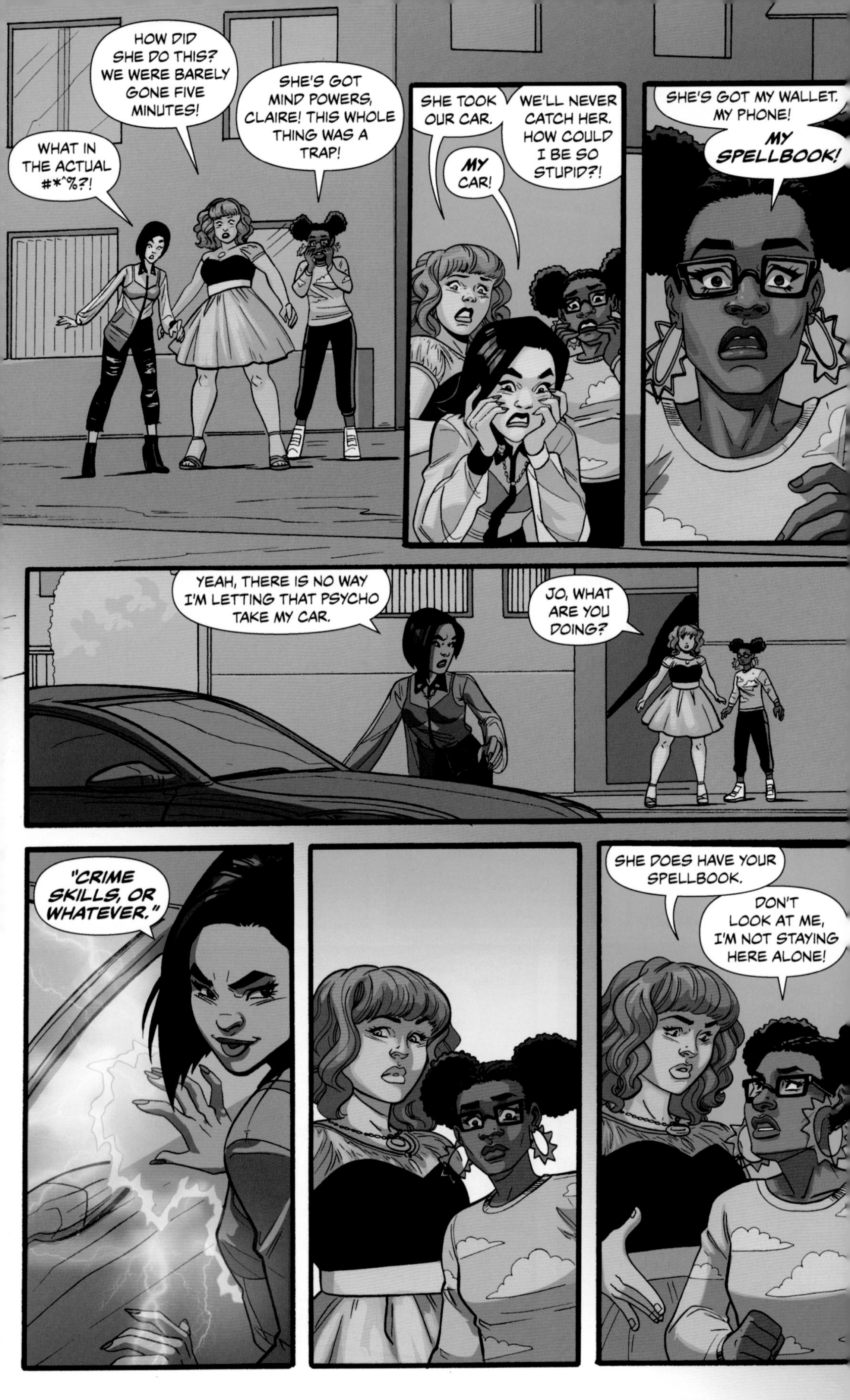
WHAT IN THE ACTUAL #*^%?!
HOW DID SHE DO THIS? WE WERE BARELY GONE FIVE MINUTES!
SHE'S GOT MIND POWERS, CLAIRE! THIS WHOLE THING WAS A TRAP!
SHE TOOK OUR CAR.
MY CAR!
WE'LL NEVER CATCH HER. HOW COULD I BE SO STUPID?!
SHE'S GOT MY WALLET. MY PHONE!
MY SPELLBOOK!
YEAH, THERE IS NO WAY I'M LETTING THAT PSYCHO TAKE MY CAR.
JO, WHAT ARE YOU DOING?
"CRIME SKILLS, OR WHATEVER."
SHE DOES HAVE YOUR SPELLBOOK.
DON'T LOOK AT ME, I'M NOT STAYING HERE ALONE!

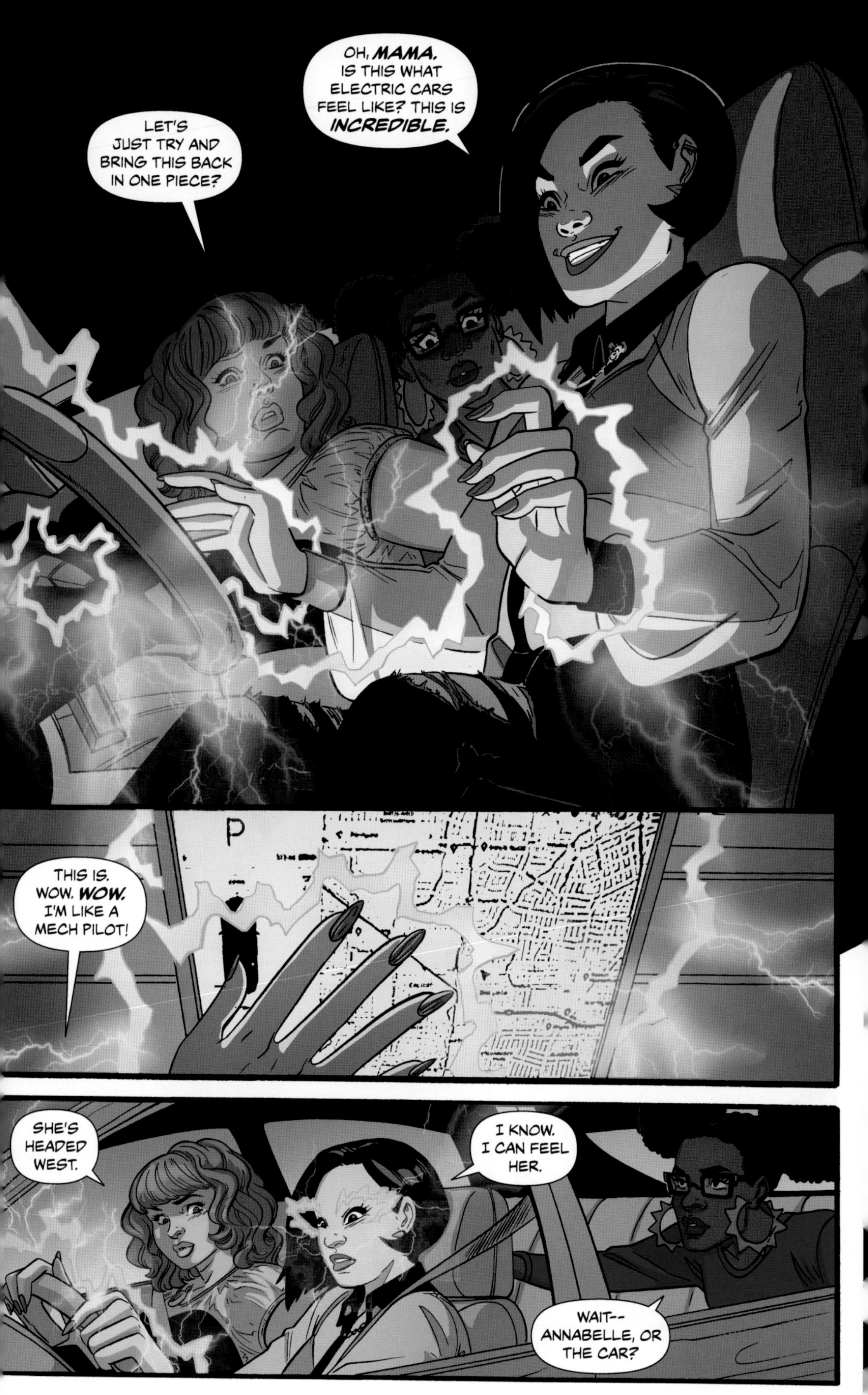
LET'S JUST TRY AND BRING THIS BACK IN ONE PIECE?
OH, MAMA. IS THIS WHAT ELECTRIC CARS FEEL LIKE? THIS IS INCREDIBLE.
THIS IS. WOW. WOW. I'M LIKE A MECH PILOT!
P
SHE'S HEADED WEST.
I KNOW. I CAN FEEL HER.
WAIT-- ANNABELLE, OR THE CAR?

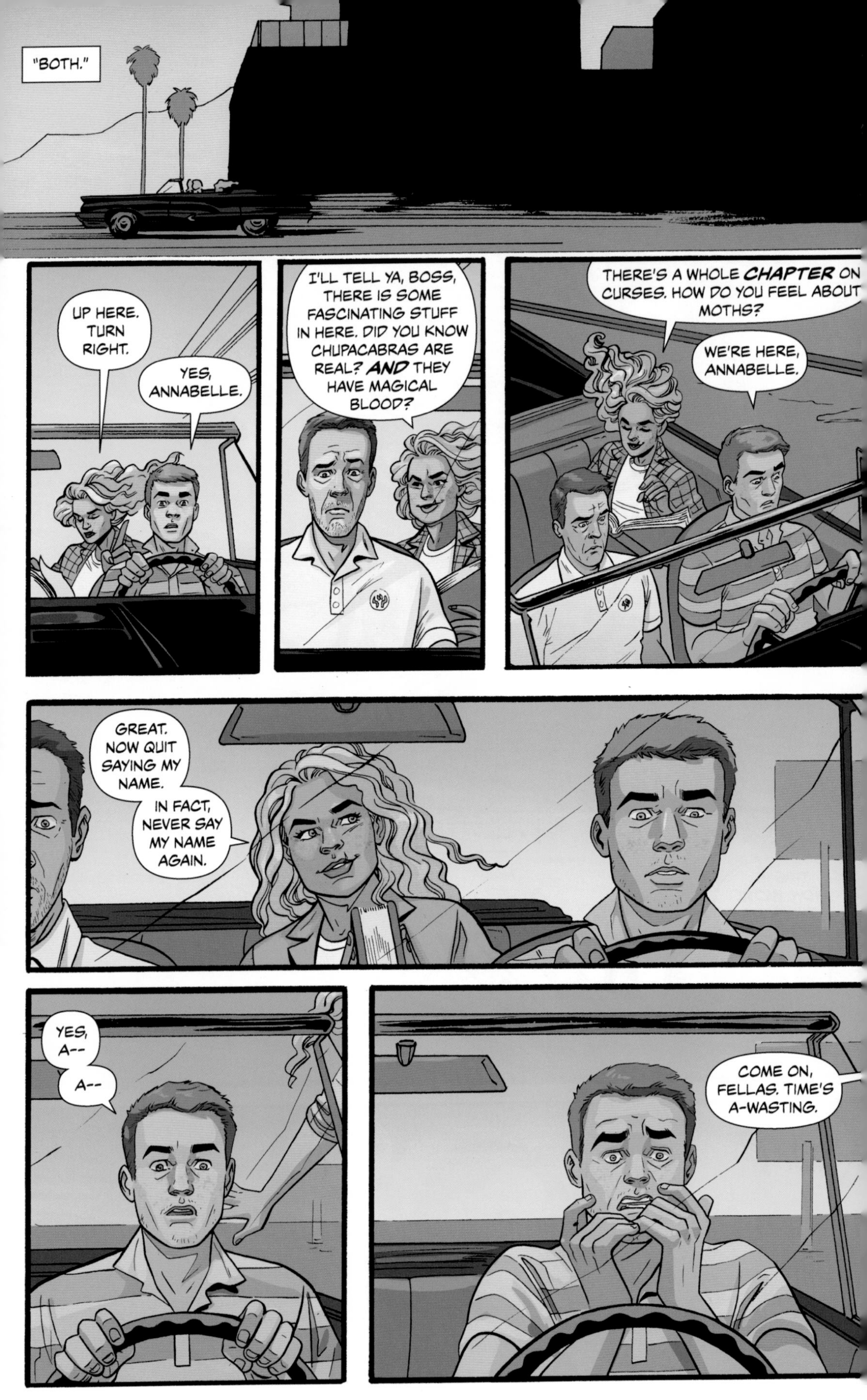
"BOTH."
UP HERE. TURN RIGHT.
YES, ANNABELLE.
I'LL TELL YA, BOSS, THERE IS SOME FASCINATING STUFF IN HERE. DID YOU KNOW CHUPACABRAS ARE REAL? AND THEY HAVE MAGICAL BLOOD?
THERE'S A WHOLE CHAPTER ON CURSES. HOW DO YOU FEEL ABOUT MOTHS?
WE'RE HERE, ANNABELLE.
GREAT. NOW QUIT SAYING MY NAME.
IN FACT, NEVER SAY MY NAME AGAIN.
YES, A--
A--
COME ON, FELLAS. TIME'S A-WASTING.

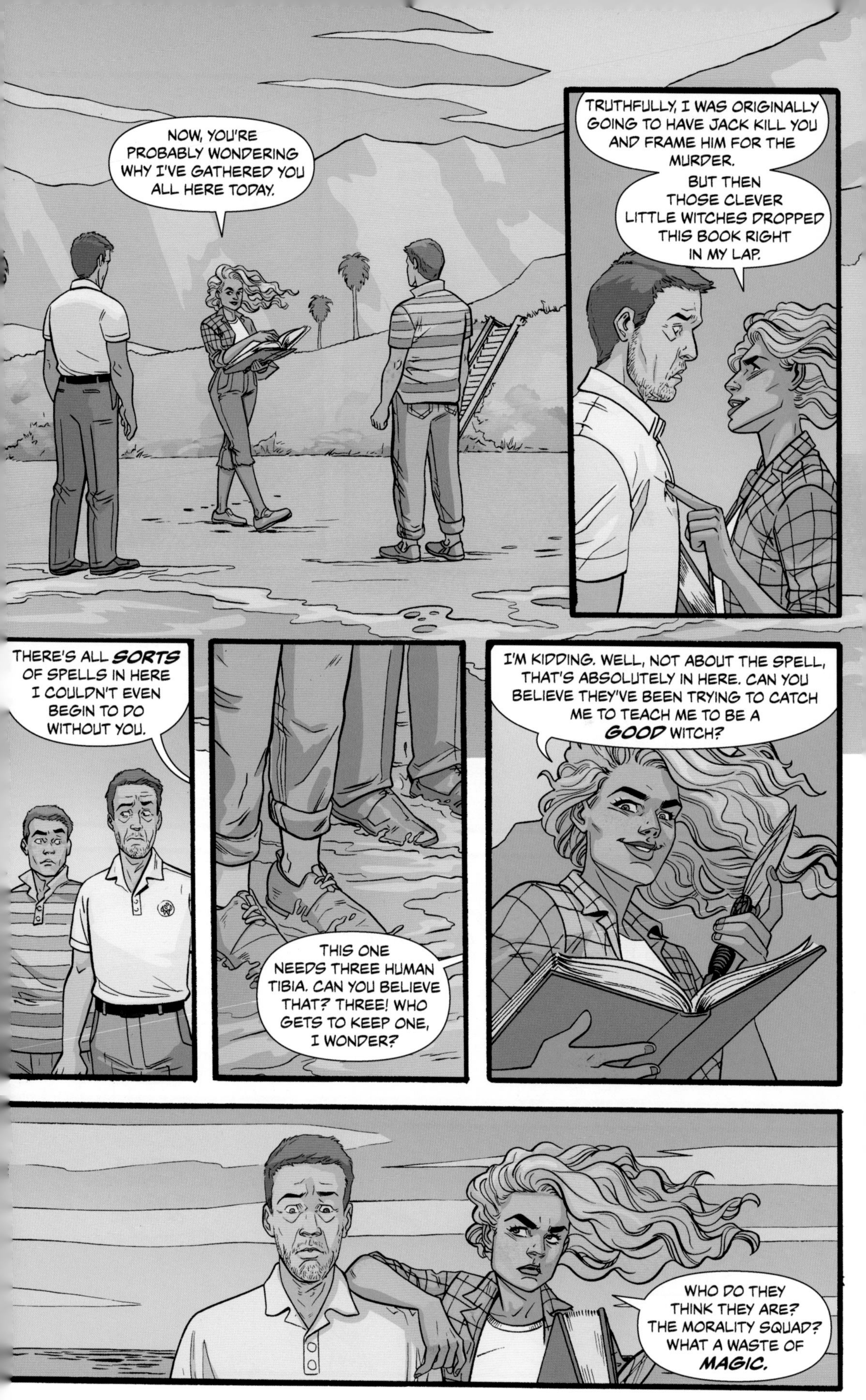
NOW, YOU'RE PROBABLY WONDERING WHY I'VE GATHERED YOU ALL HERE TODAY.
TRUTHFULLY, I WAS ORIGINALLY GOING TO HAVE JACK KILL YOU AND FRAME HIM FOR THE MURDER.
BUT THEN THOSE CLEVER LITTLE WITCHES DROPPED THIS BOOK RIGHT IN MY LAP.
THERE'S ALL SORTS OF SPELLS IN HERE I COULDN'T EVEN BEGIN TO DO WITHOUT YOU.
THIS ONE NEEDS THREE HUMAN TIBIA. CAN YOU BELIEVE THAT? THREE! WHO GETS TO KEEP ONE, I WONDER?
I'M KIDDING. WELL, NOT ABOUT THE SPELL, THAT'S ABSOLUTELY IN HERE. CAN YOU BELIEVE THEY'VE BEEN TRYING TO CATCH ME TO TEACH ME TO BE A GOOD WITCH?
WHO DO THEY THINK THEY ARE? THE MORALITY SQUAD? WHAT A WASTE OF MAGIC.

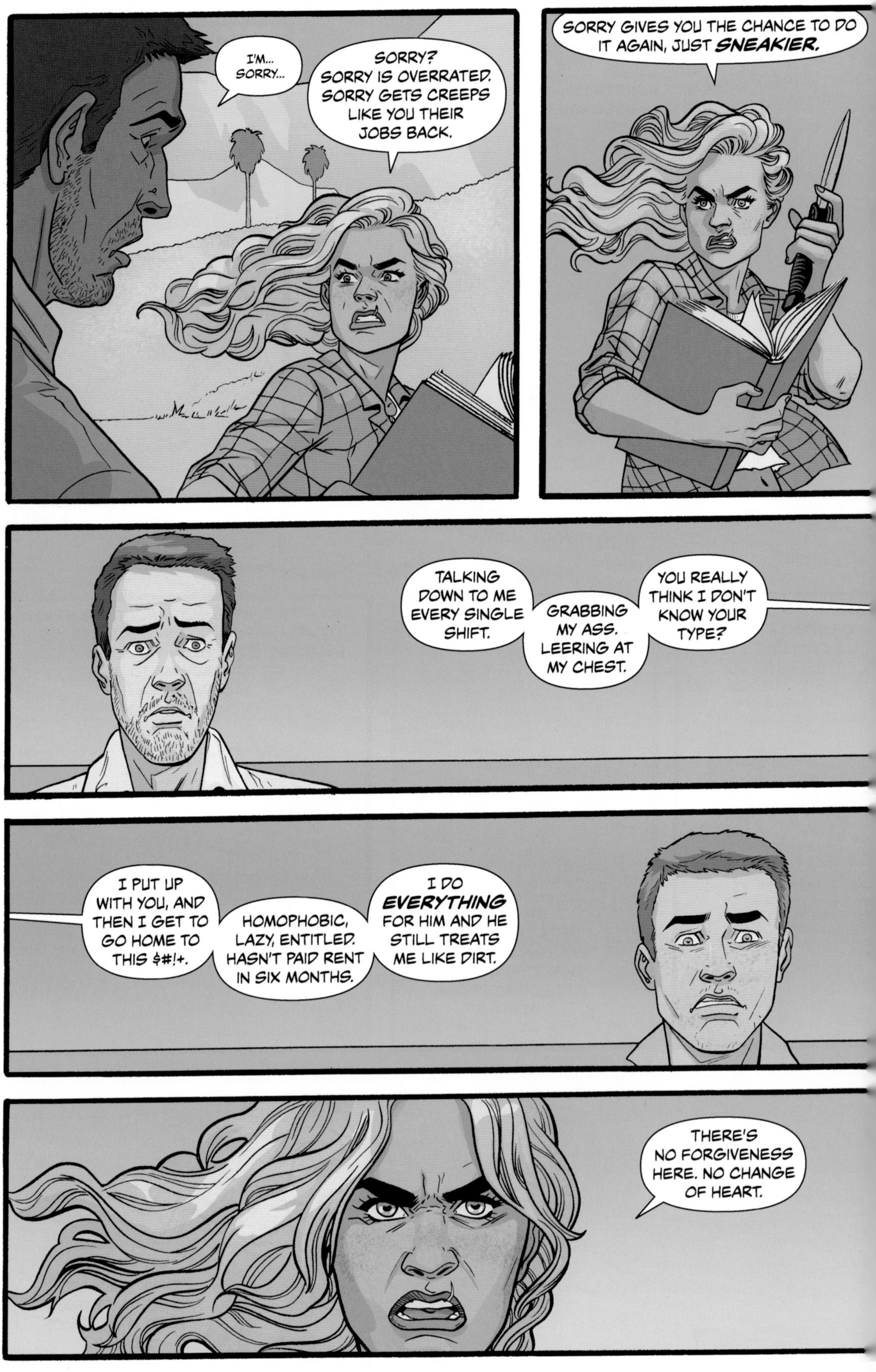
I'M... SORRY...
SORRY? SORRY IS OVERRATED. SORRY GETS CREEPS LIKE YOU THEIR JOBS BACK.
SORRY GIVES YOU THE CHANCE TO DO IT AGAIN, JUST SNEAKIER.
YOU REALLY THINK I DON'T KNOW YOUR TYPE?
GRABBING MY ASS. LEERING AT MY CHEST.
TALKING DOWN TO ME EVERY SINGLE SHIFT.
I PUT UP WITH YOU, AND THEN I GET TO GO HOME TO THIS $#!+.
HOMOPHOBIC, LAZY, ENTITLED. HASN'T PAID RENT IN SIX MONTHS.
I DO EVERYTHING FOR HIM AND HE STILL TREATS ME LIKE DIRT.
THERE'S NO FORGIVENESS HERE. NO CHANGE OF HEART.

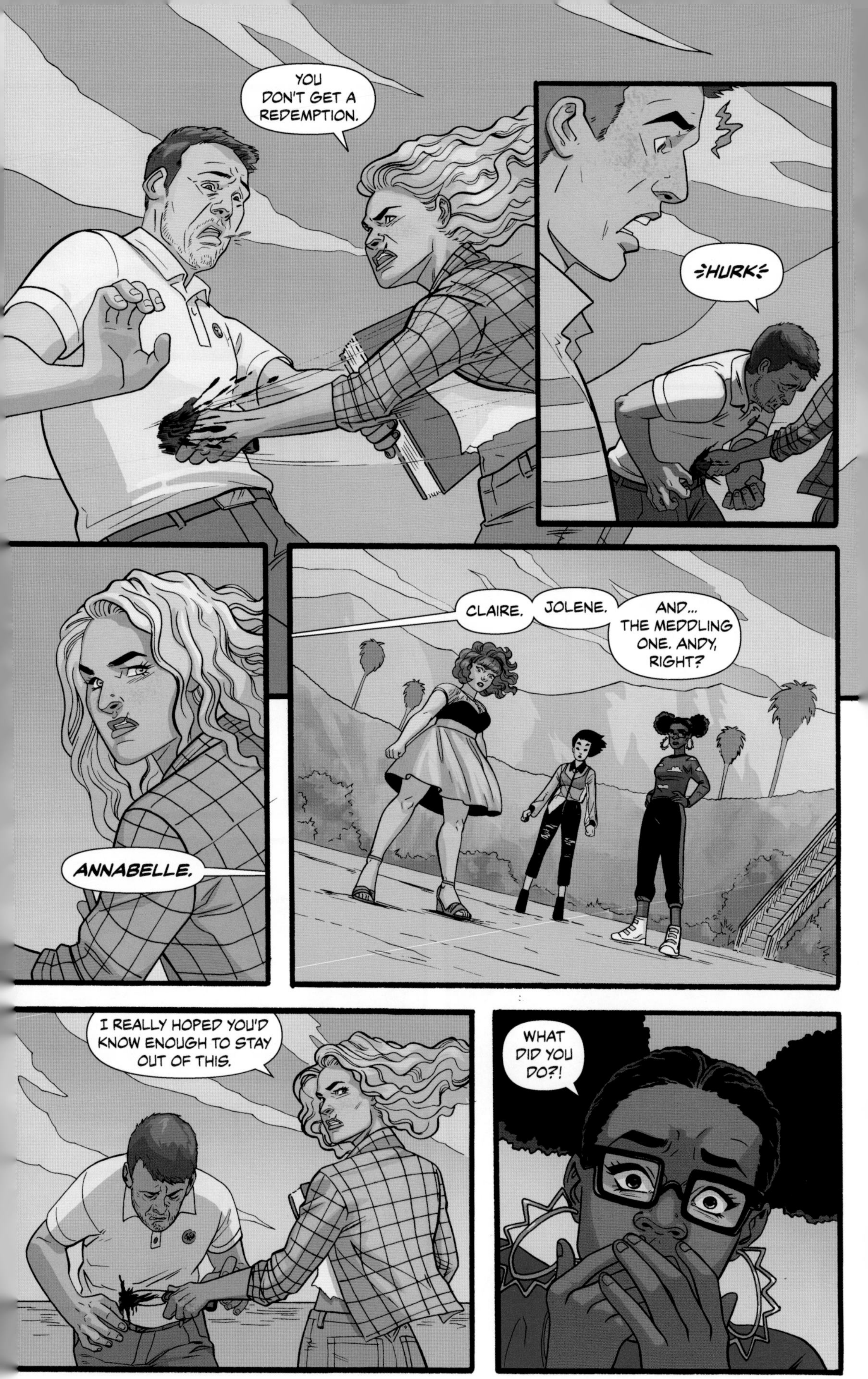
YOU DON'T GET A REDEMPTION.
HURK
ANNABELLE.
CLAIRE.
JOLENE.
AND... THE MEDDLING ONE. ANDY, RIGHT?
I REALLY HOPED YOU'D KNOW ENOUGH TO STAY OUT OF THIS.
WHAT DID YOU DO?!

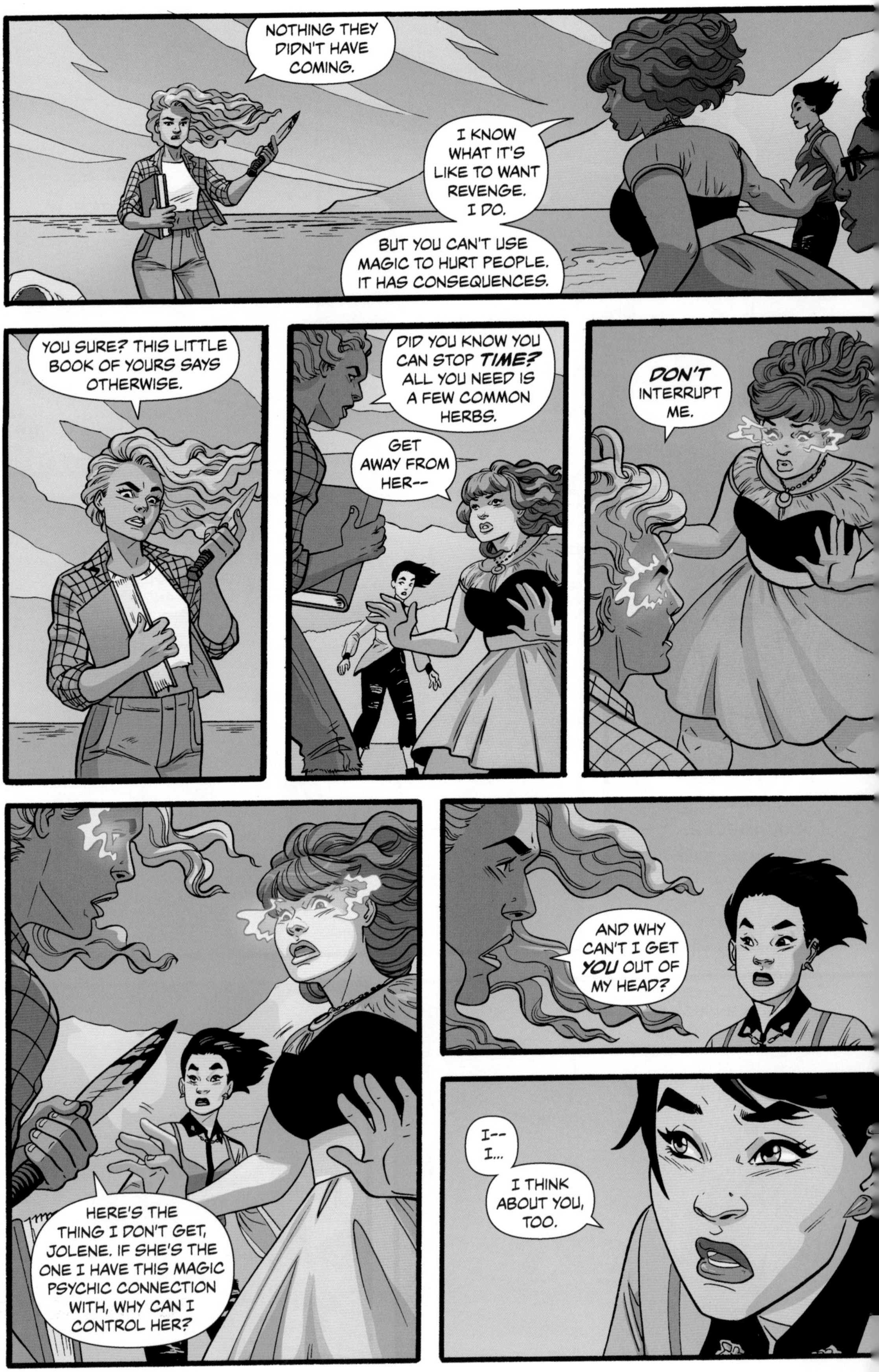
NOTHING THEY DIDN'T HAVE COMING.
I KNOW WHAT IT'S LIKE TO WANT REVENGE. I DO.
BUT YOU CAN'T USE MAGIC TO HURT PEOPLE. IT HAS CONSEQUENCES.
YOU SURE? THIS LITTLE BOOK OF YOURS SAYS OTHERWISE.
DID YOU KNOW YOU CAN STOP *TIME?* ALL YOU NEED IS A FEW COMMON HERBS.
GET AWAY FROM HER--
DON'T INTERRUPT ME.
HERE'S THE THING I DON'T GET, JOLENE. IF SHE'S THE ONE I HAVE THIS MAGIC PSYCHIC CONNECTION WITH, WHY CAN I CONTROL HER?
AND WHY CAN'T I GET *YOU* OUT OF MY HEAD?
I-- I...
I THINK ABOUT YOU, TOO.

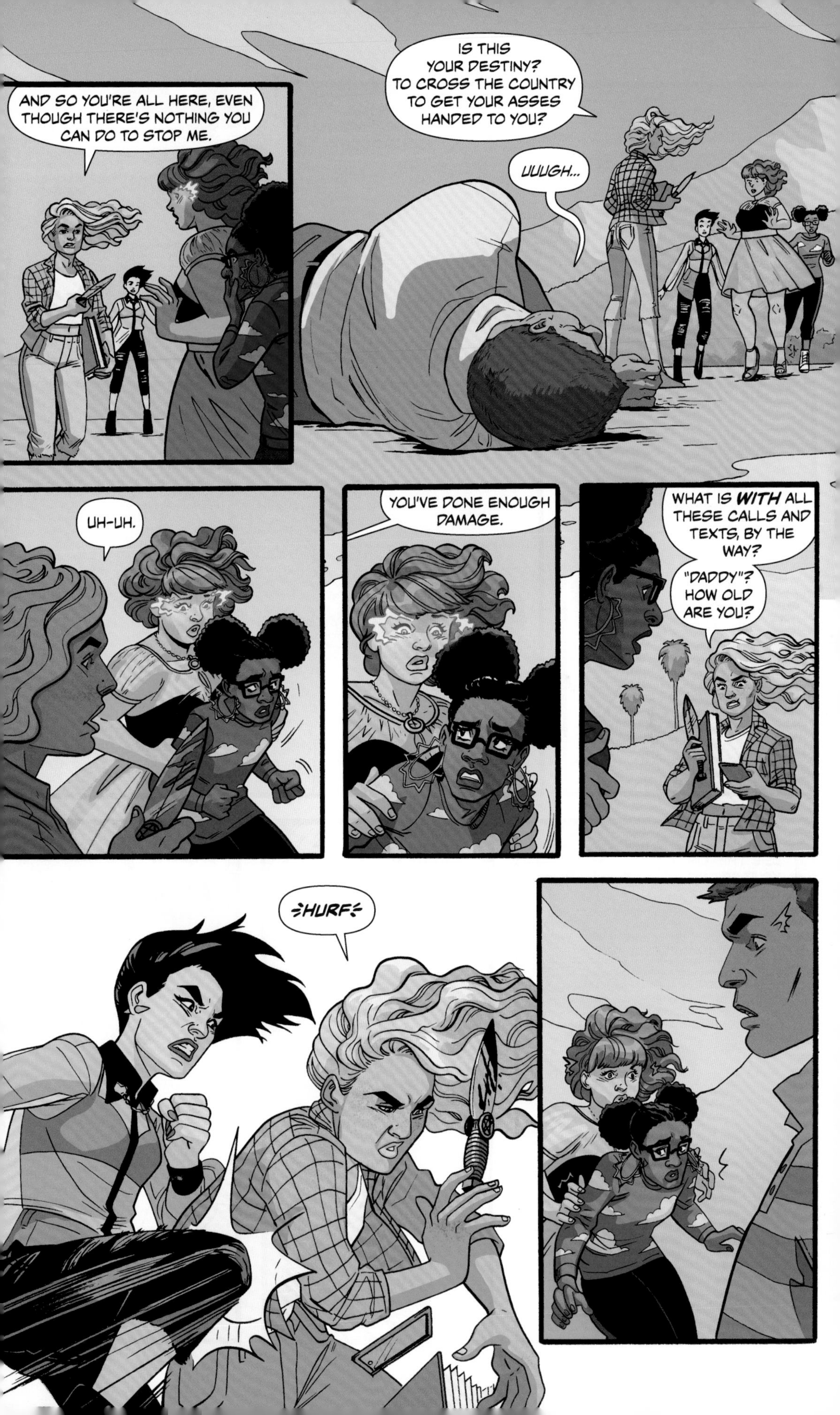
AND SO YOU'RE ALL HERE, EVEN THOUGH THERE'S NOTHING YOU CAN DO TO STOP ME.
IS THIS YOUR DESTINY? TO CROSS THE COUNTRY TO GET YOUR ASSES HANDED TO YOU?
UUUGH...
UH-UH.
YOU'VE DONE ENOUGH DAMAGE.
WHAT IS WITH ALL THESE CALLS AND TEXTS, BY THE WAY?
"DADDY"? HOW OLD ARE YOU?
HURF

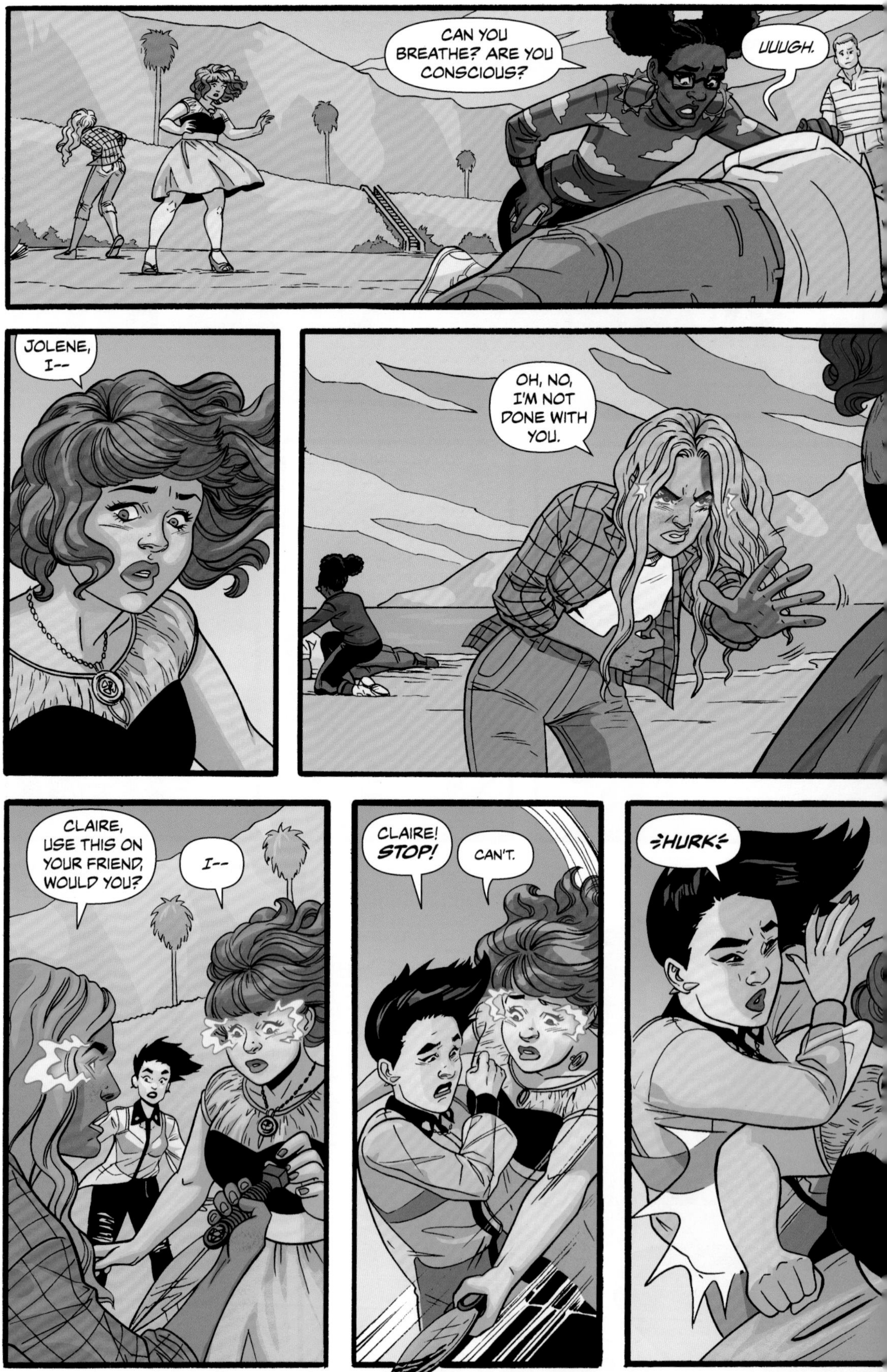
CAN YOU BREATHE? ARE YOU CONSCIOUS?
UUUGH.
JOLENE, I--
OH, NO, I'M NOT DONE WITH YOU.
CLAIRE, USE THIS ON YOUR FRIEND, WOULD YOU?
I--
CLAIRE! STOP!
CAN'T.
HURK

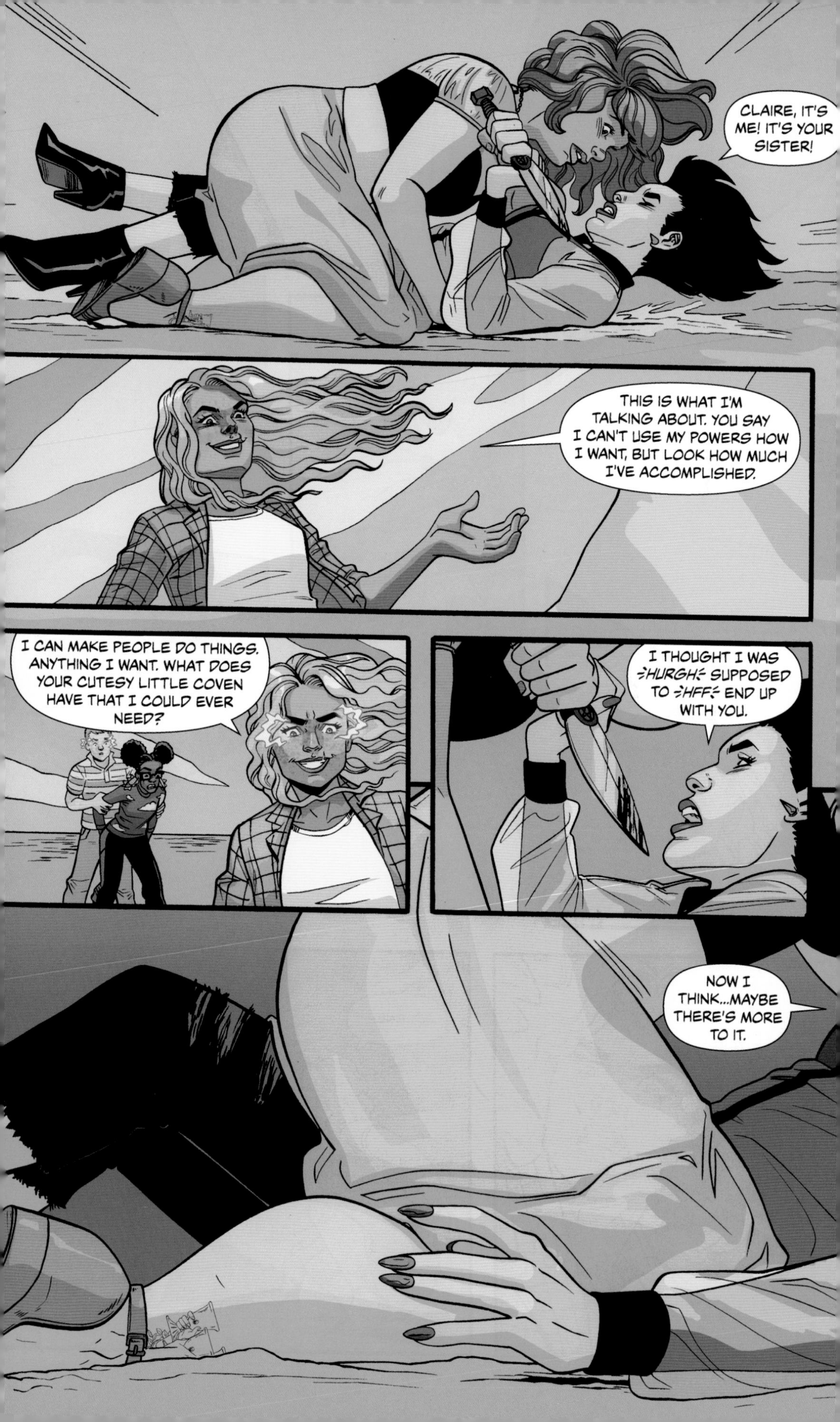
CLAIRE, IT'S ME! IT'S YOUR SISTER!
THIS IS WHAT I'M TALKING ABOUT. YOU SAY I CAN'T USE MY POWERS HOW I WANT, BUT LOOK HOW MUCH I'VE ACCOMPLISHED.
I CAN MAKE PEOPLE DO THINGS. ANYTHING I WANT. WHAT DOES YOUR CUTESY LITTLE COVEN HAVE THAT I COULD EVER NEED?
I THOUGHT I WAS =HURGH= SUPPOSED TO =HFF= END UP WITH YOU.
NOW I THINK...MAYBE THERE'S MORE TO IT.

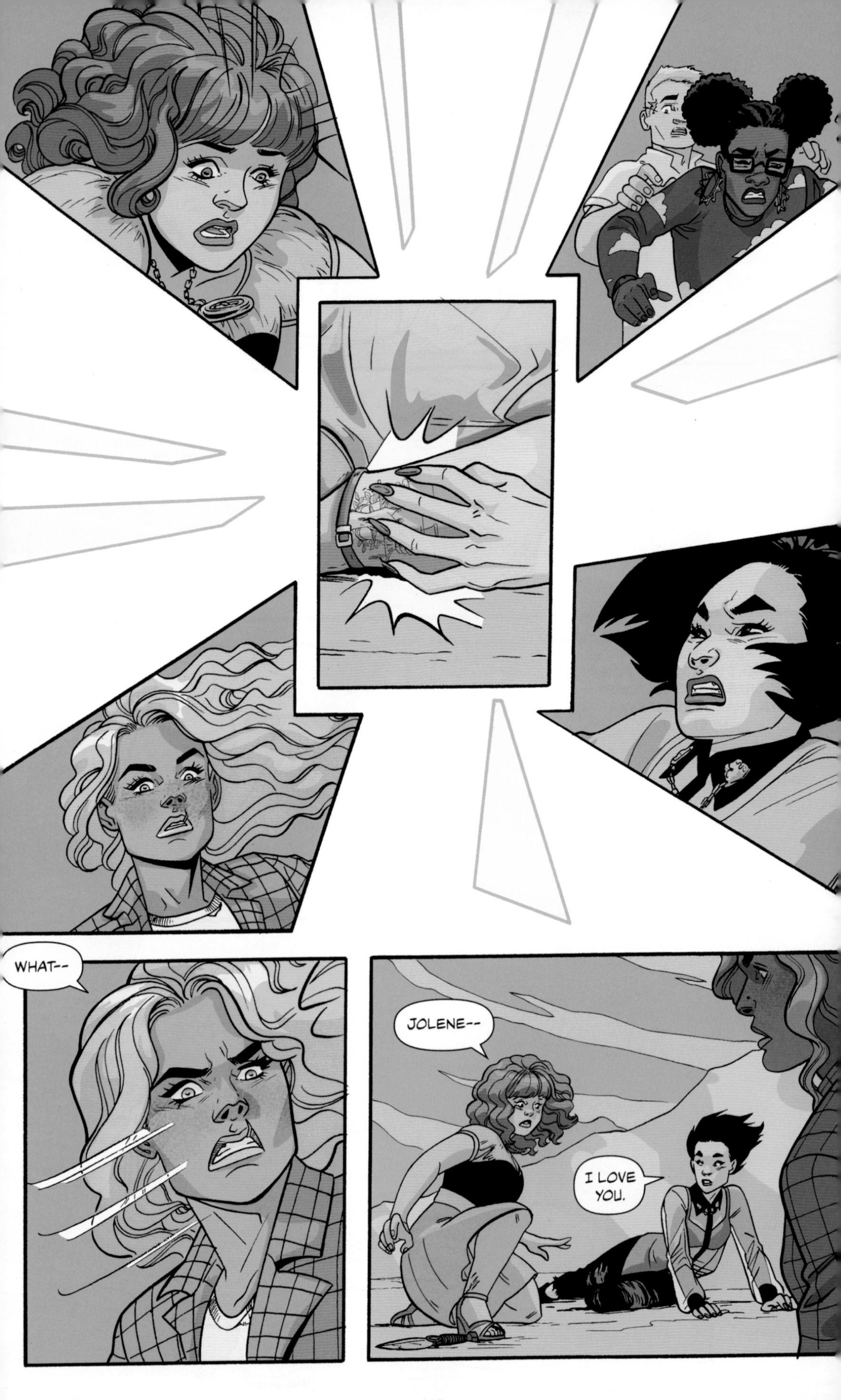
WHAT--
JOLENE--
I LOVE YOU.

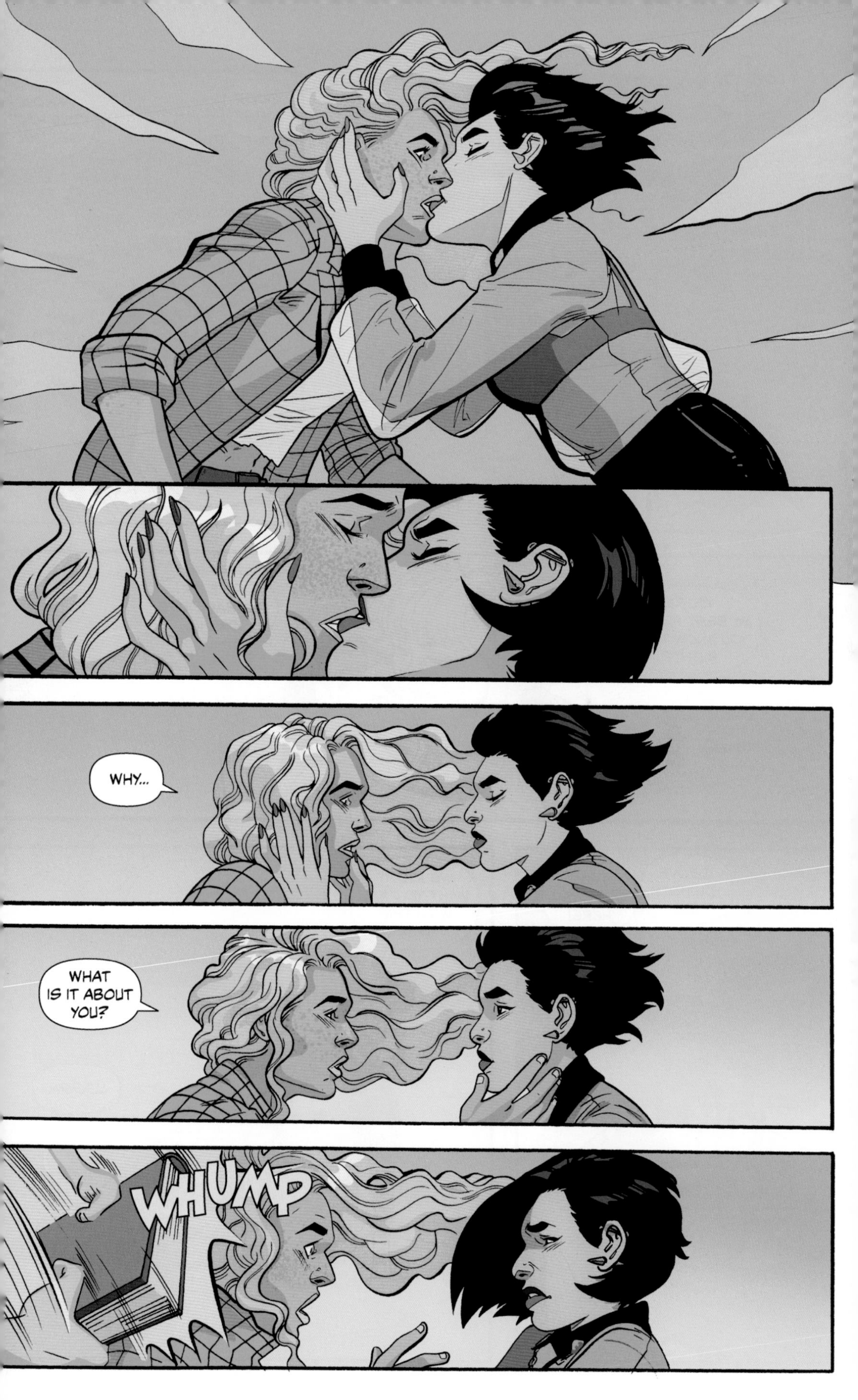
WHY...
WHAT IS IT ABOUT YOU?
WHUMP

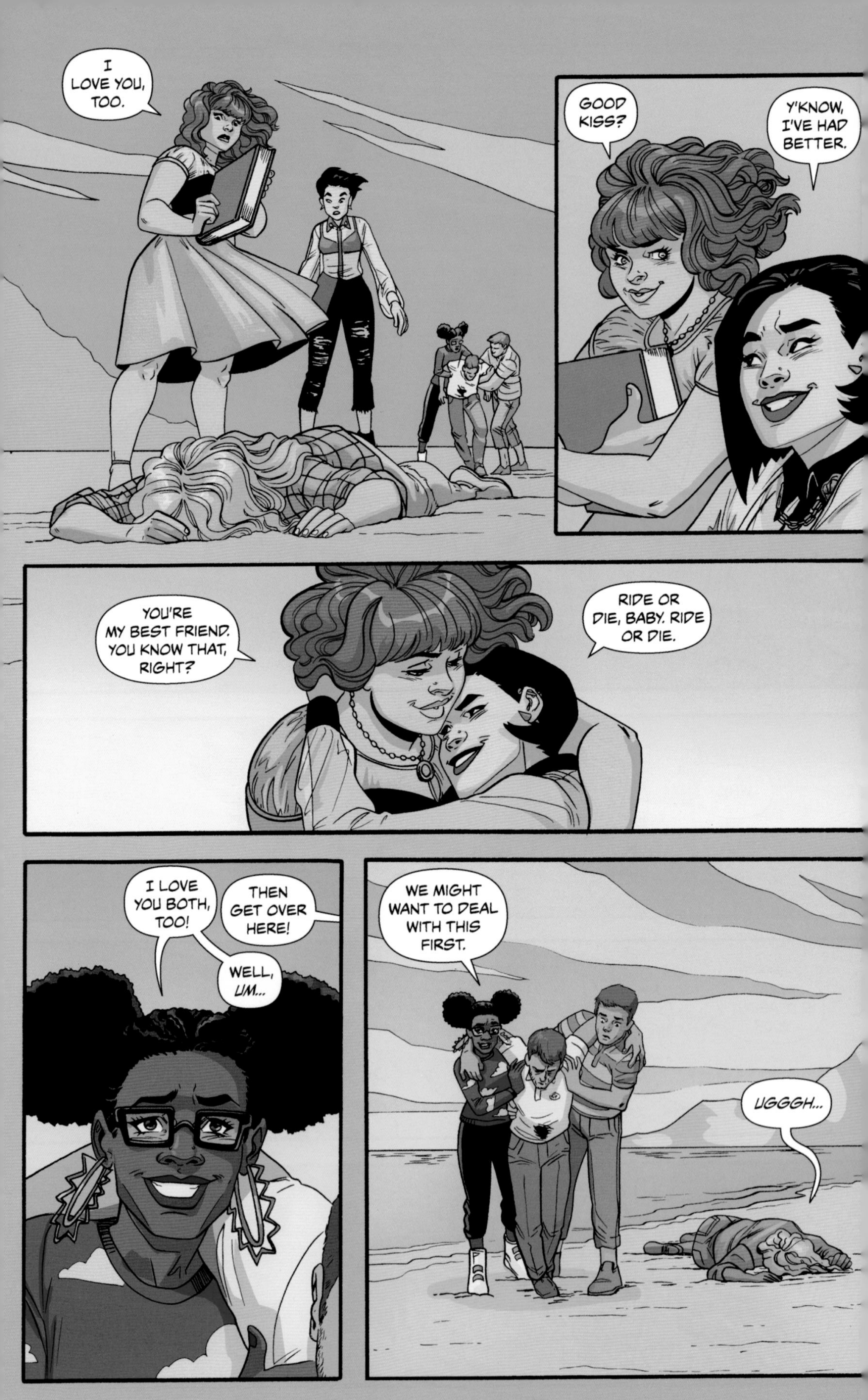
I LOVE YOU, TOO.
GOOD KISS?
Y'KNOW, I'VE HAD BETTER.
YOU'RE MY BEST FRIEND. YOU KNOW THAT, RIGHT?
RIDE OR DIE, BABY. RIDE OR DIE.
I LOVE YOU BOTH, TOO!
THEN GET OVER HERE!
WELL, UM...
WE MIGHT WANT TO DEAL WITH THIS FIRST.
UGGGH...

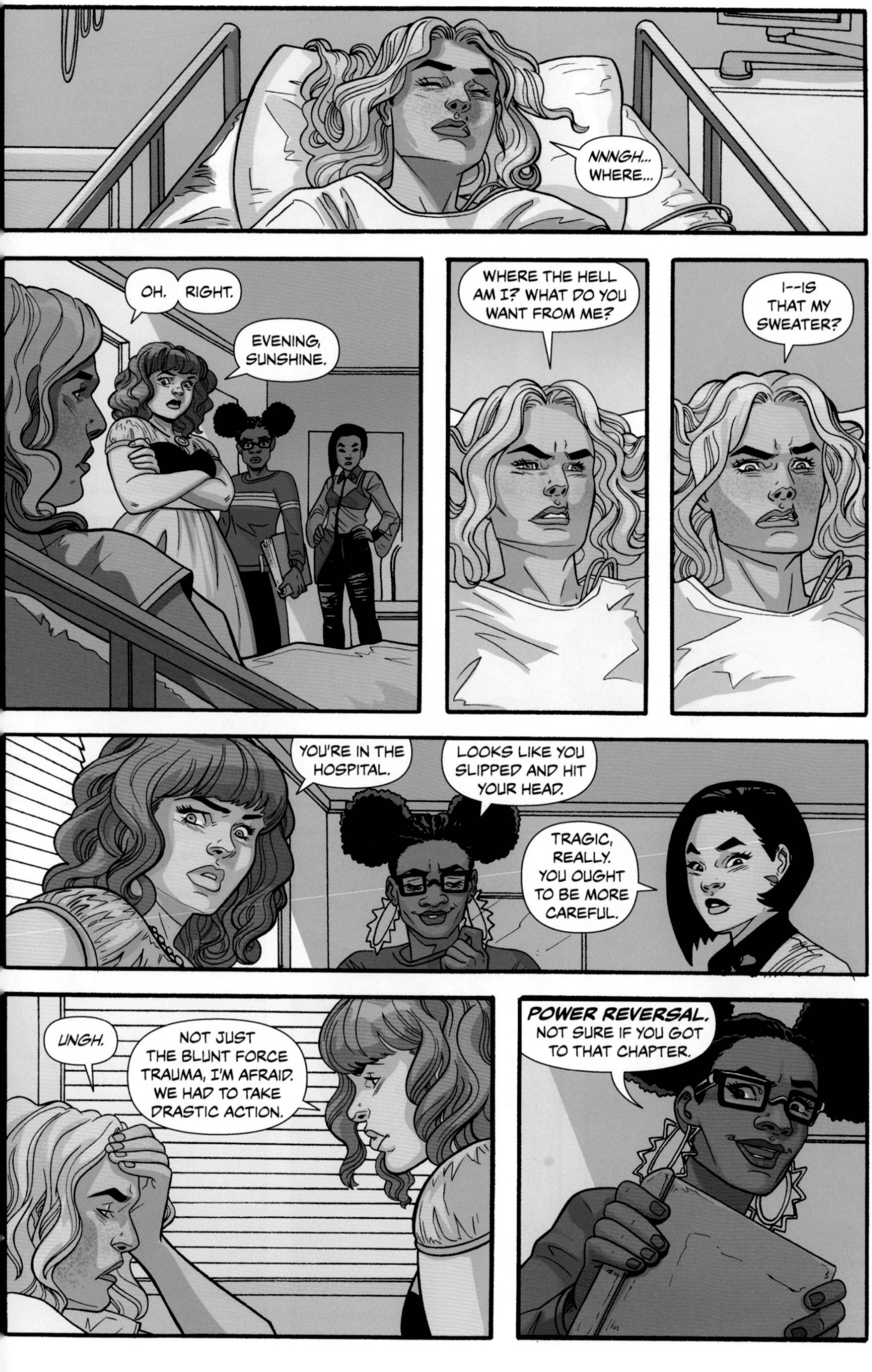
NNNGH... WHERE...
OH.
RIGHT.
EVENING, SUNSHINE.
WHERE THE HELL AM I? WHAT DO YOU WANT FROM ME?
I--IS THAT MY SWEATER?
YOU'RE IN THE HOSPITAL.
LOOKS LIKE YOU SLIPPED AND HIT YOUR HEAD.
TRAGIC, REALLY. YOU OUGHT TO BE MORE CAREFUL.
UNGH.
NOT JUST THE BLUNT FORCE TRAUMA, I'M AFRAID. WE HAD TO TAKE DRASTIC ACTION.
POWER REVERSAL. NOT SURE IF YOU GOT TO THAT CHAPTER.

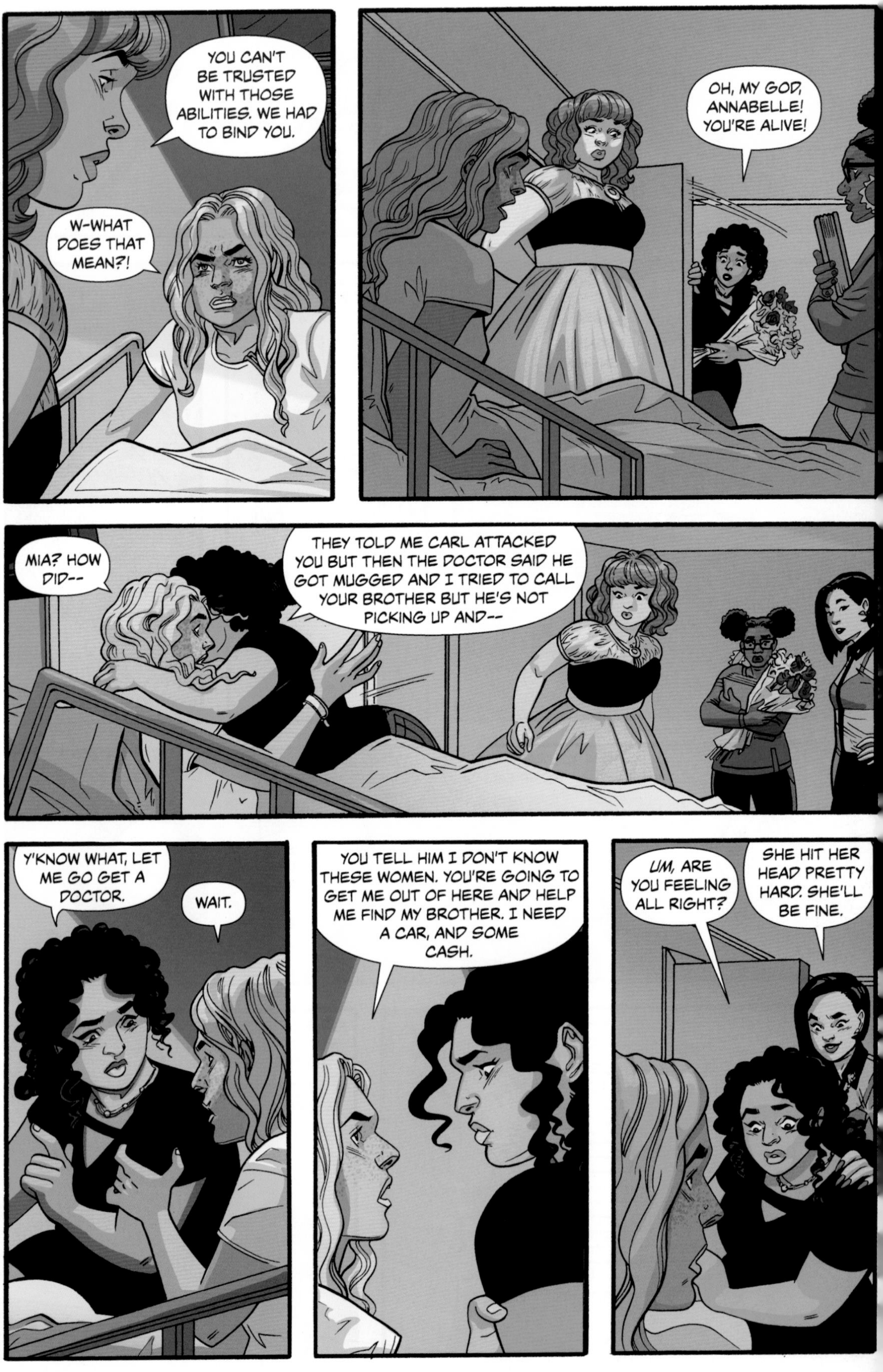
YOU CAN'T BE TRUSTED WITH THOSE ABILITIES. WE HAD TO BIND YOU.
W-WHAT DOES THAT MEAN?!
OH, MY GOD, ANNABELLE! YOU'RE ALIVE!
MIA? HOW DID--
THEY TOLD ME CARL ATTACKED YOU BUT THEN THE DOCTOR SAID HE GOT MUGGED AND I TRIED TO CALL YOUR BROTHER BUT HE'S NOT PICKING UP AND--
Y'KNOW WHAT, LET ME GO GET A DOCTOR.
WAIT.
YOU TELL HIM I DON'T KNOW THESE WOMEN. YOU'RE GOING TO GET ME OUT OF HERE AND HELP ME FIND MY BROTHER. I NEED A CAR, AND SOME CASH.
UM, ARE YOU FEELING ALL RIGHT?
SHE HIT HER HEAD PRETTY HARD. SHE'LL BE FINE.

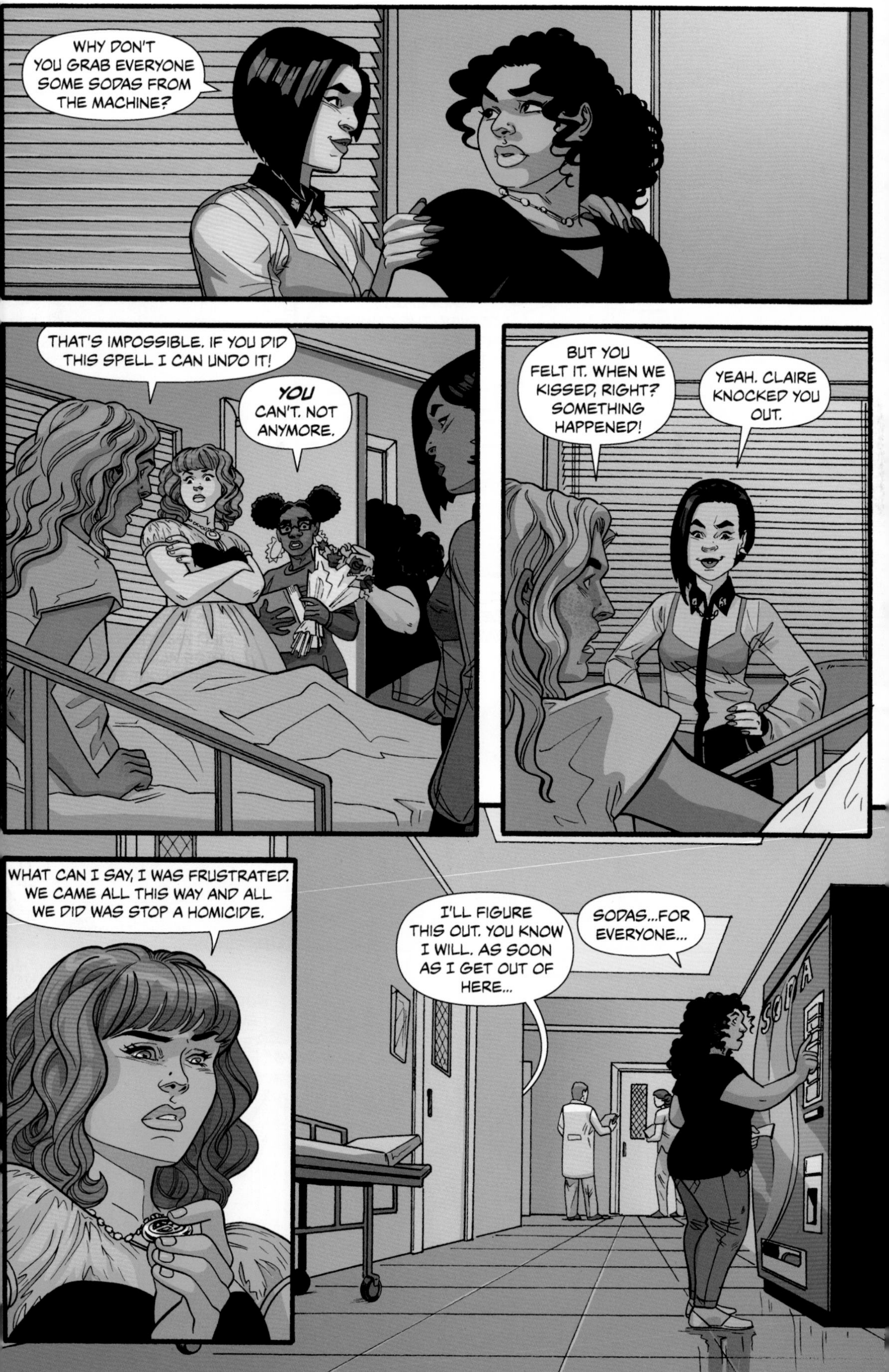
WHY DON'T YOU GRAB EVERYONE SOME SODAS FROM THE MACHINE?
THAT'S IMPOSSIBLE. IF YOU DID THIS SPELL I CAN UNDO IT!
YOU CAN'T. NOT ANYMORE.
BUT YOU FELT IT. WHEN WE KISSED, RIGHT? SOMETHING HAPPENED!
YEAH. CLAIRE KNOCKED YOU OUT.
WHAT CAN I SAY, I WAS FRUSTRATED. WE CAME ALL THIS WAY AND ALL WE DID WAS STOP A HOMICIDE.
I'LL FIGURE THIS OUT. YOU KNOW I WILL. AS SOON AS I GET OUT OF HERE...
SODAS...FOR EVERYONE...
SODA

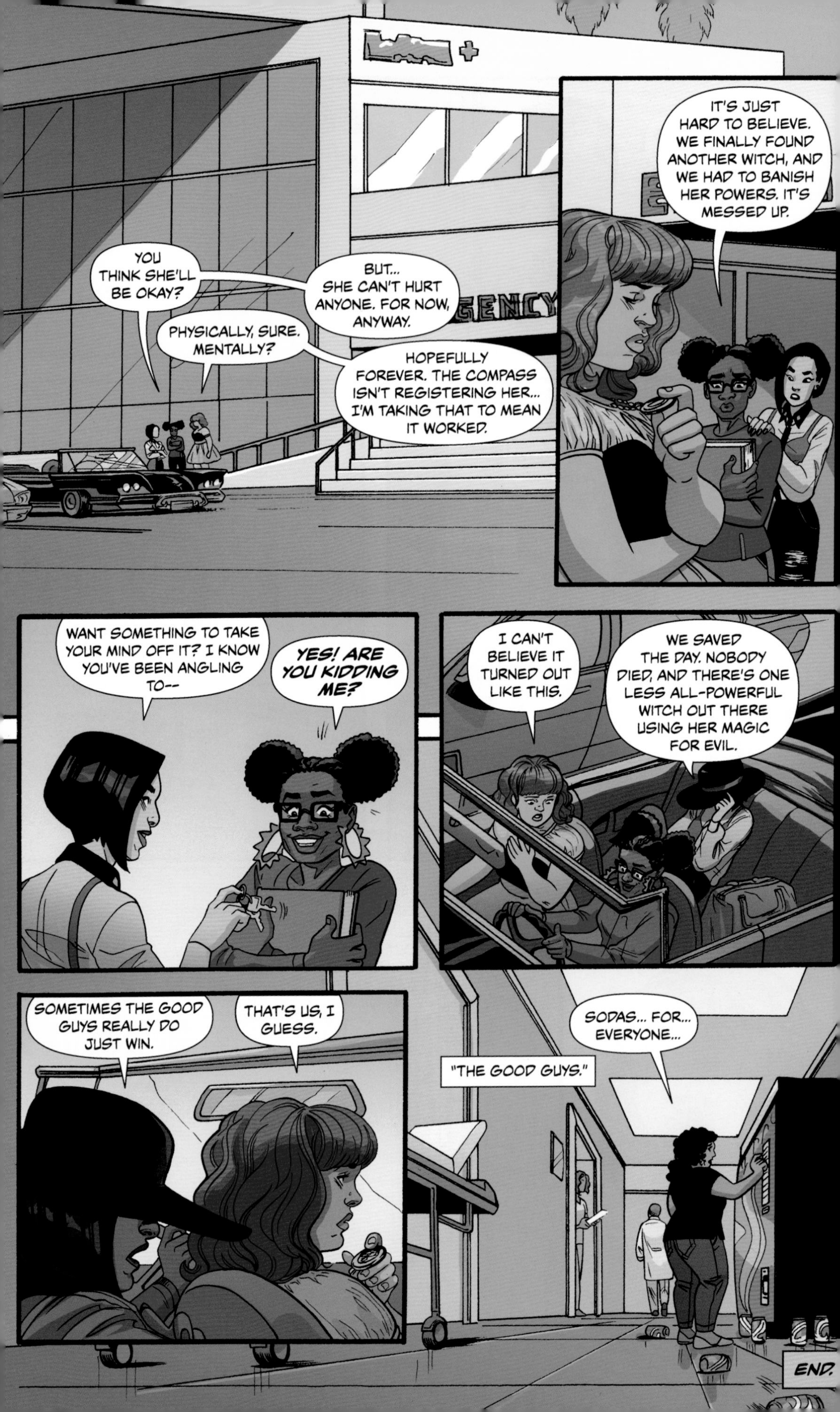

YOU THINK SHE'LL BE OKAY?
PHYSICALLY, SURE. MENTALLY?
BUT... SHE CAN'T HURT ANYONE. FOR NOW, ANYWAY.
HOPEFULLY FOREVER. THE COMPASS ISN'T REGISTERING HER... I'M TAKING THAT TO MEAN IT WORKED.
EMERGENCY
IT'S JUST HARD TO BELIEVE. WE FINALLY FOUND ANOTHER WITCH, AND WE HAD TO BANISH HER POWERS. IT'S MESSED UP.
WANT SOMETHING TO TAKE YOUR MIND OFF IT? I KNOW YOU'VE BEEN ANGLING TO--
YES! ARE YOU KIDDING ME?
I CAN'T BELIEVE IT TURNED OUT LIKE THIS.
WE SAVED THE DAY. NOBODY DIED, AND THERE'S ONE LESS ALL-POWERFUL WITCH OUT THERE USING HER MAGIC FOR EVIL.
SOMETIMES THE GOOD GUYS REALLY DO JUST WIN.
THAT'S US, I GUESS.
"THE GOOD GUYS."
SODAS... FOR... EVERYONE...
END.

SKETCHBOOK
Commentary by Kate Leth and Megan Levens

ANNABELLE LEIGH

Annabelle Leigh

Kate: Annabelle's design was one of the first things we nailed down for volume 2. I knew I wanted a traditional California beach girl, and I was listening to a LOT of Hayley Kiyoko at the time. Her hair is sun-bleached, her scar almost definitely came from skateboarding. I expect she owns upwards of a dozen pairs of sunglasses, most of them nicked from gas stations. I love her.

One of the exciting things about making your own stories is that you can do whatever you want with them. Personally, I think queer villains are a lot of fun, but it can feel pretty trope-y if they're the only representation you see. Jolene and Annabelle are two very different styles and personalities, and it's fun to have a wider spectrum. Honestly, in *Spell on Wheels*, everyone's at least a little bit queer. Claire's too much of a self-insert from both Megan and I to be *completely* straight. Andy still has a lot of growing up to do.

Megan: Annabelle's character design is sort of my love letter to the California girls I knew and befriended during my twelve years living in LA. She's hiding a lot of secrets behind all that long, beach-wavy hair!

I think what makes Annabelle such a compelling villain is that Kate's written her to be such a relatable, average young queer woman trying to survive in an unfair world . . . so these powers she comes into naturally seem like a way to balance the scales, to make up for past hurt that's been done to her.

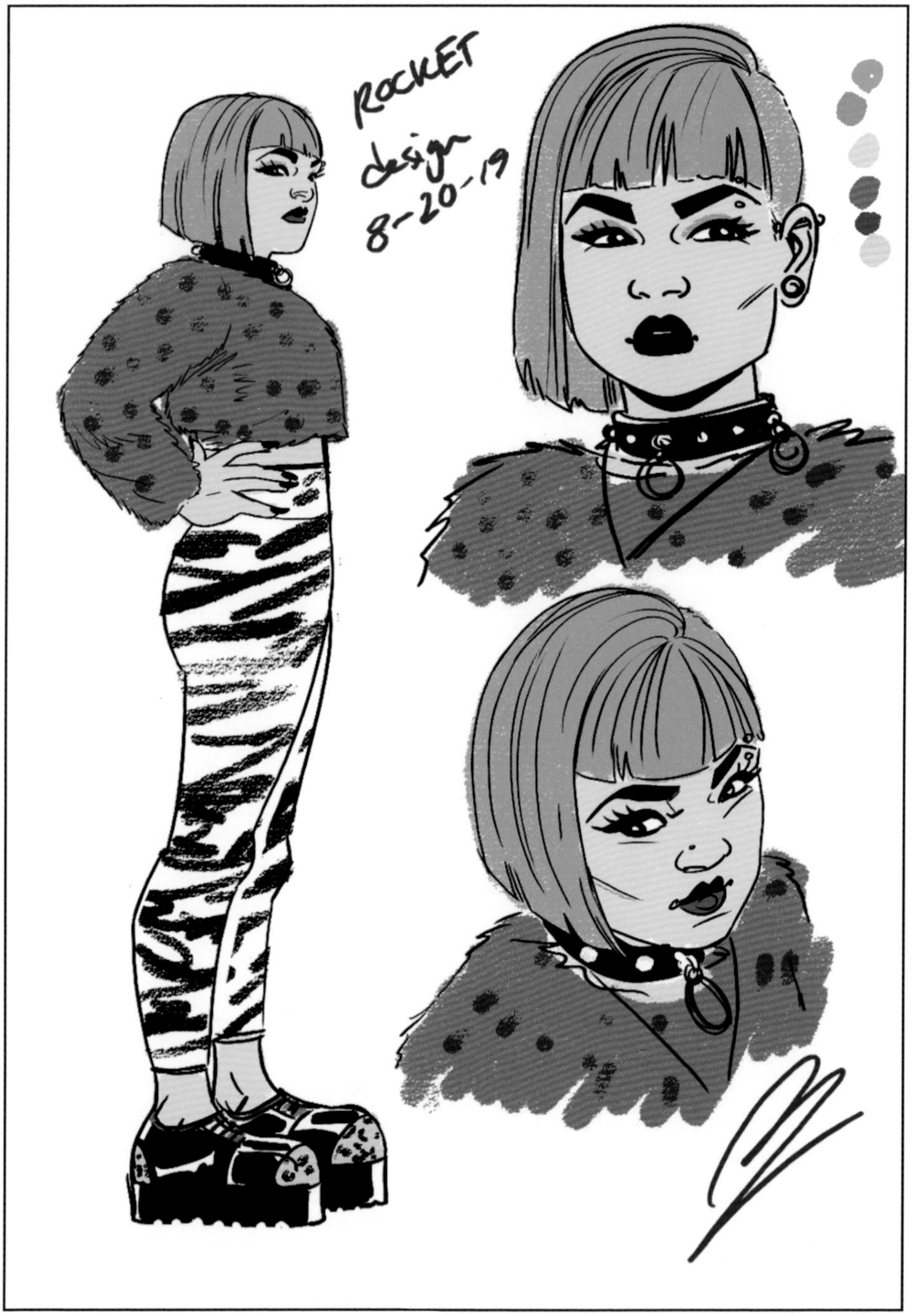
ROCKET
design
8-20-19

Rocket

Kate: Rocket, the tattoo artist Jolene apprenticed under, has the most backstory of any character we meet for just a couple of pages. In keeping with that, I had a pretty specific look in mind for their design: Japanese punk street fashion with the color palette of Jem and the Holograms. They're also influenced by Rachelle Gammon, the tattoo artist from my home town that did most of my left arm (hi, Rachelle!) whose hair is a constantly-evolving work of art. Megan and I shared a lot of concepts until Rocket, in all their queer-nonbinary-hypercolor glory, was born.

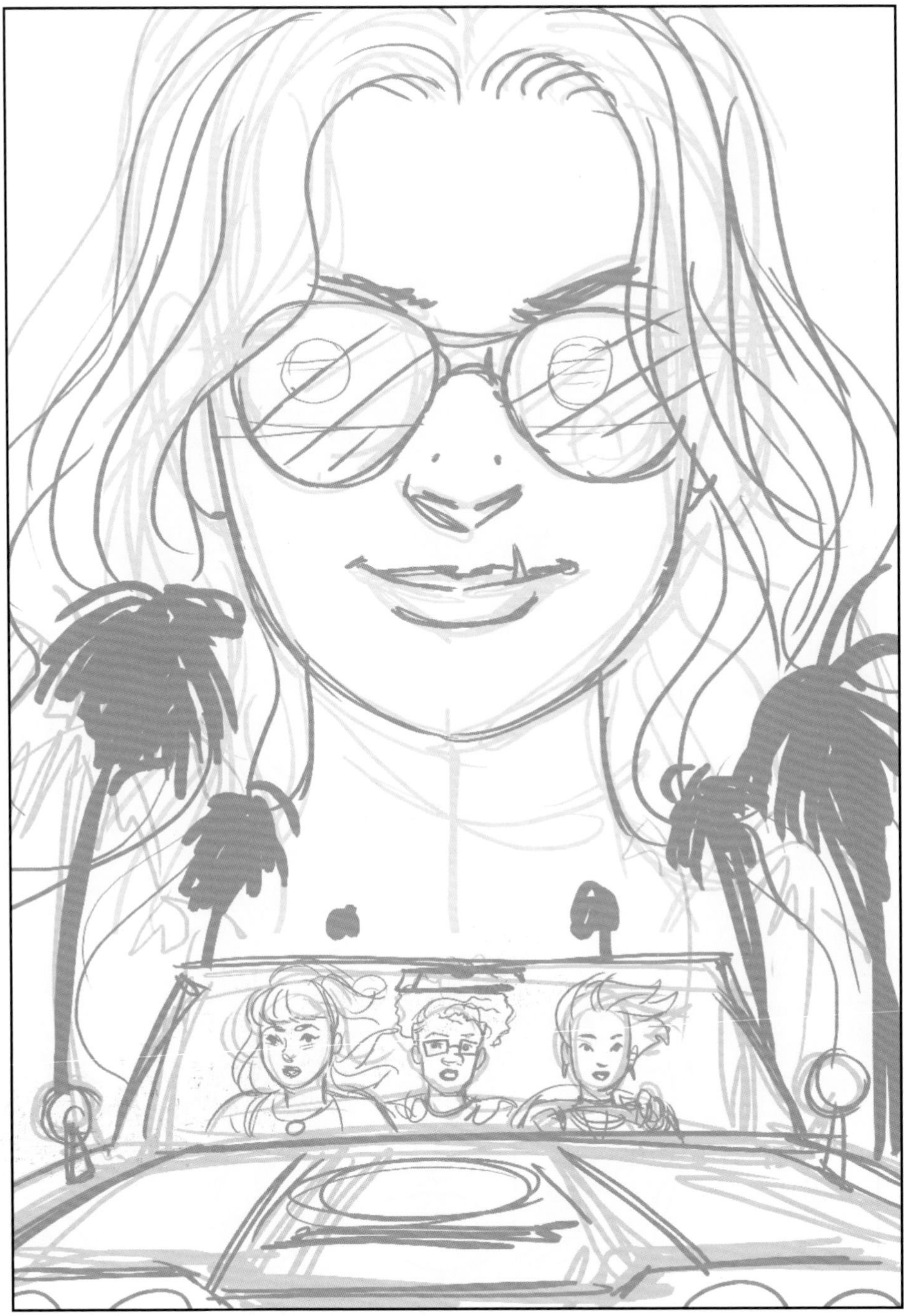

Just to Get to You ***#1 cover sketch***

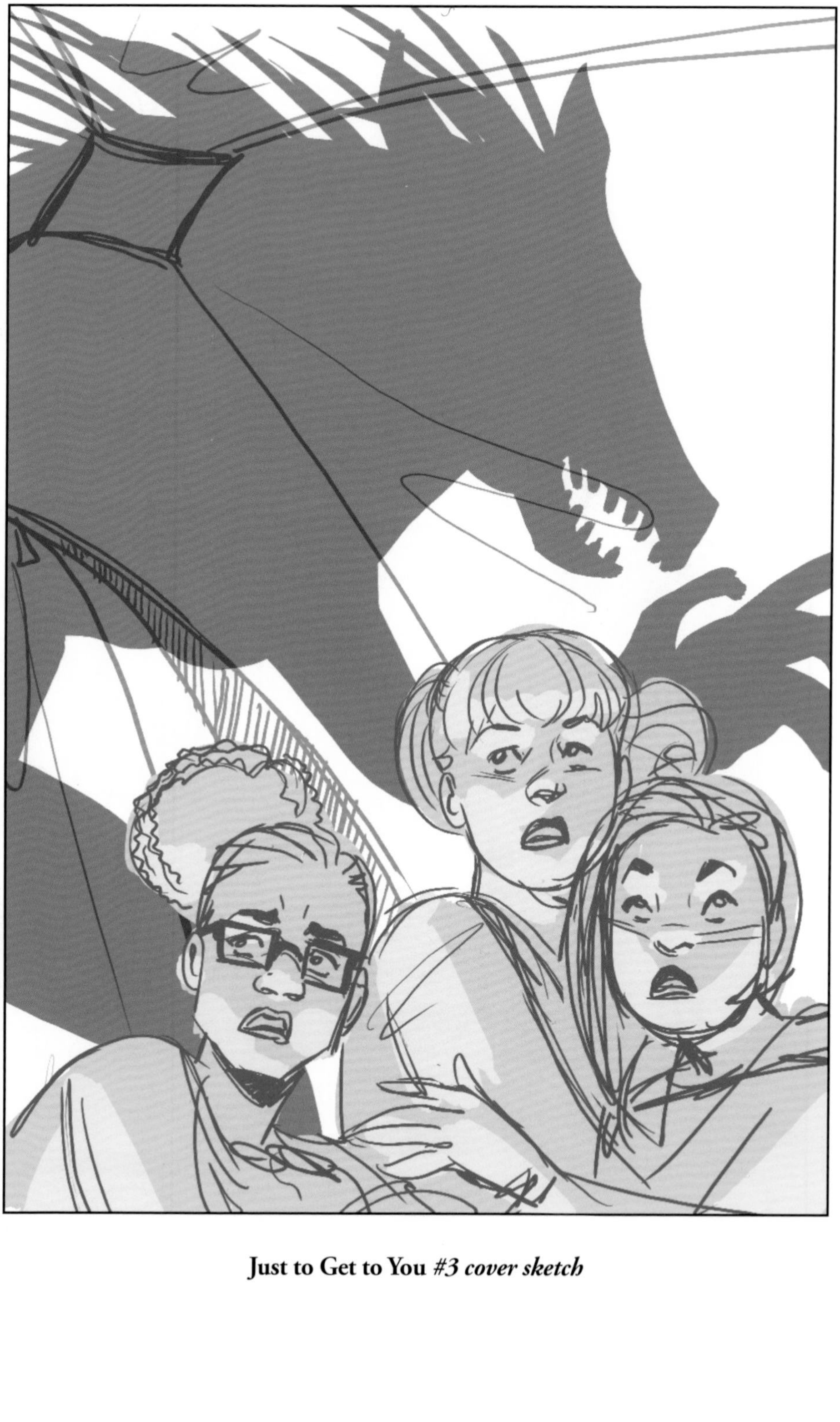

Just to Get to You ***#3 cover sketch***

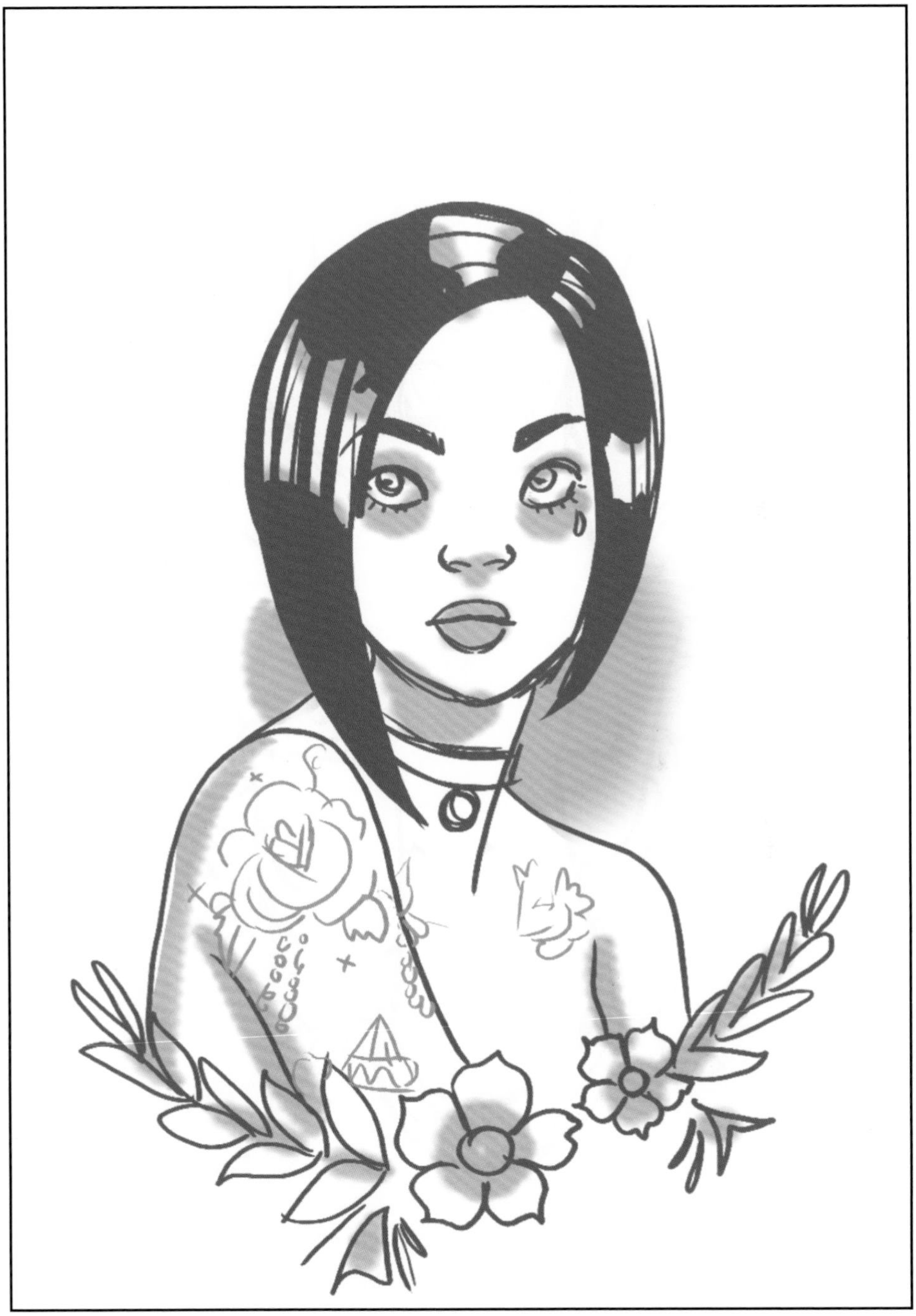

Just to Get to You *#4 cover sketch*

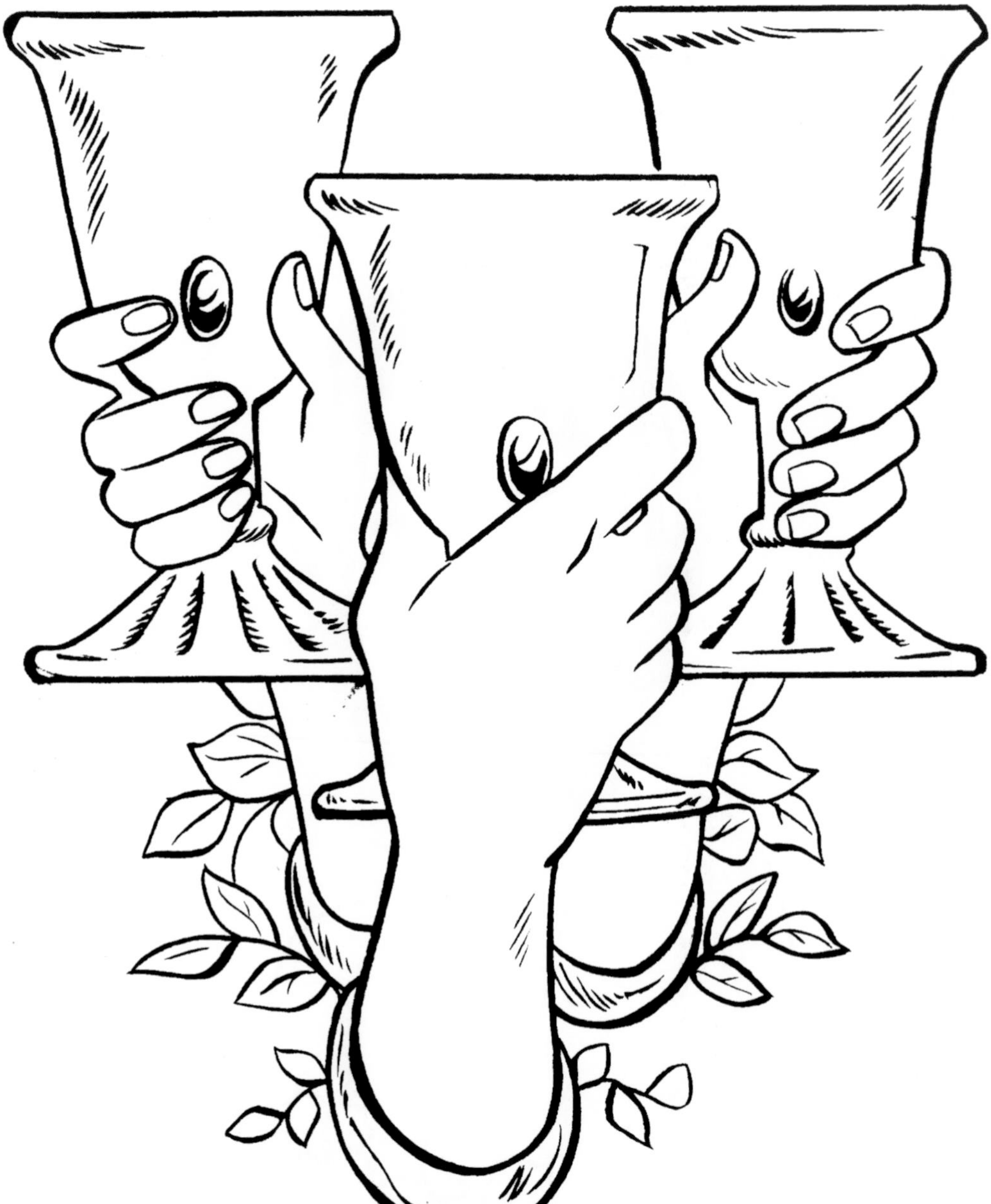

The witches' tattoo design from chapter 3

Kate: Tattoos and their symbology are endlessly fascinating to me. We used a lot of tattoo imagery in this second volume, partially because it focuses more on Jolene, partially because tattoos are just very cool. When it comes to the tattoos the three girls get together, I originally wanted a version of the original Rider-Waite-Smith tarot deck's Three of Swords, with Wands striking through the heart instead. Hilariously, I went to a tarot workshop the day after I suggested it, and the teacher laughed about how bad an omen that is and how embarrassing it is when people get tattoos of it. Live and learn.

What we landed on, and Megan did an absolute banger job of creating, was a twist on the Three of Cups. Cups are the suit of emotions, of relationships and community, and the Three of Cups represents community, sisterhood, celebration. It's usually seen as three women holding their cups aloft. Since this volume saw so much vulnerability and feeling, it made perfect sense.

Don't ask me how Jolene sanitized everything in the desert. It's MAGIC.

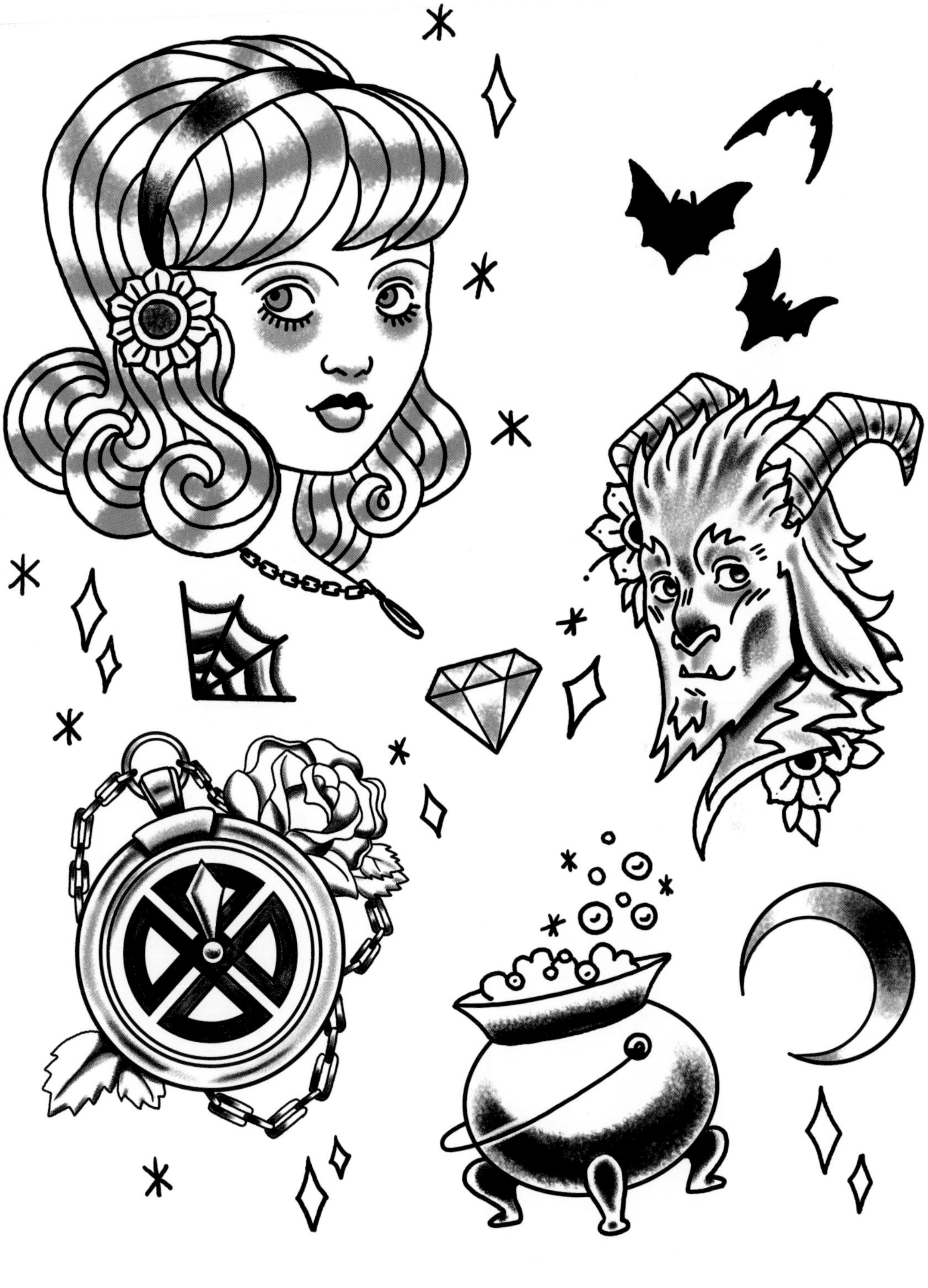

Tattoo flash designs for* Just to Get to You *#4 cover

Megan: Tattoo design is so terrifying to me! I have four myself, and plans for more, but it's such a specific art form that encompasses so many different styles, that I just don't feel I have a good grasp on. I leaned very heavily on the source reference for the sisters' Three of Cups tattoo (*facing*), and on traditional American style tattoo art for the "tattoo flash" designs on the cover illustration for chapter 4 (*page 77*).

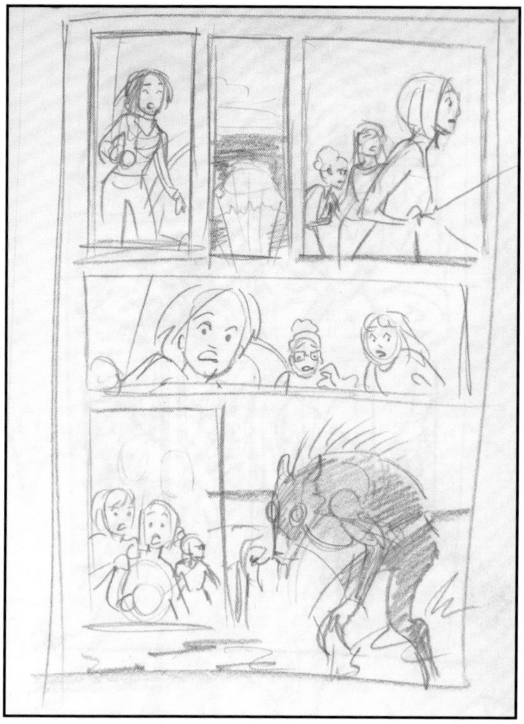

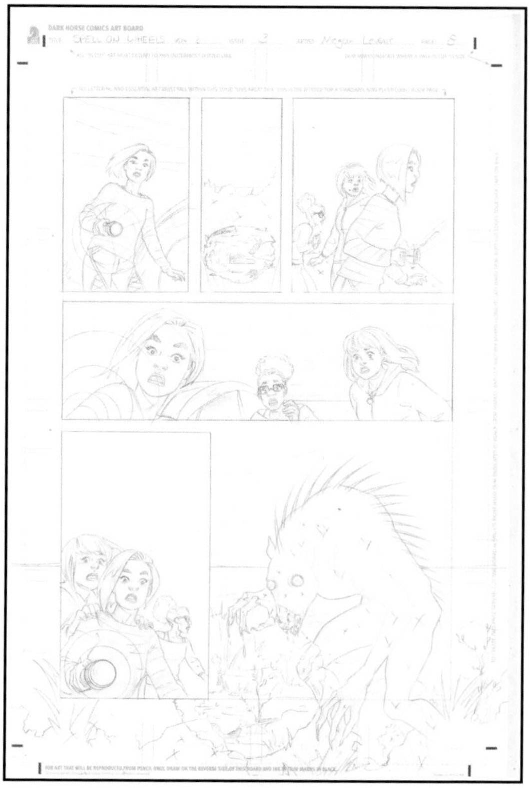

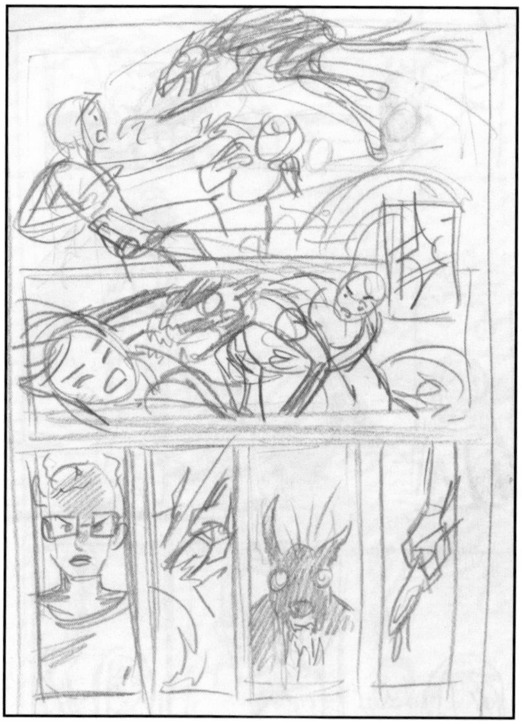

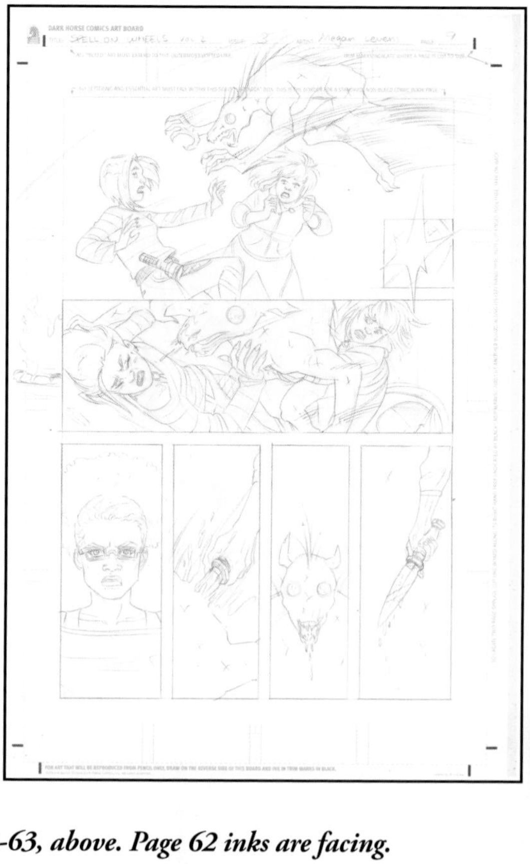

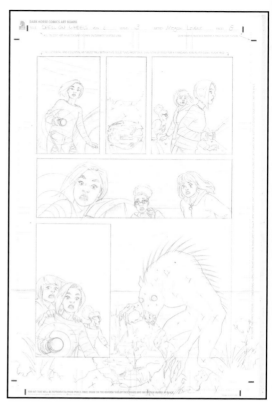

Layouts and pencil stages for pages 62-63, above. Page 62 inks are facing.

Kate: All of Megan's pages are sublime, but I was so thrilled with how this sequence came out. We didn't have as many ghouls in this story, since the journey to Annabelle takes priority, but I wanted a cryptid more than anything. Issue #3 is all about darkness and secrets coming to light, so what better way to illustrate that than with a huge, goat-sucking monster hunting them in the desert? Did I partially include it just to make room for that crass pun of Jolene's? Who could say.

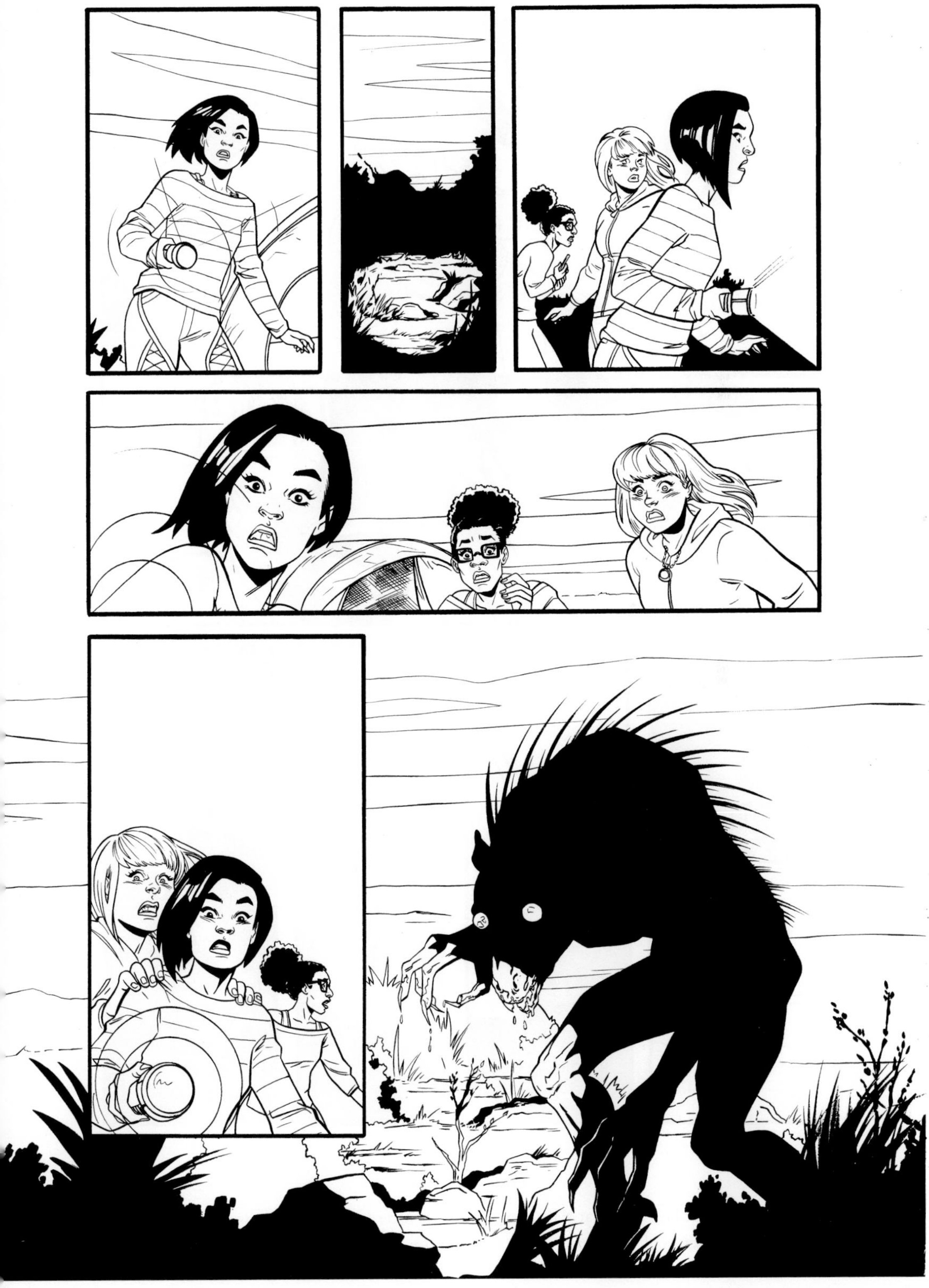

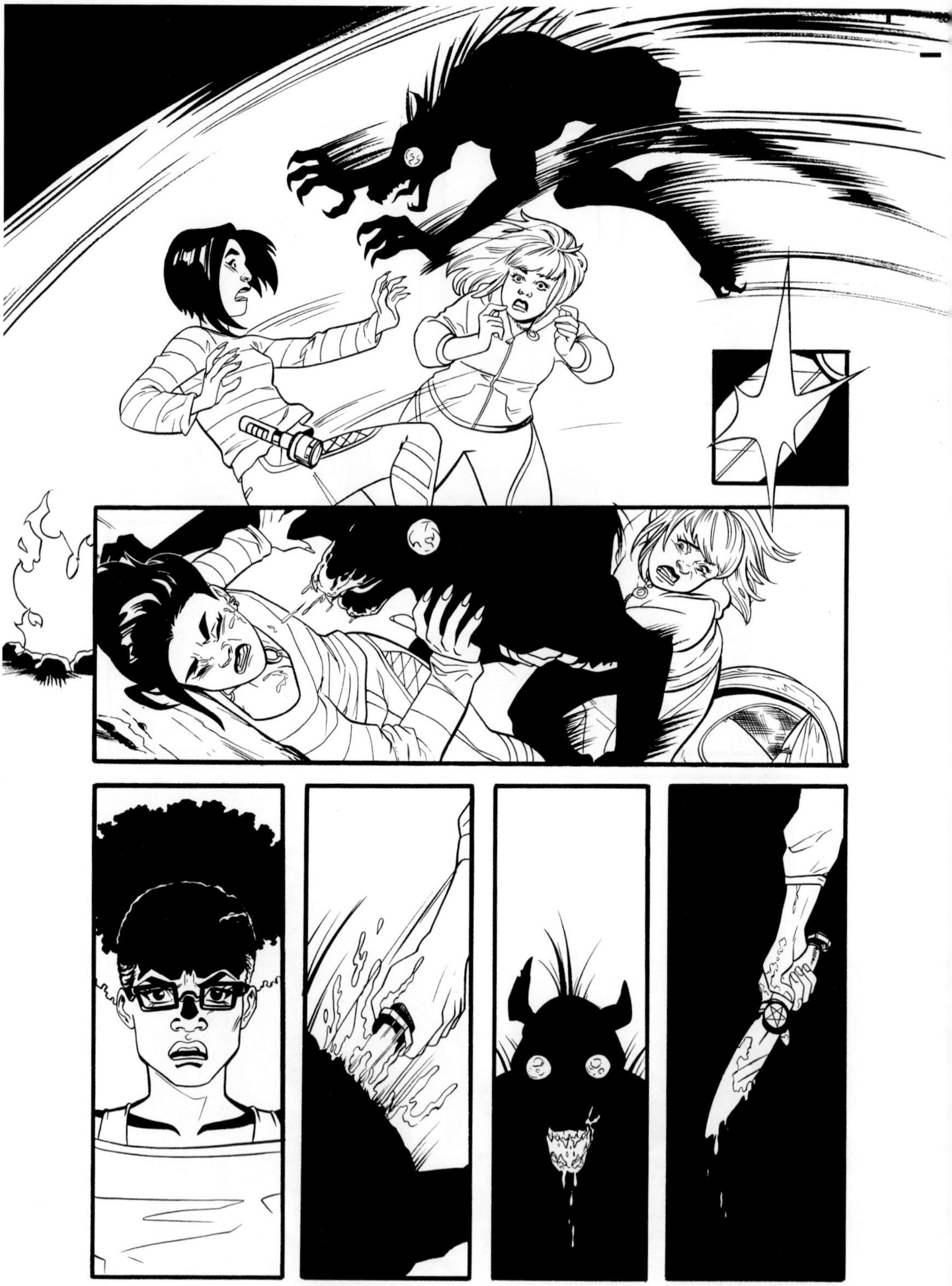

Page 63 inks

Megan: Probably the best note that Kate gave for this monster was that the less we saw, the scarier it would be . . . which is of course true of any monster! I never even really designed the chupacabra's surface details, just a structure and anatomy so I could have it move believably through the scenes. But even in my own imagination it's still hidden in shadow!

MORE TITLES YOU MIGHT ENJOY

ALENA
Kim W. Andersson
Since arriving at a snobbish boarding school, Alena's been harassed every day by the lacrosse team. But Alena's best friend Josephine is not going to accept that anymore. If Alena does not fight back, then she will take matters into her own hands. There's just one problem . . . Josephine has been dead for a year.
$17.99 | ISBN 978-1-50670-215-5

ASTRID: CULT OF THE VOLCANIC MOON
Kim W. Andersson
Formerly the Galactic Coalition's top recruit, the now-disgraced Astrid is offered a special mission from her old commander. She'll prove herself worthy of another chance at becoming a Galactic Peacekeeper . . . if she can survive.
$19.99 | ISBN 978-1-61655-690-7

BANDETTE
Paul Tobin, Colleen Coover
A costumed teen burglar by the *nome d'arte* of Bandette and her group of street urchins find equal fun in both skirting and aiding the law, in this enchanting, Eisner-nominated series!
$14.99 each
Volume 1: Presto! | ISBN 978-1-61655-279-4
Volume 2: Stealers, Keepers! | ISBN 978-1-61655-668-6
Volume 3: The House of the Green Mask | ISBN 978-1-50670-219-3

BOUNTY
Kurtis Wiebe, Mindy Lee
The Gadflies were the most wanted criminals in the galaxy. Now, with a bounty to match their reputation, the Gadflies are forced to abandon banditry for a career as bounty hunters . . . 'cause if you can't beat 'em, join 'em—then rob 'em blind!
$14.99 | ISBN 978-1-50670-044-1

HEART IN A BOX
Kelly Thompson, Meredith McClaren
In a moment of post-heartbreak weakness, Emma wishes her heart away and a mysterious stranger obliges. But emptiness is even worse than grief, and Emma sets out to collect the pieces of her heart and face the cost of recapturing it.
$14.99 | ISBN 978-1-61655-694-5

HENCHGIRL
Kristen Gudsnuk
Mary Posa hates her job. She works long hours for little pay, no insurance, and worst of all, no respect. Her coworkers are jerks, and her boss doesn't appreciate her. He's also a supervillain. Cursed with a conscience, Mary would give anything to be something other than a henchgirl.
$17.99 | ISBN 978-1-50670-144-8

THE ADVENTURES OF SUPERHERO GIRL, SECOND EDITION
Faith Erin Hicks
What if you can leap tall buildings and defeat alien monsters with your bare hands, but you buy your capes at secondhand stores and have a weakness for kittens? Faith Erin Hicks brings humor to the trials and tribulations of a young, female superhero, battling monsters both supernatural and mundane in an all-too-ordinary world.
$16.99 each | ISBN 978-1-61655-084-4
Expanded Edition | ISBN 978-1-50670-336-7

DARKHORSE.COM AVAILABLE AT YOUR LOCAL COMICS SHOP OR BOOKSTORE • TO FIND A COMICS SHOP IN YOUR AREA, VISIT COMICSHOPLOCATOR.COM
For more information or to order direct, visit DarkHorse.com

Alena™, Astrid™ © Kim W. Andersson, by agreement with Grand Agency. Bandette™ © Paul Tobin and Colleen Coover. Bounty™ © Kurtis Wiebe and Mindy Lee. Heart in a Box™ © 1979 Semi-Finalist, Inc., and Meredith McClaren. Henchgirl™ © Kristen Gudsnuk. The Adventures of Superhero Girl™ © Faith Erin Hicks. Dark Horse Books® and the Dark Horse logo are registered trademarks of Dark Horse Comics LLC. All rights reserved. (BL 6041 P1)

THE SECRET LOVES OF GEEK GIRLS

Hope Nicholson, Margaret Atwood,
Mariko Tamaki, and more

The Secret Loves of Geek Girls is a nonfiction anthology mixing prose, comics, and illustrated stories on the lives and loves of an amazing cast of female creators.
$14.99 | ISBN 978-1-50670-099-1

THE SECRET LOVES OF GEEKS

Gerard Way, Dana Simpson, Hope Larson, and more
The follow-up to the smash hit *The Secret Loves of Geek Girls*, this brand new anthology features comic and prose stories from cartoonists and professional geeks about their most intimate, heartbreaking, and inspiring tales of love, sex, and dating. This volume includes creators of diverse genders, orientations, and cultural backgrounds.
$14.99 | ISBN 978-1-50670-473-9

MISFITS OF AVALON

Kel McDonald
Four misfit teens are reluctant recruits to save the mystical isle of Avalon. Magically empowered and directed by a talking dog, they must stop the rise of King Arthur. As they struggle to become a team, they're faced with the discovery that they may not be the good guys.
$14.99 each
Volume 1: The Queen of Air and Delinquency | ISBN 978-1-61655-538-2
Volume 2: The Ill-Made Guardian | ISBN 978-1-61655-748-5
Volume 3: The Future in the Wind | ISBN 978-1-61655-749-2

ZODIAC STARFORCE: BY THE POWER OF ASTRA

Kevin Panetta, Paulina Ganucheau
A group of teenage girls with magical powers have sworn to protect our planet against dark creatures. Known as the Zodiac Starforce, these high-school girls aren't just combating math tests—they're also battling monsters!
$12.99 | ISBN 978-1-61655-913-7

ZODIAC STARFORCE: CRIES OF THE FIRE PRINCE

Kevin Panetta, Paulina Ganucheau
A new Big Bad has come out to play and demons are overrunning the town! The UK team's secrets are causing a rift in the Zodiac alliance, and divided they may fall!
$17.99 | ISBN 978-1-50670-310-7

SPELL ON WHEELS

Kate Leth, Megan Levens, Marissa Louise
A road trip story. A magical revenge fantasy. A sisters-over-misters tale of three witches out to get back what was taken from them.
$14.99 | ISBN 978-1-50670-183-7

SPELL ON WHEELS: JUST TO GET TO YOU

Kate Leth, Megan Levens, Marissa Louise
As they make their way along the highway toward the strange presence possessing Claire, the witches find you can't go home again. And they're running out of time.
$19.99 | ISBN 978-1-50671-477-6

THE ONCE AND FUTURE QUEEN

Adam P. Knave, D.J. Kirkbride,
Nick Brokenshire, Frank Cvetkovic
It's out with the old myths and in with the new as a nineteen-year-old chess prodigy pulls Excalibur from the stone and becomes queen. Now, magic, romance, Fae, Merlin, and more await her!
$14.99 | ISBN 978-1-50670-250-6

DARKHORSE.COM AVAILABLE AT YOUR LOCAL COMICS SHOP OR BOOKSTORE • TO FIND A COMICS SHOP IN YOUR AREA, VISIT COMICSHOPLOCATOR.COM
For more information or to order direct, visit DarkHorse.com